T0146036

Cybersecurity and Human Rights in the Age of Cyberveillance

Cybersecurity and Human Rights in the Age of Cyberveillance

Edited by
Joanna Kulesza
Roy Balleste

ROWMAN & LITTLEFIELD
Lanham • Boulder • New York • London

Published by Rowman & Littlefield
A wholly owned subsidiary of The Rowman & Littlefield Publishing Group, Inc.
4501 Forbes Boulevard, Suite 200, Lanham, Maryland 20706
www.rowman.com

Unit A, Whitacre Mews, 26-34 Stannary Street, London SE11 4AB

British Library Cataloguing in Publication Information Available

Library of Congress Cataloging-in-Publication Data

Names: Kulesza, Joanna, editor. | Balleste, Roy, editor.
Title: Cybersecurity and human rights in the age of cyberveillance / edited by Joanna Kulesza, Roy
Balleste.
Description: Lanham : Rowman & Littlefield, 2016. | Includes bibliographical references and index.
Identifiers: LCCN 2015030976| ISBN 9781442260412 (cloth : alk. paper) | ISBN 9781442260429
(ebook)
Subjects: LCSH: Computer networks–Security measures. | Computer security. | Human rights. |
Cyberspace–Social aspects.
Classification: LCC TK5105.59 .C88 2016 | DDC 303.48/34–dc23 LC record available at http://
lccn.loc.gov/2015030976

∞ ™ The paper used in this publication meets the minimum requirements of American
National Standard for Information Sciences Permanence of Paper for Printed Library
Materials, ANSI/NISO Z39.48-1992.

Printed in the United States of America

To the students of international law.

Contents

Foreword

Cybersecurity: Its Many Actors and the Human Rights Message

This book offers a captivating insight into some of the most crucial cybersecurity issues. Under the perspective of human rights, it is structured as a collection of chapters covering research on various current questions. Due to their complexity, the answers provided are far from simple. They are rather extensive and multifaceted. The book should be of particular interest not only to lawyers and legal researchers but also to Internet policy professionals and criminologists.

Chapter 1, "Defining Cybersecurity: Critical Infrastructure and Public-Private Partnerships," authored by Joanna Kulesza, extensively analyzes the double-edged notion of "cybersecurity," its meaning and goals: it expresses both a particular need for the adoption of certain measures and at the same time a safeguard for opportunities and liberties. In order to be effective, cybersecurity has to be connected with the notions of "cyberthreat" and "cybercrime" in order to provide security requirements and obligations related to them under the prism of global cooperation and universal standards. It also refers to the meaning of critical infrastructure and identifies the actors under particular cybersecurity obligations. It finally stresses the role of private actors in ensuring cybersecurity, the role of the governments to facilitate a public-private cooperation, and the need for a thorough reference to international human rights standards.

Dimitrios Delibasis's "Cybersecurity and State Responsibility: Identifying a Due Diligence Standard for Prevention of Transboundary Threats" in chapter 2 then moves from the role of the private actors to the principle of state responsibility and how it can be set as a reference point to address and

regulate computer network attacks as entailed in the new term of "cyberwarfare." This new form of warfare is more informal, decentralized, and outsourcing based. The principle of the legal international obligations is highlighted, as it can be used as one of the main foundations for the creation of a
regulatory framework. Any countermeasures, though, must be in accordance
with the proportionality principle and must be distinguished from the "plea
of necessity," which must be applied in cases of emergency only. Based on
the state responsibility and sovereignty paradigm, therefore, certain obligations can be extracted not only toward a state's own people but also toward
the rest of the international community.

Chapter 3, "In Harm's Way: Harmonizing Security and Human Rights in
the Internet Age," written by Roy Balleste, deals with the challenging issue
of harmonizing security and human rights in the digital era. In order to
achieve that, the protection of social and democratic values must be considered a prerequisite in order to reconcile this "social contract" and cybersecurity. The issue of proportionality when security measures have to be applied is
also highlighted, along with the necessity of cooperation between governments and all stakeholders. The Internet and its security must be studied from
the prism of international human standards and not merely addressed with
criminal law principles.

Chapter 4, "Privacy versus Security: Identifying the Challenges in a Global Information Society," written by Rolf H. Weber and Dominic N. Staiger,
builds further on this perspective and identifies the challenges and tensions
between privacy and security and the need to maintain a balance in order to
avoid privacy abuses. The main question, therefore, is whether the measures
that limit privacy are proportionate to the purpose they want to achieve. The
new technological developments have grown up the gap between technical
capabilities and privacy laws, and a new framework is required. An extensive
analysis is provided with all the risks that privacy encounters in the light of
security in the areas of data collection and use, identification, and surveillance. The need to adjust the legal frameworks to these technological challenges is more pressing than ever, and the best way to achieve this is through
the conclusion of an international agreement.

Chapter 5, "Freedom of Expression, Human Rights Standards, and Private Online Censorship," authored by Monica Horten, focuses on the conflict
of copyright enforcement and freedom of expression online and answers the
question of how to interpret the duty of states with regard to private actors
when applying content restrictions. Underlying network technologies on the
one hand enable free speech but on the other hand hinder it, as they can be
used to restrict Internet users' activities. This restrictive functionality must,
first of all, be in compliance with human rights law, and it is a state's duty to
provide adequate safeguards and have special duties with regard to private
actors.

Chapter 6, "(Global) Internet Governance and Its Discontents," written by Marianne I. Franklin, illuminates Internet governance as an international and geopolitical undertaking, in contrast with a conception that characterizes it as a place of minimal state intervention. It is increasingly regarded as an international human rights affair. Starting from some historical and definitional points, the discussion moves to more organizational and participatory issues. It concludes on the political character of Internet governance and the fact that many of the political and sociocultural issues arising for the future of Internet policy making are not new as such but only in relation to their techno-legal implications.

Francesca Musiani's "Walled Gardens or a Global Network?: Tensions, (De-)centralizations, and Pluralities of the Internet Model" has a more technical character. Starting from the Internet history, its architecture, and the principle of decentralization that qualified Internet genesis, it continues with new alternative Internet service approaches. Trying to identify how the Internet is technically shaped, it comes to the conclusion that it is based not on a single principle but rather on the coexistence of various actors.

Chapter 8, "National Security and U.S. Constitutional Rights: The Road to Snowden," examines the legislative and diplomatic scenery between cybersecurity and citizens' rights four years before the Snowden revelations. Richard B. Andres characterizes this scenery as one dominated by a classic "national security" versus "civil and property rights" debate, attempting on the one hand to determine to what extent concessions would be necessary for the U.S. protection and on the other hand who would make these concessions. This resulted in the militarization of cyberspace in the United States instead of finding a practical solution to the problem.

In chapter 9, "Attribution Policy in Cyberwar," Kalliopi Chainoglou examines how international law meets the twenty-first-century concerns regarding cyber attacks. The starting point is the cyber challenges posed to state sovereignty and state responsibility, and the technical and legal issues on state attribution. It moves on with the jus ad bellum perspective. The challenges to national sovereigns are crucial and not susceptible to a pure legal analysis. The ongoing discussions, however, on the applicability of the already existing rules are expected to provide the necessary clarifications.

Taking all the above into consideration, the analysis and reflection of this book's articles provide a constructive and holistic perspective to the reader regarding the challenges that cybersecurity faces in the light of human rights issues. If the term "cybersecurity" has no fixed meaning, but depends for its definition on the actor using it, this book does just the right thing: by showing the plurality of actors involved in this issue, but by repeating the human rights message throughout most pages, in particular the one about proper balancing and proportionality, it makes sure the message reaches its target. Given these facts, this book is qualified as a precious contribution to the ever-increasing and evolving cybersecurity issues, creating a field not only for academic reflection and discussion but also for practical solutions and answers in policy requests.

Paul De Hert, Vrije Universiteit Brussel, Tilburg University
codirector, Brussels Privacy Hub

Preface

The twenty-first century is the age of the global information society. It is a society in desperate need of rules and standards that will allow it to keep growing in peaceful coexistence. Without those the arguably greatest invention of the previous centennial, the World Wide Web, and the community that grew with it, is doomed to perish. Faced with the decentralized architecture of the network, all humans were once again proved equal, with no central power to stand guard of the agreed consensus on individual values, rights, and obligations. The decentralized network, designed to withstand a nuclear attack, proved resilient also to governmental influence or central management. While the expressive John Perry Barlow's 1996 *Declaration of the Independence of Cyberspace* can no longer be considered accurate, its notions of liberty and peer democracy still raise the hearts of the young and old alike, even more so when state authorities, including those representing nondemocratic regimes, reach out to hold Internet governance in their hand.

The global information community, formed of individuals, businesses, and authorities acting within their respective roles and limited capabilities, needs to find a new model for governance, one tailor-made for this unique network. While the search for the best Internet-governance model is still on, international human rights law has a solid foundation to offer for its operation. Because of the challenges posed by Internet governance in recent years, the human rights catalog gained arguably the most attention in the world's political agendas since its official recognition in 1948. Created to identify the basic traits of human dignity protected by laws everywhere, it gained new significance when those traits were under threat from new technologies. This is primarily seen in governments that introduce new tools to limit individual rights, such as the right to protect one's private information from unauthorized disclosure or to freely share one's opinions and ideas throughout all media. As was always the case in history, those restrictions are said to be put in place for the sake of protecting national interests and security. The new element of this age-old struggle is the fact that governments can no longer effectively introduce those restrictions alone—they need the help of other Internet-governance actors, above all, large Internet service providers. And as was always the case, individuals stand up against restrictions on their liberties. The new element in the contemporary global community, which is better organized than ever—whether it is the Arab Spring, fueled by social media, or the losing battle against alleged copyright infringers—is that individuals find effective ways to resist excessive restrictions of their liberties all over the world. A new balance between protecting national interests and individual liberties needs to be found for the global information society. This book is meant as a humble contribution to that pursuit. Indeed, human rights are sacrosanct, and any assertion that these could not exist in a particular setting is absolutely incorrect. Any doubt about their existence, even as a simple suggestion, is a mere attempt to deny existing rights to those who cannot defend or protect what belongs to them by birth. In the end, all stakeholders, but particularly governments, must exhibit authority with stewardship on behalf of all Internet users. Only by protecting that arrangement will history attest to the legitimacy of the governance process.

The book starts off with identifying the scope and limits of the overall term used as justification for new restrictions on individual freedoms: cybersecurity. Originally it was a technology term referring to the protection of electronic networks from security threats. According to the U.S. National Science and Technology Council, cybersecurity means the protection from unauthorized modification or destruction of systems, networks, or information, including systems of information authentication. The term also covers the assurance and the confidentiality of data transfers, meaning their protection from unauthorized access or disclosure of information, including also "timely and reliable access to and use of systems, networks and information."[1] Cybersecurity raises not only technical issues, such as identifying the systems and hardware in need of particular protection from cyberthreats (often referred to as "critical infrastructure"), but also crucial legal questions primarily relating to threats prevention and human rights, including the right to privacy and freedom of speech. This book aims to identify the thin line between cybersecurity measures required from states and nonstate parties, primarily private companies and the international law catalog of human rights as shaped by the late twentieth-century practice and jurisprudence. Particular emphasis is put on tracing the limits of individual human rights, such as the right to privacy or the right to access information and the contemporary state and company practice of data retention or content filtering. The contributors of this book have undertaken the demanding challenge to confront the rich academic work, jurisprudence, and practice in the area of human rights from the last sixty-five years with the most recent events that shook up global politics through the use of the Internet. As a result, the book offers unique contemporary perspectives on the limits of human rights online referring to the latest political events and case law, including the PRISM controversy, the planned European Union (EU) data-protection amendments, as well as the rich Internet-related case law of the European Court of Human Rights. It provides a freeze-frame legal analysis of the ongoing legal discourse on limits of global cyberveillance while serving as a reference for any future debate on the issue. The book is meant as an invitation to the ongoing discussion on the desired and needed shape of human rights online. The contributors hope that this invitation will be accepted by all those who care about the safety and liberty in the global network that revolutionized the world as we knew it.

NOTE

1. U.S. National Science and Technology Council, Interagency Working Group (IWG) on Cyber Security and Information Assurance (CSIA), *Federal Plan for Cyber Security and Information Assurance Research and Development: A Report* (Washington, DC: National Coordination Office for Networking and Information Technology Research and Development 2006), 3.

Acknowledgments

It is a pleasure to thank those who supported the work on this book and our work in the field of Internet law. To them we owe a debt of gratitude.

First, we would like to thank the editorial and production staff at Rowman & Littlefield. In particular, we want to thank Martin Dillon, consulting editor, and Lara Graham, associate editor, for all their help and guidance during the entire process.

We are indebted to the following individuals for their support: Jan Kulesza, assistant professor, Department of Criminal Law, University of Lodz, Poland; Paul De Hert, chair of criminal law, International and European Criminal Law, Vrije Universiteit Brussel, Belgium; Alfredo Garcia, dean and professor of law; Cecile Dykas, associate dean for academic affairs; and Sonia Luna-Lamas, associate director and head of technical services, St. Thomas University School of Law, Miami Gardens, Florida.

Lastly, we offer our deepest regards and gratitude to all of those not mentioned that supported us in any manner during the completion of the book.

Chapter One

Defining Cybersecurity

Critical Infrastructure and Public-Private Partnerships

Joanna Kulesza

CYBERSECURITY: AN AMBIGUOUS TERM

Cybersecurity is a notorious term on the mouths of everyone: from military officials, state politicians, and local media to private businesses—global, small, and medium—and everyday Internet users, concerned about their personal data and safety of personal banking online. While everyone uses it, as it has a serious and knowledgeable feel to it, they all mean different things when referring to "cybersecurity." For military personnel, cyberspace is yet another battlefield, and cybersecurity is a natural consequence of the need for national and international security, resilience, and capacity building. For politicians, it is a chance to show their awareness of raising challenges and care for national and global peace and security. For media, any cybersecurity breach is a pretext for predicting daunting future scenarios, attracting ever more readers, listeners, or viewers. For businesses, it is the necessity to effectively secure their resources, be it strictly monetary or any other digitized data, indispensable for running a business in the twenty-first century. Finally, for everyday Internet users, cybersecurity means the freedom to interact through the global network without threats to their property, privacy, or other personal rights. In this very brief introduction, it is clear that cybersecurity can be defined as both: a particular need or even a necessity for certain measures to be introduced and at the same time as a safeguard for particular opportunities and liberties. It is also clear that the problem touches upon nearly all actors of the international arena: state authorities, armies, international organizations, media, business, and individuals. It is a given that not only their visions of cybersecurity but also, most importantly, their needs and expectations toward it vary or directly contradict. While state authorities usually support the recommendations from the military and aim at designing and executing the most tightly knit network of technical and legal safeguards, considering security at the cost of individual freedoms, businesses, and individuals opt only for the necessary security measures, allowing for a relatively unrestrained exercise of personal liberties, such as freedom of speech, privacy, or economic liberties, including freedom of contract.

From a practical point of view, the problem of effective cybersecurity measures poses questions not only on the scope of subjects bound by security requirements and the contents of their obligations but also on the very definition of a cybersecurity threat, one that engages the necessary cybersecurity procedures. This chapter seeks to answer those questions, attempting to define the critical elements of the global network that need particular care and attention in order to prevent grave cyberthreats. At the time of the global war on terror in which the world finds itself at the beginning of the twenty-first century, one thing about cybersecurity is clear: it cannot be effectively achieved without global cooperation and universal standards enforced by all those potentially subjected to cyberthreats. While other chapters in this book are devoted to particular challenges posed by cybersecurity threats, this one will start off by identifying the intended goal behind "cybersecurity" and what it actually means. This will be done by looking at the existing notions of cybersecurity and the consequences they hold for international policies as well as for national laws.

CYBERCRIME, CYBERTHREATS, AND CYBERSECURITY

When discussing the notion of cybersecurity, two neighboring terms need to be mentioned: cybercrime and cyberthreats. Ideally a clear distinction among the three terms should be drawn. While the latter is a difficult task, one could generally rely on two criteria when attempting to identify such a distinction: the legal status of a certain activity, that is, whether it is penalized by national laws or not, and the fact that such an activity is exercised with the use of computers or computer networks.

Cybercrime

With that distinction in mind, one could say that the term "cybercrime" covers all those activities that have been sanctioned by national laws and involve the use of computers and/or computer networks. With numerous, multilateral or bilateral,[1] international agreements on cybercrime in place, no particular definition of a cybercrime exists, simply due to the fast-paced evolution of the Internet itself and, effectively, Internet-related crimes. The only international treaty dealing directly with cybercrime—the 2001 CoE

Cybercrime Convention[2]—also does not contain a definition of a cybercrime, referring solely to a number of activities considered "cybercrimes," as a representative, yet open, catalog. That was done intentionally by the treaty drafters, as they were well aware of the fast-paced evolution, specific to this particular sort of offenses. The individual "cybercrimes" named and defined in the convention include offenses against the "confidentiality, integrity and availability of computer data and systems" (title 1), including illegal access (article 2) and interception of computer data (article 3), interference of data (article 4) and system (article 5) interference, and production, distribution, and possession of devices used for committing such offenses (article 6); computer-related offenses (title 2), including computer forgery (article 7) and fraud (article 8); content-related offenses (title 3) that cover offenses related to child pornography (article 9); and, most controversial, offenses related to infringements of copyright and related rights (title 4, article 10).[3] Yet, as already mentioned, this catalog is an open one with ever more new crimes, or rather new ways of committing well-known offenses, being added thereto by national legislators.[4] With the domain of criminal law resting at the hands of national governments, one must refer to national laws when identifying an activity as a crime. Also, criminal prosecution remains the domain of national executive, regardless of enhanced international cooperation, such as that of the Europol or Interpol in place.[5] Therefore, when dealing with cybercrime one must keep in mind two crucial factors: the notions of cybercrime differ in individual jurisdictions, and their prosecution depends directly on effective international cooperation.[6] It is through unification of national laws and enhanced international cooperation that any success in the fight against cybercrime may be achieved.

Cybersecurity

Regardless of their national or regional definitions, all cybercrimes pose a direct threat to cybersecurity. Cybersecurity may be therefore defined as the need to undertake certain measures to protect computer networks and digital data from cybercrimes. Yet this seemingly simple definition is deficient for two reasons. First, not all states have introduced cybercrime regulations, and those introduced vary in scope, definitions, and above all, the level of enforcement. Moreover, there are other threats that involve computer networks and cause harm to individuals and businesses, which are not penalized by national legal systems, with the varying perceptions on spam, including phishing messages, serving as a prime example.[7] One of the key future challenges in fighting cybercrime is the effective protection of critical infrastructure, which can only be effective when executed in solid alliance with the private sector.[8]

Based on this brief analysis, one could define cybersecurity as all measures aimed at protecting computer networks and digitized data from cyberthreats, including cybercrimes and other harmful activities. This definition might however seem too broad for the purpose of this book. While introducing a national, regional, or global standard for national authorities to protect their residents and nationals online or for companies to protect the data of their customers may rightfully be considered a legitimate cybersecurity measure, installing antivirus software on a teenager's computer by their parents ought not, even though both serve the same purpose. It seems therefore that the definition of cybersecurity, should it be useful, ought to cover only those threats that potentially bring harm to more than one individual—preferably a large number of people—or hold the potential to inflict significant material damage. Those are the security measures that are discussed when national or international cybersecurity is at stake, and those should attract our attention in this book. Therefore cybersecurity may be defined as all measures aimed at protecting computer networks and digitized data from cyberthreats, including cybercrimes and other harmful activities, which may bring harm to a large number of individuals or hold a risk of significant material damage.

CYBERSECURITY AND CRITICAL INFRASTRUCTURE: THE ACTORS

Critical Infrastructure

When defining cybersecurity, the biggest challenge is identifying the entities under particular cybersecurity obligations. This can only be done once the potential targets of such cyberthreats are named. As explained above, when referring to "significant" damage or a large number of individuals at risk as a necessary precondition for defining cybersecurity, one naturally turns to such infrastructure and systems the malfunction of which imminently meets this criterion. There is no need however to seek elements of this infrastructure anew, solely for the purpose of this chapter. National civil defense theory and practice have long recognized what is being referred to as "critical infrastructure," a term covering means of mass transportation, water, or electricity supplies and the like.

The European Commission refers to critical infrastructure as "an asset or system which is essential for the maintenance of vital societal functions."[9] The legal definition used in EU law describes "critical infrastructure" as "asset, system or part thereof located in Member States which is essential for the maintenance of vital societal functions, health, safety, security, economic or social well-being of people, and the disruption or destruction of which would have a significant impact in a Member State as a result of the failure to maintain those functions."[10]

The European Critical Infrastructure (ECIs) Directive provides detailed guidelines on identifying elements of critical infrastructure and setting particular obligations on its operators, including running a risk analysis for those particularly vulnerable assets.[11] Those obligations are set to provide the maximum level of security and resiliency of systems crucial for European security.

Critical infrastructure is similarly defined for the purposes of the U.S. Homeland Security Office, which describes it as "the assets, systems, and networks," both physical and digital, which are so important to the state that "their incapacitation or destruction would have a debilitating effect on security, national economic security, national public health or safety, or any combination thereof."[12] In the United States, the protection of critical infrastructure is guided by the 2013 Presidential Policy Directive 21 (PPD-21) on "Critical Infrastructure Security and Resilience," which refers to sixteen distinct sectors of critical infrastructure.[13]

The Organisation for Economic Cooperation and Development (OECD) takes on a somewhat different approach, looking cumulatively at threats to critical infrastructure, regardless of their origin, be it natural disasters or illicit online activities. The latest in a series of OECD documents on critical infrastructure protection includes a broad definition of "critical risks" that covers "threats and hazards" resulting in "the most strategically significant risk," yet originate from "sudden onset events" such as "earthquakes, industrial accidents, terrorist attacks, pandemics, illicit trade or organized crime."[14] It recommends a "whole-of-society approach" requiring the participation of governments, business, and individuals in actions aimed at preventing threats to critical infrastructure. This description seems well fitted to the multistakeholder model reflective of the online environment discussed in this chapter. A specific recommendation refers to "creating models for public-private partnerships" in order to create reliable models of exchanging information crucial to maintaining security, with a particularly significant role granted to private, rather than public, actors.[15]

Among the infrastructures requiring scrupulous attention, the OECD Recommendation names "critical infrastructure networks" that include "energy, transportation, telecommunications and information systems."[16] Encouraging business to enhance their security preparedness, the documents reference risk analysis and joint development of security standards.[17] Although non-binding, the OECD document can serve as a prime example of the current trend in cybersecurity—the emphasis placed on private actors and the crucial need for enhanced multistakeholder cooperation. Even more so than in matters of policy setting, the definition of "critical infrastructure" raises controversy in academia. Some authors go as far as to link "critical infrastructure" directly to "industrial networks," defining the former as "critical *systems and assets* used within" any network "operating some sort of automated control system that communicates digitally over a network."[18] Yet as evidently not all critical infrastructure is equipped with an Internet connection, one ought to clarify that only parts of open networks, such as the Internet, would fall within the scope of this analysis, leaving all internal networks (intranets) beyond the scope of this chapter. While online connectivity may play a minor role in the operation of an industrial network, possibly added solely for the convenience of the employees running it, still all equipment connected to the Internet and used for operating critical infrastructure should automatically be subject to enhanced (cyber) security concerns. That is due to the fact that any Internet connectivity of a critical industrial network enables potential attackers to directly access and debilitate it.[19]

INDUSTRIAL MECHANICS

When addressing critical infrastructure operated within industrial networks,[20] Supervisory Control and Data Acquisition (SCADA) and Distributed Control System (DCS) systems, most often deployed for rendering mass services, ought to be given particular attention.[21] As some authors argue, it is the SCADA systems in particular that are most vulnerable to cyberthreats, more so than any other element of critical infrastructure.[22] Clay Wilson argues that since SCADA vulnerabilities and exploits are openly published, they are the easiest target for possible attacks. This fact is also being used for state-sponsored intrusions, with countries developing weapons targeted at SCADA systems in particular.[23] The risk is often enhanced because of the fact that highly skilled cybersecurity and software experts are rarely employed on SCADA systems directly,[24] with crucial competence left at the hands of mechanical, rather than computer, engineers. Moreover, the cybersecurity services offered by SCADA producers fall significantly behind those provided by other software companies, with updates and patches published infrequently and requiring extensive testing.[25] Hence when cybersecurity is being discussed, it is the SCADA-based industrial systems that ought to be given particular care along with the entities operating them endowed with their respective security obligations.[26] SCADA systems security should therefore lie at the heart rather than at the outskirts of all cybersecurity plans. It is this particular kind of controls that are used for the majority of systems deployed for critical infrastructures, including those applied for delivering water, energy, or manage mass communications.

INTERNET SERVICE PROVIDERS

Beyond industrial mechanics the second group of businesses obliged to undertake particular cybersecurity measures are those providing Internet services, in particular those responsible for Internet connectivity. This broad category referred to as Internet service providers (ISPs) is most discussed when cybersecurity is at stake, primarily because they are the obvious actors to be held responsible for any Internet security breaches. This instinctive reaction, although often not justified—because it is the users, private or corporate, who are to blame for intrusions—has significantly changed the legal and technical situation of ISPs in recent years, with enhanced cybersecurity and cyber resilience legislation as well as growing expectations targeted at their activities.[27]

For academic purposes, providers offering Internet-related services may be identified as access providers, caching providers, host providers, and content providers, depending on the kind of service or services they enable, where clearly one entity can play two or more roles simultaneously.[28] While detailing individual obligations of each ISP group would provide material for a separate chapter, it suffices to say that they all are under growing pressure and increasing obligations to introduce appropriate cybersecurity measures. The ongoing discussion covers three crucial points:

1. *The potential need for a conclusive rather than an open list of ISPs obliged to introduce particular cybersecurity measures.* The current trend is for creating open lists of such entities, ones referring to categories of services or operated infrastructures considered critical, rather than a conclusive list of business sectors, services, or service providers. This is due to two factors: the fast-changing nature of all Internet-related issues—a conclusive list risks becoming outdated by the time it is completed; and a significant resilience from the ISP community itself, not willing to be subjected to additional, costly security obligations, going beyond what the business itself finds sufficient. Those arguments are well justified: an open list of cybersecurity-bound entities leaves much room for speculation on the scope and content of actually required measures and, primarily, their subjects. Practical solutions come rather from national, regional, and international business practices, than state legislation that is limited to setting general obligations and nonbinding, inconclusive guidelines.[29]

2. *The question of particular cybersecurity measures to be enacted by ISPs in respective business areas.* While it remains clear that all ISPs must undertake certain network resiliency and data-protection measures, with particular emphasis on users' data and privacy, there remains the challenge of identifying the manner in which information

significant for cybersecurity measures ought to be exchanged.[30] Businesses are reluctant to share information about vulnerabilities used by the attackers for conducting cyber attacks against them as well as about methods of identifying such threats or breaches. Sharing the latter might give undesired business advantage to the competition or reveal trade secrets.

3. *The problem of operational costs brought about by enhanced cybersecurity measures, with ISPs requesting financial support from governments in order to facilitate the growing demand for new cybersecurity tools, procedures, software, and hardware.* So far governments have been reluctant in offering any financial support to ISPs, laying the material burden of cybersecurity measures on the business and, indirectly, on the users. An exemplary list of businesses endowed with particular cybersecurity obligations may be derived from, for example, currently drafted EU regulations. The prime example of such eagerly discussed regulation is the 2013 draft Directive on Network and Information Security (NIS Directive).[31] The general goal of the regulation, declared by the European Commission is that of "requiring the Member States to increase their preparedness and improve their cooperation with each other, and by requiring operators of critical infrastructures, such as energy, transport, and key providers of information society services (e-commerce platforms, social networks, etc.), as well as public administrations to adopt appropriate steps to manage security risks and report serious incidents to the national competent authorities."[32]

The proposal refers to entities endowed with particular cybersecurity obligations as "market operators," a term that covers "providers of information society services which enable the provision of other information society services" as well as "operators of critical infrastructure that are essential for the maintenance of vital economic and societal activities in the fields of energy, transport, banking, stock exchanges, and health."[33] A nonexhaustive list of elements of both those categories is annexed to the draft and includes "e-commerce platforms, Internet payment gateways, social networks, search engines, cloud computing services, [and] application stores"; businesses dealing with energy, including electricity and gas suppliers; distribution system operators and retailers; storage operators; transmission system operators in electricity; "oil transmission pipelines and oil storage" as well as "operators of oil and natural gas production, refining and treatment facilities"; transportation, such as air and maritime carriers, railways, airports, ports, traffic management control operators; and auxiliary logistics services, including warehousing, storage, and cargo handling.[34] The list also includes banking services, covering credit institutions, stock exchanges, and health-sector facilities, such as hospitals, private clinics, and other health-care facilities.[35]

CYBERSECURITY ACTORS AND OBJECTIVES

As stated above, cybersecurity is of crucial concern to critical infrastructure operators. With enhancing legal obligations laid upon them by national laws and international business practice, those operating infrastructure used for offering mass services, such as water or energy supplies, mass transportation, banking, or telecommunication services need to introduce appropriate risk-assessment tools and keep up with latest security developments in their field. When those infrastructures are connected to any open computer network, such as the Internet, their security concerns are enhanced by their cyber dimension. They need to secure the assets and data they use not only from unauthorized intrusion by, for example, a disgruntled former employee, or unforeseen circumstances such as natural disasters, but also from unauthorized online access. Appropriate software and cybersecurity procedures need to be introduced by all those operating critical infrastructure with an open network connectivity.

Network Architecture, Multistakeholderism, and Cybersecurity

The *Tallinn Manual*, a fundamental publication for the legal analysis of cybersecurity and international law, defines critical infrastructure as all systems and assets, physical and virtual, within a nation-state's jurisdiction that "are so vital that their incapacitation or destruction may debilitate a State's security, economy, public health or safety or the environment."[36] It differentiates however "critical infrastructure" from "cyber infrastructure," whereas the latter covers all "communication, storage and computing resources upon which information systems operate," including the Internet, as an example of "global information infrastructure."[37] Effectively, critical Internet infrastructure covers all "communication, storage and computing resources," comprising the Internet, which are crucial to a state's security, its economy, public safety, or environment. The term can and ought to be understood in the context of critical infrastructure, discussed above, yet as its additional, significant element. As already mentioned, the notion of national and international security is dynamically changing. What once was the domain of state military is now being confronted with enhanced privatization. Whether one looks at the U.S. PRISM program, aimed at gathering intelligence on telecommunications users, or at international espionage, all the crucial information lies at the hands of private companies, ISPs, in particular, those operating critical cyber infrastructure. With the fall of the Berlin Wall, nation-state involvement in all business sectors, including telecommunication services, declined in many countries around the world. One might even risk saying that governments holding a firm grip on national telecommunication and media are in decline.[38] The role of states in running national telecommunication services was further limited by enhancing globalization, which brought the liberation of the telecommunications market, now largely owned by a few global providers. At the same time, global companies shape their policies not only to reflect national laws but also more significantly to mirror global customer demand and economic trends. This tendency is particularly visible when it comes to the Internet and online services. Whether one looks at notice-and-takedown procedures or privacy policies introduced by market leaders such as YouTube or Facebook, operating on the global market, it is primarily consumer demand rather than shifting jurisdictional capacity of nation-states that influences executive decisions.[39] This unique crowdsourcing of company policies is a direct result of the distributed architecture of the network. Designed with resilience against a central attack, the Internet has no headquarters from where it can be "steered" or managed. Therefore the term "Internet governance" rather than "management" is commonly used to describe the complex processes behind the running code. While the notion of Internet governance and multistakeholderism is subject to a separate chapter in this volume, to fully understand the need for cooperation in the field of cybersecurity one ought to briefly summarize those two key terms.[40]

In 2005, the World Summit on the Information Society (WSIS) defined Internet governance as "the development and application by governments, the private sector and civil society, in their respective roles, of shared principles, norms, rules, decision-making procedures, and programs that shape the evolution and use of the Internet."[41] Despite its deficiencies, such as the practical difficulty in separating those "respective roles" of the three key actors, the definition is a just reflection of the complexity held by the decentralized network architecture. In order to effectively introduce and execute any efficient "principles, norms, rules, decision-making procedures, and programmes" for the online environment, it is necessary to grant an active involvement for those three crucial groups of actors: "governments, the private sector and civil society."[42] With this characteristic in mind, the basic principle of Internet governance—the principle of multistakeholderism—is easy to describe. As some authors have explained, the network might be seen as a composite of concentric layers.[43] The innermost of the physical layers consist of telecommunication cables, satellites, and computer hardware, indispensable for an Internet connection to physically work.

Such infrastructure is usually subject to private ownership by telecommunication companies. Despite interesting academic proposals to ensure Internet connectivity by expropriating those companies for the sake of making the Internet part of the common heritage of mankind,[44] private ownership of the Internet backbone must be considered a preliminary condition for securing any online communication. The middle, logical layer on the other hand is quite different in its structure. It is comprised of software enabling the hardware to connect and runs on Internet standards proposed and enacted by the Internet community itself—with only some input from telecommunication companies and governments. This process is well visible in the work of the Internet Engineering Task Force (IETF), initially called upon by the U.S. government to solve technical issues of the network's everyday operation. Any standard setting done by the IETF is through the voluntary Requests for Comments (RFCs). Those working recommendations deal with individual problems encountered by members of the community. When a particular challenge is identified, a request for comments on how it might be solved is issued on the IETF website. An ensuing discussion allows to identify a consensus on a particular technical standard applicable to all the devices working online. In the context of this volume it is important to note that the RFCs are not legal acts. They are developed and deployed solely as technical standards, although their status has been compared to that of the law of cyberspace.[45] If users or application developers wish for their device or software to work online, they need to follow the technical recommendations included in the RFCs. The IETF, formally an element of the Internet Society, operates primarily on a voluntary basis, with income from membership fees, and remains open to all those interested in how the global network operates.[46] Despite having no legal subjectivity, it is one of the key players on the Internet governance arena, representative of how the middle layer of code operates. It clearly shows that the power to introduce technical standards cannot be monopolized by national authorities or international organizations. Neither can it be run by telecommunication companies, who may encourage their agents to follow the IETF and take active part in its works; yet it must meet the rules of the forum in order to effectively shape its guidelines. At the same time it must be noted that the IETF is not the only entity creating telecommunications standards. Other key actors in the field include the ITU-T,[47] a section of the International Telecommunication Union, an intergovernmental organization, which is reluctant to introduce nongovernmental bodies into its system, and ICANN—the Internet Corporation for Assigned Names and Numbers, a California based nonprofit corporation that is currently the best representation of how multistakeholder governance works in practice. ICANN has been designed to include all Internet-governance actors in the process of shaping Internet-related policies, including those who focus primarily on the most outer, content layer of the Internet. The content layer covers all the information and data available online, the aspect of the network most valuable to Internet users and governments alike. The former is interested in getting access to as much content as possible, while the latter is on the lookout for any content that might represent a threat to state security, local notions of morality, public order, or what is being described with the popular yet vague term *raison d'état*. Those two groups represent clearly conflicting interests and, as has been noted above, those interests can only be catered for through the involvement of the key actors in the technical and logical sphere of the Internet. It is impossible to shape Internet content without the understanding and supervision over the networks standards and its hardware. Since there is no central control point for the Internet, any attempt at regulating online activity can only be affected by the joint efforts of all the actors named above. That is also true in the case of cybersecurity—any effective security measure must meet the approval of and be followed by all actors involved in the operation of the network. Effective cybersecurity requires a comprehensive and operational multistakeholder model.

SUMMARY: CYBERSECURITY THROUGH PUBLIC-PRIVATE PARTNERSHIPS

The term "multistakeholderism" has become a dreaded word in the Internet-governance circles: among academics, telecommunication professionals, and civil society activists alike. Not only is it vague, but also implementing any form of a fully functional, transparent, and comprehensive multistakeholder governance model has proven nearly impossible in the almost twenty years since the creation of ICANN—the flagship for multistakeholder Internet governance.[48] It seems as if creating one single multistakeholder forum for solving all Internet-related matters is a tale of the past. The Internet Governance Forum was created by the United Nations in 2006 to serve this very purpose. Nearly a decade after its creation, one may safely say it has not gained the key role of the main discussion forum for all the Internet-governance-related matters it was initially designed to serve. Its open-talk-shop formula works as far as discussing ideas and values is concerned; it fails however when any significant decisions are to be taken. Those are usually affected in the old-fashioned way: during diplomatic conferences or through international organizations. Yet with the growing role of private actors in governing the network, the private-public partnership model for Internet-governance-related decisions cannot be disregarded. This also seems to be the case for cybersecurity. All the documents referred to above emphasize the role of private actors in ensuring cybersecurity. International practice clearly proves that without the cooperation among public authorities and private Internet service providers no effective security measures can be introduced. The "all necessary measures" required from states and businesses alike to ensure cybersecurity refers to a notion well known to international law and relations. It is a term most common to international environmental law, which operates primarily through public-private partnerships.[49] Any standard setting is based on expert reviews and is made through industry participation. The due diligence required from states and businesses in the area of environmental law is a well-designed paradigm, put into much detail by academia, jurisprudence, and international practice.[50] Private-public partnerships are also one of the pillars of international business law, where good-business-practice sharing and benchmarking are primary tools for international cooperation and standard setting.[51] To follow the OECD guideline on cybersecurity, what is needed is a "whole-of-society approach," with the active participation "of all stakeholders, from individuals to government entities, businesses, non-governmental organisations and the third sector."[52] The organization recommends enhancing the creation of public-private partnerships by developing "trusted information sharing networks . . . and supply chains," while "taking advantage of private sector capability and expertise to develop new technologies, build resilient infrastructure and deliver financial mechanisms." With cybersecurity clearly at the top of national and international agendas of all Internet-governance-related issues, this sectored approach to Internet governance, with a focus on enhancing network resilience, is best suited to the needs of the early twenty-first century. Effective cybersecurity cannot be enforced by governments alone—it must be ensured through public-private cooperation. At the same time it must be kept in mind that there is no security without liberty. Any cybersecurity standard-setting must include a thorough reference to international human rights standards, both general and those referring to particular individual rights and liberties, such as privacy or free speech. The rich body of international law provides detailed guidelines on both: necessary due diligence measures in preventing transboundary cyberthreats and necessary minimum standards for individual human rights. Any model for cybersecurity protection must therefore, next to detailed technical standards and practical obligations, reflect the need for human rights guarantees.[53]

NOTES

1. The only multilateral treaty in force dealing directly with cybercrime is the Council of Europe Convention on Cybercrime, 2001, ETS No. 185 (hereafter the CoE Cybercrime Convention). Yet other forms of international cooperation in various fields deal with the very issue, just to mention the Europol unit on cybercrime: European Cybercrime Centre (EC3) or the Interpol program on cybercrime. There are also numerous bilateral treaties on police and crime enforcement cooperation covering the issue of cybercrime, with the most recent trend of cybercrime related in bilateral investment treaties; see, for example, Scott J. Shackelford, Eric L. Richards, Anjanette H. Raymond, and Amanda N. Craig, "Using BITs to Protect Bytes: Promoting Cyber Peace by Safeguarding Trade Secrets through Bilateral Investment Treaties," *American Business Law Journal* 52, no. 1 (2015): 1–74.

2. See note 1.

3. The controversy surrounding title 4 of the CoE Cybercrime Convention originates from a strong conviction of some state authorities and civil society representatives that a criminal persecution of copyright offenses ought not be enforced in the same way as, for example, child pornography or identity theft, as the former covers primarily material damage, while the latter

deals with protecting individual rights, such as one's dignity or personal identity. The inclusion of a copyright regulation in the body of the convention, pushed for by the United States, was one of the reasons the convention never achieved a high level of ratifications (as per February 26, 2015, the treaty has been ratified by forty-five countries, including six non-CoE members, as the treaty is open to signature also to states not represented in the council). It ought to be noted that the original controversies, including the one mentioned, as well as the growing and changing threat of new cybercrimes, are the key reasons behind the current work of the council aimed at amending the treaty.

4. For a detailed analysis of new cyberthreats, see, for example, Babak Akhgar, Andrew Staniforth, and Francesca Bosco, *Cyber Crime and Cyber Terrorism Investigator's Handbook* (Waltham, MA: Syngress, 2014), 24–29.

5. See note 1.

6. Vogel names six key challenges to fighting cybercrime that include (1) its definition, (2) the question of applicable jurisdiction, resulting in (3) the need for well-coordinated transnational investigations as well as (4) the need for enhanced international cooperation, (5) the necessity to recognize the significance of public-private partnerships, and (6) the growing demand for effective prevention. See Joachim Vogel, "Towards a Global Convention against Cybercrime," *ReAIDP/e-RIAPL* C-07 (2008): 1–10.

7. National approaches to unsolicited commercial e-mail can be identified as either "opt in" or "opt out," requesting the recipients to explicitly agree to (opt in) or protest against (opt out) receiving such commercial messages. While the first option is enforced in European Union law in, for example, European Commission Directive 2002/58/EC of the European Parliament and of the Council of July 12, 2002, concerning the Processing of Personal Data and the Protection of Privacy in the Electronic Communications Sector (Directive on Privacy and Electronic Communications, OJ L 201, 2002), article 13, the latter is the legislative standard for, for example, the United States with its 2003 CAN-SPAM Act (15 U.S.C. chap. 103). Spam takes up over a half of global e-mail traffic, raising costs for service providers and users alike.

8. See, for example, Robert Anderson Jr., "Cyber Security, Terrorism, and Beyond: Addressing Evolving Threats to the Homeland," Statement before the Senate Committee on Homeland Security and Governmental Affairs, September 10, 2014, http://www.fbi.gov/.

9. European Commission, Critical Infrastructure, Migration and Home Affairs, last updated June 23, 2015, http://ec.europa.eu/; see also European Commission, Communication from the Commission on a European Programme for Critical Infrastructure Protection (2006), final and documents mentioned therein, in particular the Commission Staff Working Document on the Review of the European Programme for Critical Infrastructure Protection (EPCIP) (2012) and the Council Directive 2008/114/EC of December 8, 2008, on the Identification and Designation of European Critical Infrastructures and the Assessment of the Need to Improve Their Protection, OJ L 345, 23.12 (2008), 75–82 (hereafter ECIs Directive).

10. ECIs Directive, article 2.

11. ECIs Directive, articles 3–5. Effectively, the European critical infrastructures include "1) energy installations and networks; 2) communications and information technology; 3) finance; 4) health care; 5) food; 6) water (dams, storage, treatment and networks); 7) transport (airports, ports, intermodal facilities, railway and mass transit networks and traffic control systems); 8) production, storage and transport of dangerous goods (e.g., chemical, biological, radiological and nuclear materials); [and] 9) government (e.g., critical services, facilities, information networks, assets and key national sites and monuments)." See European Commission, Critical Infrastructure Protection (2004), http://europa.eu/.

12. U.S. Office of Homeland Security, "What Is Critical Infrastructure?" 2013, last updated August 26, 2015, http://www.dhs.gov/.

13. Those critical sectors include the chemical sector; commercial facilities; communications; "critical manufacturing"; dams; defense industrial base; emergency services; energy; financial services; food and agriculture; government facilities; healthcare and public health; information technology; nuclear reactors, materials, and waste; transportation systems; and water and wastewater systems. See White House, Office of the Press Secretary, "Presidential Policy Directive: Critical Infrastructure Security and Resilience," February 12, 2013, http://

www.whitehouse.gov/. Those are almost identical as those defined by the ECIs Directive (see article 2).

14. OECD, Recommendation of the Council on the Governance of Critical Risks (2014; hereafter OECD GCR). Earlier documents include the Recommendation on the Protection of Critical Information Infrastructures (2008), the Recommendation of the Council concerning Chemical Accident Prevention, Preparedness and Response (1988), and the Recommendation of the Council concerning Guidelines for the Security of Information Systems and Networks: Towards a Culture of Security (2002).

15. OECD GCR, para. III.5 i).

16. OECD GCR, para. IV.2. i).

17. OECD GCR, para. IV.3.

18. See Eric D. Knapp and Joel Thomas Langill, *Industrial Network Security: Securing Critical Infrastructure Networks for Smart Grid, Scada, and Other Industrial Control Systems* (Waltham, MA: Elsevier, 2015), 26.

19. One might point however to the 2010 Stuxnet worm incident, which caused substantial damage to Iranian uranium enrichment facilities. The virus was distributed online, yet the very infrastructure at Natanz, which it was designed to target, had no direct Internet connection. As is often the case, it was the human factor that failed with one of the employees infecting the network with malware they unwarily imported through an infected USB stick. See David E. Sanger, "Obama Order Sped Up Wave of Cyberattacks against Iran," *New York Times*, June 1, 2012, http://www.nytimes.com/; and John Markoff, "Malware Aimed at Iran Hit Five Sites, Report Says," *New York Times*, February 11, 2011, http://www.nytimes.com/.

20. Knapp and Langill refer to Industrial Control Systems (ICS) as covering both: SCADA and DCS (Knapp and Langill, *Industrial Network Security*, 1).

21. For a detailed analysis of these kinds of systems, which include natural gas pipelines, nuclear plants, water systems, and oil refineries, see, for example, Ronald L. Krutz, *Securing SCADA Systems* (Indianapolis: Wiley, 2005), 23–41.

22. I. N. Fovino, A. Coletta, A. Carcano, and M. Masera, "Critical State-Based Filtering System for Securing SCADA Network Protocols," *IEEE Transactions on Industrial Electronics* 59, no. 10 (2012): 3943–50; Clay Wilson, "Industrial and SCADA Systems May Be Increasingly Targeted for Cyberattack," University of Maryland University College, December 22, 2012, http://www.pesolutions-it.com/.

23. Wilson, "Industrial and SCADA Systems," 5. The allegedly U.S.- and Israeli-sponsored 2010 Stuxnet worm attack against Iran was a SCADA-aimed one (see Sanger, "Obama Order").

24. Wilson, "Industrial and SCADA Systems," 7.

25. Ibid.

26. For similar argument, see also Krutz, *Securing SCADA Systems*, 73–88, arguing that SCADA-operated industrial facilities are highly vulnerable to terrorist attacks or those enacted by rogue/former employees.

27. For a detailed discussion on the role of Internet intermediaries, see chapter 5, by Monica Horten, in this book.

28. For a discussion on the significance of such a categorization, see, for example, Thomas Hoeren, "The European Liability and Responsibility of Providers of Online Platforms such as 'Second Life,'" *Journal of Information Law and Technology* 1 (2009), http://www2.warwick.ac.uk/. A similar distinction was introduced in the EU Directive on e-commerce. See Directive 2000/31/EC of the European Parliament and of the Council of June 8, 2000, on Certain Legal Aspects of Information Society Services, in Particular Electronic Commerce, in the Internal Market (Directive on electronic commerce, OJ L 178, 17.7.2000), articles 12–15.

29. For an example of good business practice, see the work provided by Vangelis Ouzounis, "Resilience of Networks and Services and Critical Information Infrastructure Protection," European Union Agency for Network and Information Security (ENISA), accessed August 28, 2015, https://www.enisa.europa.eu/. Good business practice is being facilitated through non-binding cybersecurity standards offered also by the International Standardisation Organisation (ISO standards 27001 and 27002), Information Security Forum (ISF; the regularly updated "Standard of Good Practice"), and the Internet Engineering Task Force (IETF); through their

Requests for Comments (RFCs), starting with the 1997 RFC 2196. The above-named activities and documents are only meant to serve as examples and are not intended as a complete or a representative list.

30. For a discussion on cybersecurity threats to privacy, see chapter 4, by Rolf H. Weber and Dominic N. Staiger, in this book.

31. European Commission Proposal for a Directive of the European Parliament and of the Council concerning Measures to Ensure a High Common Level of Network and Information Security across the Union, COM (2013), 48 (hereafter NIS).

32. NIS, explanatory memorandum, p. 2.

33. NIS, article 3, part (8).

34. NIS, annex II.

35. Ibid.

36. Michael N. Schmitt, ed., *Tallinn Manual on the International Law Applicable to Cyberwarfare* (Cambridge: Cambridge University Press, 2013), 258.

37. Ibid.

38. That is not to say that the notion of state propaganda is no longer accurate. It was the German chancellor Otto von Bismarck who back in the nineteenth century coined the term "Reptilienfonds" ("reptile fund," slush fund) to signify state funds dispensed to sponsor seemingly objective media publications favorable to the government. The concept of "reptile funds" and "reptile press" is still very much alive, just as any other form of state propaganda. There is however a difference between state-owned media or a legal ban on access to any "unauthorized" news sources and a particular economic policy enforced by media outlets, choosing to serve the government in a particular way within a democratic society. For a detailed analysis on media freedom around the world, the annual report by Reporters without Borders is a trustworthy resource: "World Press Freedom Index 2014," accessed August 29, 2015, http://rsf.org/.

39. The United States, the base for many Internet companies, is the exception to this rule, being able to enforce its laws onto numerous Internet leaders such as Google or AT&T, as proven by the PRISM controversy.

40. For a discussion on multistakeholderism, see chapter 6, by M. I. Franklin, in this book.

41. WSIS, "Tunis Agenda for the Information Society," November 18, 2005, http://www.itu.int/.

42. Ibid.

43. Yochai Benkler, *The Wealth of Networks: How Social Production Transforms Markets and Freedom* (New Haven, CT: Yale University Press, 2006), 392; Janet Abbate, *Inventing the Internet* (Cambridge, MA: MIT Press, 1999), 151–53; L. Lessig, *Code: Version 2.0* (New York: Basic Books, 2006), 144.

44. Antonio Segura-Serrano, "Internet Regulation: A Hard-Law Proposal," New York University School of Law, Jean Monnet Working Paper 10 (2006): 31–51.

45. Lawrence Lessig, *Code: And Other Laws of Cyberspace* (New York: Ashgate, 1999), 5.

46. H. Alvestrand, "Request for Comments: 3935; A Mission Statement for the IETF," Cisco Systems, October 2004, http://www.ietf.org/.

47. The ITU Telecommunication Standardization Sector (ITU-T) works through Recommendations (ITU-T Recs). See "ITU-T Recommendations," International Telecommunication Union (ITU), accessed September 1, 2015, http://www.itu.int/.

48. For a discussion on multistakeholderism, see chapter 6, by M. I. Franklin, in this book.

49. K. Bäckstrand, "Accountability of Networked Climate Governance: The Rise of Transnational Climate Partnerships," *Global Environmental Politics* 8, no. 3 (2008): 74–102.

50. Riccardo Pisillo Mazzeschi, "The Due Diligence Rule and the Nature of the International Responsibility of States," *German Yearbook of International Law* 35 (1992). 9.

51. Tanja A. Börzel and Thomas Risse, "Public-Private Partnerships: Effective and Legitimate Tools of International Governance?" in *Complex Sovereignty: On the Reconstitution of Political Authority in the 21st Century*, ed. Edgar Grande and Louis W. Pauly (Toronto: University of Toronto Press, 2007), 205.

52. OECD GCR, para. I.

53. On the interconnection between cybersecurity and human rights, see chapter 3, by Roy Balleste, in this volume.

Chapter Two

Cybersecurity and State Responsibility

Identifying a Due Diligence Standard for Prevention of Transboundary Threats

Dimitrios Delibasis

Cyber attacks defeat the basic national security paradigm that has existed in our country since the early nineteenth century.
—Colonel Chester H. Morgan (SJA/USAF Office of Special Investigations) [1]

In this chapter, I will attempt to establish a link between the rules on state responsibility and computer network attacks and assess the potential for using it as a possible reference point for developing a set of rules specifically tailored to regulate such attacks.

CYBERWARFARE AND THE AGE OF THE MARKET STATE

As the world enters the second decade of the twenty-first century, the "nation-state" and, along with it, the specific form of warfare it has given rise to appears to have practically completed its cycle. The end of the Cold War, which brought the great ideological confrontations of the twentieth century to a close, combined with the rapid advancements in technology that gave birth to the "global village," have marked the initial stage of a transition to a new international legal order. This new order could be best defined as the era of the technologically advanced and globally networked "market state," [2] which is almost totally dependent for its existence on the international capital markets and the modern multinational business network. [3]

This new transition is also being reflected in the rise of cyberwarfare activity, which has become global, networked, and decentralized and above all is no more constrained by any physical borders, or domestic jurisdictions, similar to the market state it resembles. We are essentially facing a new form of warfare, which capitalizes on the market state's ability to empower individual opportunity through outsourcing and global networking, and that at the same time renders modern societies vulnerable by also allowing access to their critical infrastructures. Due to the fact that they are now interconnected and can also be accessed by third parties, such infrastructures are now more vulnerable than they have ever been.[4] Along with the economic context, globalization has also transformed the strategic and legal context in which states operate by giving rise to a new threat against which there can be very little defense, even if a state's borders are secured. The advent of the market state has redefined the traditional concept of warfare by providing state and nonstate actors with an opportunity to employ weapons, tactics, and strategies that historically used to be a state monopoly. Advances in modern technology, especially in modern information technology, have allowed even small and isolated private groups to deliver devastating attacks against national critical infrastructures and more importantly against civilian populations, even in the world's most powerful countries.

As part of this latest evolutionary phase, warfare is currently moving from activities that were almost entirely state sponsored and therefore led to an often strong leverage on the part of their sponsors, to activities that can now comprise a global networked aspect as a result of which they now have more power than ever before to influence the various states they are linked to, with Al-Qaeda being perhaps the best example of this newly appeared situation.[5] Furthermore, by having to rely for their existence on the same global networks that have given rise to the market state and not anymore on state support, modern cyberspace warriors have finally managed to release themselves from the various constraints that states used to impose upon them in order to keep their activities under check, thus avoiding any unnecessary political complications. This has led to a new form of warfare that is supposedly more violent and more unpredictable than ever before.

These are the most important features that distinguish cyberwarfare operations from previous evolutionary phases of warfare. As Rand senior analyst Brian Michael Jenkins notes,[6] in the era of the nation-state, both state and nonstate actors of aggression wanted a lot of people watching, not a lot of people dead. In direct analogy with the international legal order that gave birth to it, "nation-state" warfare, deeply embedded in its ideological identity, which often took many shapes and forms, always depending on where relevant allegiances laid, was more intent on delivering a political message rather than causing great amounts of civilian casualties.[7] As a matter of fact, civilian casualties, especially if they were excessive, could undermine not only the long-term goals nation-state actors of aggression were trying to achieve but also their cohesiveness and even their very own existence, as it could make them unpopular to their respective governments or to those sponsoring their activities. In the era of nation-state warfare, any activities resulting in large civilian losses would be counterproductive at best. They would only result in internal friction with members of the international community that were not in approval of this sort of action; the potential loss of support from potential sponsors, which during the Cold War had always been careful not to exceed a particular threshold of violence; and lastly, the inevitable crackdown from the governments that may find themselves at the receiving end of any such activities.

The exact opposite is true with regard to cyberwarfare, the most important characteristic of which is its great potential for causing civilian casualties. In fact, the first signs of this shift had become evident in the last three decades that marked the transition from the previous international legal order to the current one.[8] Today's actors of aggression are no more limited by financing from specific sources such as organized crime or their traditional state sponsors. Global networking allows financing to come from multiple sources, such as nonprofit and nongovernmental organizations, charities, websites, and above all a variety of enterprises and businesses, which can operate under a pretext of legitimacy and are being used as cover so that their profits can be diverted to other more shady activities.[9] Computer networking has allowed both states and private entities to outsource their operations and as a result achieve a longer reach and better results than ever before. This new generation of warfare that in a sense was pioneered by Al-Qaeda[10] is mainly structured around a vast network of local operatives that are provided with ample funding for their respective training, logistics needs, and services, along with guidance from representatives of their mother organization. As a consequence, global networking has offered unprecedented access to resources, training, and operational flexibility, which is evident in the growing complexity and effectiveness of the cyberwarfare attacks launched.[11]

Twenty-first-century computer-networked warfare has abandoned the centralized and hierarchical structure of traditional warfare for a new one that is largely informal, is highly decentralized, and gives emphasis to outsourcing. Twenty-first-century actors of aggression are now relying on a large number of independent cells that are loosely connected to one another and that follow the operating principles of any other modern globalized networks.[12] As a consequence, they are now able not only to branch out their activities but also to provide logistics support for such activities to be executed by local groups that are scattered all over the world. The newest and most dangerous aspect of this structure is that it can easily utilize groups that used to be at odds with each other and unite them under a common purpose, allowing market state actors of aggression to tap into a constituency that is much broader than ever before.[13] In the same way that newly emerging market states are now increasingly defined by their transnational character and interests and less by their territorial sovereignty and physical borders, this new generation of warfare is being increasingly defined by its adaptation of traits such as outsourcing, global networking, redundancy, diversity, interoperability, and decentralization.

The greatest advantage enjoyed by this new form of warfare is that reliance on global networking and the abandoning of the physical domain in favor of the virtual domain of the Internet has maximized its potential for success, while minimizing the risks involved.[14] It is now much easier to recruit new operatives, free from the constraints of physical recruiting, and it is also much easier to rely on a multitude of open sources to collect and disseminate information in a manner that has historically been the exclusive domain of states. Moreover, it is now easier than ever before for actors of aggression to conceal themselves and to evade detection and capture by operating in a virtual transnational world, which allows the moving from one legal jurisdiction to another with virtual impunity. As a result, proper investigation and prosecution of any cyberwarfare activities has become an extremely complicated affair that requires a closer cooperation than ever before between states whose laws with regard to arrest, prosecution, and extradition can usually vary greatly.

This enhanced efficiency and global reach does not come completely free of risk. Global networking can act as "a two-way mirror," not only allowing an accurate insight in the ideas, tactics, and actual strategy of potential aggressors but also providing a means of tracking them down and eventually of bringing them to justice,[15] as it can turn their own strengths against them. The true question we face with regard to cyberwarfare is whether we can realize that we are facing a period of transition and the advent of a new form of warfare that has nothing to do with what we dealt with for the greatest part of the twentieth century. If we fail to answer the aforementioned question properly, we are also likely to fail to appreciate the most important as well as dangerous difference of this new generation of warfare from the previous one: computer networking has made easier the access and potential deployment of weapons of mass destruction than ever before. The advent of computer networking appears to have coincided with a steady rise of terrorist attacks, by an order of magnitude in the last fifteen years, which is probably a strong indication in itself about the shape that the future is likely going to take.[16] The only mitigating factor, at least for the time being, is that the actual means needed for carrying out the most deadly of these types of attacks still fall within the realm of weapons of mass destruction (WMD) and as such are difficult to obtain, develop, and deploy effectively.

The end of the Cold War and the multipolar world that followed it combined with the advent of the "global information village" has made proliferation more of an issue than ever before, as it has allowed for an unprecedented commodification of WMD/WMD research and development components not only for states but also for private entities. This has led in turn to a significant growth of the black market that relates to such materials, thus making their potential proliferation, especially with regard to the aforementioned groups and their respective ability to gain access to them a more serious threat than ever before.[17] The relevant risk becomes even greater by the ability of modern information technology and global networking to magnify the activities of market state actors of aggression and present them to a worldwide audience in a theatrical and dramatic way, which could be rather appealing to them. It presents them with an ideal means of recruitment and above all an ideal means of getting their message through and spreading their terror. Even more potentially dangerous here is the ability of global networking to make it extremely difficult to establish a link between actors of aggression and twenty-first-century market states, even where such a link actually exists, thus fueling further the potential incentive to cause as many civilian casualties as possible. Combined with an inherent and increasingly potent ability to offer access to sensitive technologies and to the national critical infrastructures of states, it gradually makes the notion of a major and potentially catastrophic attack more likely and certainly more technologically feasible than ever before in history.[18]

Every generation of warfare has had a specific international constitutional order to direct its activities against and has always been defined not only by this international order but also and primarily so by its own stance against it. In the period of the nation-state, warfare in all its forms had been defined by the principle of absolute territorial and state sovereignty. In the era of the market state and globalized networks, the traditional concept of sovereignty, which had been synonymous with clearly marked territory and physical borders, is steadily losing ground in favor of a new international legal and economic order, which increasingly transcends national territories and interests in their traditional sense. Eventually and in order for the international constitutional order to successfully adapt to the new legal and security challenges it faces, the traditional concept of absolute state sovereignty will likely have to be reformed so that when states are engaged in certain activities, for example, cyberwarfare operations, which may be in breach of their international obligations, they would be liable to the international community and could face specific measures, including the possibility of military force. Existing legal norms on state responsibility could form the basis for such a reform, and it is therefore essential to assess their potential applicability to cyberwarfare activities.

CYBERSECURITY AND STATE RESPONSIBILITY

General Rules and Application

It is a long-established norm of customary international law that any breach on the part of a state, through an internationally wrongful act, of an obligation it may be subject to, under international law, entails its international legal responsibility.[19] Such an internationally wrongful act, which may very well fall in the realm of cyberwarfare operations, can comprise an action or omission (or any combination of the two). At the same time, the actual characterization of an action or omission as an internationally wrongful act would essentially depend on the specific requirements of the obligation that has been breached, as these requirements are set forth in international law. This principle was affirmed for the first time in 1938 by the predecessor of the United Nations International Court of Justice, the Permanent Court of International Justice, in the *Phosphates in Morocco* case. In its ruling, which has been confirmed in the deliberations of several more cases and arbitrary tribunals, since 1938, the court asserted that when a state commits an internationally wrongful act against another, then international responsibility is established immediately between the two states.[20]

Within the context of cyberwarfare operations, an internationally wrongful act could comprise a potential violation of the UN charter, for example, in the form of a forcible action committed through cyber means, or alternatively, a contravention of an obligation stemming from the legal norms of armed conflict, such as a cyberwarfare attack against a civilian target. It could also consist of a breach of peacetime regulations that may not necessarily involve conflict,[21] such as a violation of the law of the sea or of the nonintervention principle. A typical example of that latter case could be an incident during which a warship of a state that is exercising its right of innocent passage conducts a cyberwarfare operation against the coastal state's interests. On the other hand, a potential act of espionage that is conducted through cyberwarfare means, for example, one that targets the information and communication networks of another nation, would not likely violate any international legal obligation per se, as long as it does not encroach upon any specific prohibitions. This is due to the fact that the law of international state responsibility is not applicable to acts that are not specifically prohibited, or that are simply left unregulated by international law.[22] It is also essential to remember that causing damage is not a prerequisite for an activity, irrespective of whether it actually falls in the realm of cyberwarfare or not, to be deemed as an internationally wrongful act.[23] It goes without question that there are cases in which causing damage may be required as a prerequisite, or a *conditio sine qua non*, as it is more commonly known, for giving rise to the law of state responsibility with regard to a state's actions.

Within this context, it is also essential to explore the parameters of the legal relationship that a potential internationally wrongful act would likely establish between any wrongdoing state and the state(s) that may have been supposedly injured by its actions.[24] According to one view, this legal relationship is one of a mostly bilateral nature, in which the obligation of the former state to make reparations is set against a subjective right of the latter state to demand such reparations. A second school of thought supports a theory, according to which the primary legal consequence of an internationally wrongful act is an actual authorization, on part of the international legal order, whose character is mainly coercive, to the injured state to resort to coercive sanctions against the state(s) that have committed such an act. A third view, which seems to have prevailed in the international community, argues that in international law a wrongful act can give rise to various types of legal relations, depending on the specific circumstances of each case, which cannot be limited to reparations or sanctions.

Even more importantly, there has been a rather heated discussion with regard to the issue of whether the legal relationships that may arise between states after a violation of an international obligation are of a bilateral or multilateral nature. The matter was eventually resolved by the International Court of Justice (ICJ), which in its Barcelona Traction Case ruling held that every state, by virtue of being a member of the international community, has a legal interest in the protection of certain essential obligations, which are obligations *erga omnes*.[25] As the court has clearly pointed out in many follow-up rulings, the legal norms of international responsibility cover all relations that may arise from an internationally wrongful act, and their respective jurisdiction extends beyond the relationship between the state that has committed the act and the state that has been injured by its commission (or its omission, as the case may be) to include all other states that may be subjects of international law. In the end, it has been deemed immaterial whether the resulting relations are with regard to a potential obligation of restitution, compensation, or whether they give rise to a right on the part of the injured state to respond with countermeasures.

The aforementioned analysis is likely to prove of extreme importance in the context of cyberwarfare operations and not only with regard to their characterization as internationally wrongful acts under the law of state responsibility. The principle of the international legal obligations, which are obligations *erga omnes*, could be used as one of the main foundations for the development of a specifically tailored, regulatory framework, which will make it plain to all members of the international community that any direct or indirect involvement in cyberwarfare activity that would be above a certain threshold would entail an international responsibility against all other states, thus making them liable to countermeasures, including the possibility of military action. The next step in the development of such a specialized set of rules is likely going to be the ability to determine whether a given cyber-warfare activity, apart from being internationally wrongful, is also attribut-able to the state that is supposedly responsible for it. [26] The relevant legal test can be either subjective or objective, depending on the particular circum-stances of the international obligation that is being breached by a given activity or omission. To be more precise, a potential breach that may depend on the intention or knowledge of the official organs of a state would be subjective. In contrast, in cases where the intention or knowledge might be irrelevant, then the actual breach would rather be an objective one. [27]

On occasion a conduct that may lead to a breach of an international obligation may very well comprise both the commission and the omission of an act or acts, just as it happened during the factual situation that formed the basis of the *Corfu Channel* case. In that instance, the fact that the authorities of Albania knew, or should have known, of the presence of mines in Alba-nian territorial waters and had nevertheless done nothing to warn other states of the impending danger was a sufficient basis for establishing that the coun-try was in breach of an international obligation, thus entailing its internation-al responsibility. [28] In a similar fashion, in the deliberations for the *Tehran* case, the court based its decision on the actual knowledge on the part of the Iranian authorities of the existence of a set of circumstances that called for the taking of specific steps in order to prevent a breach of an international obligation and the subsequent failure on their part to proceed with these steps. [29] The correlation with activities that fall in the realm of cyberwarfare is obvious here, as there could be cases, for example, in which a state might be aware of the fact that its territory or information networks are being used by another state or by a group of private actors as a means of illegal cyber-warfare activities against another state, or states, and still takes no action whatsoever to prevent these activities or at least warn the state, or states, against which they are being conducted.

Each state has its own distinct legal personality, which is in fact what allows it to act under international law. However, no state can act except by and through its own agents and representatives, more commonly known as "the organs of the State." [30] This concept is an extremely broad one, and it is deemed to comprise any and all persons or entities that have been enjoying such status under a state's internal legislation, irrespective of their actual function or position in the governmental hierarchy. It therefore stands to reason that any cyberwarfare activities that are undertaken by state agencies or by any official or person that acts under the authority of the state, thus representing *pro tanto* the government, will entail state responsibility if it violates an international legal obligation. [31] Once again, this rule must be understood in the broadest sense possible, and it should be applied to all acts or omissions of the organs of a state, so far as they have performed them in an official capacity, without any distinction whatsoever between legislative, executive, or judicial organs of that same state. [32]

It is immaterial whether the aforementioned organs of a state have acted in compliance with specific instructions or whether they have simply done so as a result of the existence of a factual relationship that links their relevant conduct to the state in question. In such circumstances, even ultra vires acts that may breach an international obligation can give rise to international responsibility. [33] More often than not, private persons or entities that are not official organs of a state may be given the power by domestic legislation to exercise governmental authority and can therefore be equated to ordinary state organs. In this capacity, the private entities are usually recruited to act as auxiliaries in order to supplement the activities of governmental hierarchy, while still remaining outside this hierarchy. However, it is essential that there is a real link between these entities and the state for their activities to be attributable to it. [34] For example, and with regard to cyberwarfare, private corporations could be granted the authority by a government to conduct offensive or defensive information warfare operations; to be engaged in cyber intelligence or counterintelligence activities; or to provide Computer Emergency Response Teams (CERTs) in relation with certain information security roles. Additionally, a state may call upon private actors, either individuals or groups, to conduct cyberwarfare operations against other states or specific targets abroad. In this final case, if the activities of such nonstate actors are being performed on the instructions of, or under the direction or the effective control of, a given state, then they could be considered to be attributable to the state in question. [35]

The key factor here is the actual degree of the control exercised rather than the control itself. On the whole, the mere existence of a general situation of dependence and support is not considered sufficient to justify attribution of the conduct of nonstate actors to a state. According to the established legal test, in most cases, the relevant control would need to go beyond the mere financing and equipping of any nonstate actors and must also involve participation in the planning and supervision of military operations. [36] The UN International Court of Justice has generally advocated a low "overall control" threshold, by indicating that these matters should be largely decided on a case-by-case basis, even though it would not apply to individuals or unorganized groups, except in cases where they have acted under specific instructions or directives, aimed at the commission of specific acts, or had received public approval of their actions after their commission. [37] It therefore stands to reason that in situations involving illegal cyberwarfare activities, which are being conducted by private actors on their own initiative and without instructions, direction, or control, on the part of a state, there is no conduct that is attributable to a state and no subsequent issue of state responsibility. Also, merely encouraging or simply expressing support for the actions of such independently acting private parties is not enough to satisfy the requirements of the "overall control" test.

It is also important to remember, especially with regard to cyberwarfare operations, that the question of the actual locale of a given activity that may be in breach of one or more of a state's international obligations is totally irrelevant to a potential determination of whether there is an issue of international responsibility.[38] For example, there might be a group of nonstate actors that, based in state A, assimilates computers located in state B into its botnet, which is then being used to overload computers in a third state, while under instructions from a fourth state. Obviously, this conduct would be attributable, under the legal norms of state responsibility, to the state under the overall control of which the aforementioned group has been conducting its activities. It goes without question that in such a scenario the state, in the territory of which the aforementioned nonstate actors are located, would bear international responsibility only if it knew or should have known of their conduct and still took no steps whatsoever to prevent them from continuing their activities or warn the state in the receiving end of such activities.[39] On the other hand, there may be cases where even when the legal requirements for establishing a state's responsibility for internationally wrongful acts have not been met, such acts may still be retroactively attributable. This can happen when a state acknowledges and adopts conduct that was not originally attributed to it as its own.[40] Once again this is directly relevant to cyberwarfare activities, as, for example, we may have a group of nonstate actors conducting activities against a state and another state, which originally had no connection whatsoever with them, that not only expresses support for their actions but also proceeds to offer them direct support, either in order to enhance the effects of their actions or to protect them from possible retaliation or arrest. From that point on that other state has effectively acknowledged and adopted the conduct of these actors as its own, thus giving rise to its international responsibility.[41]

Countermeasures and Reparations

As provided by the International Law Commission's Articles on State Responsibility, any state that is injured by an international wrongful act is entitled to resort to countermeasures, which may also include cyberwarfare means, always provided that such countermeasures are proportionate with the injury suffered.[42] The term "countermeasures" is traditionally being used in reference to certain activities that would normally be unlawful in the context of international law but that could legitimately be resorted to in response to a conduct that is also in violation of international legal norms. The purpose of countermeasures is to encourage the offender to cease its illegal activities and comply with international law with the added and rather strict limitation that they must be necessary and proportionate.[43] It therefore stands to reason that as soon as the offending state desists its illegal conduct and things return to the previous status quo, the injured state is no longer entitled to persist in any countermeasures it may have initiated. It is also important to keep in mind that before a state is liable to resort to counter-measures, it first has to appeal to the offending state to cease its unlawful conduct and restore the previous situation. This requirement is not absolute, as states are still entitled to resort to countermeasures, as a matter of urgency when they are faced with wrongful acts that pose a serious threat to their interests and leave no time for deliberation.[44] In order to be lawful, counter-measures must also satisfy a few additional requirements, such as (a) the obligation to refrain from the threat or use of force; (b) the obligation to protect fundamental human rights; (c) the prohibition of reprisals; and (d) the need to comply with any obligation that may exist under peremptory norms of general international law.[45]

With regard to the obligation of states to refrain from the threat or use of force, it must be remembered that proportionate countermeasures could involve a limited degree of military force, even in response to circumstances that may not reach the threshold of what would be deemed an armed attack.[46] Countermeasures, irrespective of their nature, shall always comprise means that could only have temporary or reversible effects and be taken in such a way as to permit the resumption of performance of the obligations in question.[47] With regard to cyberwarfare operations, this means that the actual effects of any countermeasures must be temporary or reversible, unless there is no other real alternative.[48] This is in accord with the legal test of proportionality, as it has been set forth by the ICJ, which in its rulings has specifically stated (a) that countermeasures must be proportionate to the gravity of the initiating breach;[49] and (b) that countermeasures must be commensurate with the injury suffered, taking into account the gravity of the internationally wrongful act and the rights in question.[50] Within this context, cyberspace warfare capabilities could prove extremely useful as a countermeasures tool, as they can provide states with additional options to respond to a given situation and, even more importantly, can usually take place in a controlled environment and are therefore far more likely to satisfy the proportionality requirement than more conventional means. According to article 48 of the articles on state responsibility, which is considered to reflect international customary law, a state other than the injured state is entitled to invoke the responsibility of another state if (a) the obligation breached is owed to a group of states including that state and is established for the protection of a collective interest of the group; or (b) the obligation breached is owed to the international community as a whole.[51] Based on the fact that the principle of article 48 is considered to reflect international customary law, it could be used as a starting point for the regulation of cyberwarfare activities, which if resorted to would likely breach a state's international obligations and would also pose a serious threat to the interests and security of another.

It is also important to make a distinction between countermeasures and actions taken on the "plea of necessity," which are protective measures of a cyber or other nature that may violate the interests of other states and that may be invoked only in exceptional cases of emergency.[52] The plea of necessity is still a rather controversial matter that is the subject of debate in the international legal community; however, it could also prove useful with regard to the potential regulation of cyberwarfare activities, especially if such activities eventually evolve into a serious threat for the actual maintenance of peace and security. On the other hand and despite any existing controversy, it is generally recognized that each case of a plea of necessity must be judged after a careful balancing of the overall interests involved. As a result, any relevant protective measures that may be taken under these circumstances must be the only means of redressing the situation and must also not seriously impair the essential interests of the states affected by them or those of the international community. This principle is also likely to be useful in cases where states are faced with serious cyberwarfare threats, which call for immediate action, as it could justify a potential resort to such action, even in cases where it would cause interference with the interests of other members of the international community, as, for example, when a state is forced to shut down a number of Internet service providers (ISPs) or is forced to resort to counterhacking.

States responsible for the commission of an internationally wrongful act are under the obligation to make full reparation for any injury caused.[53] This principle was first defined in detail by the Permanent Court of International Justice in the *Chorzow Factory* case.[54] The court, in a ruling that was reaffirmed several times since, has been very specific about the fact that the term must be used in a most general sense and that reparation must attempt to wipe out all consequences of an illegal situation and reestablish the situation that would have existed if the illegal act in question had not been committed.[55] On certain occasions it may not be realistically possible to restore the *status quo ante* and bring about a *restitutio in integrum*. In these cases, reparation takes the form of financial compensation, which must correspond to the value of restitution in kind and if necessary may also include damages for any losses sustained.[56] Reparation may also take the form of moral satisfaction, especially in cases where an injury may not be made good by any other means.[57] Moral satisfaction may comprise an acknowledgment of the breach, an expression of regret, a formal apology, and/or punishment of any guilty parties, on the part of the offending state, or any other appropriate modality as it may be agreed upon. This principle may often lead to disproportionate and even crippling requirements so far as the responsible state is concerned. As a result, restitution is excluded if it involves a burden out of all proportions to the actual benefit gained or if it is materially impossible.[58]

When a wrongful act that involves a use of force gives rise to international responsibility, especially in cases where the use of force amounts to a war of aggression, the obligation to make reparation may be difficult to meet. The problem is that more often than not unlawful recourse to force can cause death and destruction on a vast scale, thus ruling out the option of satisfaction or restitution in kind, except in cases where the aggressor has appropriated property at least part of which is traceable.[59] In such circumstances, the most effective form of reparation may be a payment of compensation that should relate to all losses and injuries suffered by the victim states and their nationals. States parties to a conflict could reach an agreement, according to which the issue of compensation will be resolved in court or through arbitration. In some cases the ICJ may acquire the relevant jurisdiction, even in the absence of a specific agreement to that effect, and proceed to settle not only the form but also the amount of reparation, either of which it is free to do during the trial or at a later stage.[60] Within the context of reparations it is essential not to confuse the obligation to make reparations for a breach of the *jus ad bellum* with the totally different and independent liability of a belligerent party to pay compensation for a breach of the *jus in bello*. The latter obligation encompasses infractions, which may be committed by both the aggressor state and by the victim state, in which case the compensation paid by the aggressor may be reduced.[61]

CONCLUSION

State Responsibility and Sovereignty

The advent of the "market state" appears to be casting some very serious doubt not only on the most fundamental elements of the traditional notion of state sovereignty but also on the ability of current international legal norms to effectively regulate efforts to cope with the new challenges posed by the "global networked terrorism" of the twenty-first century.[62] This is mainly due to the fact that these legal norms have been tailored to serve an international community consisting of states with a clearly defined sovereignty. They are also structured in a way that almost totally rules out potential precautionary threats, thus making anticipatory self-defense unlawful, unless it takes place with the approval of the UN Security Council. Even specialized international legal instruments, such as the Geneva Conventions, were conceived with the classic paradigm of war in mind, which involves sovereign states, employing regular armies that confront each other on clearly drawn out battlefields. As a result, they are not capable of regulating cyberwarfare activities and other forms of global networked warfare, which are mostly about defying physical borders, having no regular army or uniforms, and operating mostly by stealth, often committing crimes that do not fall into the same category as those committed by ordinary criminals and who more often than not attack foreign states without being parties to an internal conflict.[63]

In most cases, operatives involved in cyberwarfare activities fall within neither the Geneva Conventions' article 4 definition of a prisoner of war nor the definition of article 2, which applies to armed conflicts between states that are parties to the convention. On the other hand, article 3, which attempts to guarantee protection at a level lower than that reserved for regular armed forces, is only applicable to "non-international conflicts," thus leaving out organizations like Al-Qaeda.[64] Even where interstate judicial cooperation is not a problem, ordinary prosecutions and rules of procedure can usually only provide a less than satisfactory answer, as in the vast majority of cases where existing rules of evidence are inappropriate to deal with the novelties of the issue at hand; for example, they often do not take into consideration the need to protect sensitive information as well as the sources and means through which such information may be gathered. This is not to mention the additional requirement according to which a crime needs to be actually committed before, or at the very least in, the process of being committed before detention and prosecution can take place.[65]

These issues are not simply about just a few problematic elements of the current legal order, which might be repaired through any sort of haphazard means. Instead, they appear to be systemic in nature, indicating the period of evolutionary transition that the international community is currently entering, which irrespective of whether we choose to ignore it or not, is eventually bound to include the properties of international law. This is not something unheard off; it has happened several times before in the course of history and often in a dramatic fashion, as a direct consequence of the fact that law has always followed closely any changes in the fundamental nature of the international constitutional and social order. Key in this evolutionary process has always been the ability of the law of nations to evolve in unison with the specific challenges ushered in by each new historical era. The transformation of warfare, which is currently taking place in the wake of the advent of the "market state," is a typical example of this process.

The problem at hand becomes even more apparent with a close look at the traditional concept of sovereignty that the international legal order still abides by and by assessing its potential ability to respond to the new security challenges brought forth by the era of the "market state" and of cyberwarfare. This principle has to satisfy the following test: first, it must be fully vested; second, it must be territorial; and last but not least, it must not be shared, so that its respective holder is superior to any and all other authorities under its jurisdiction.[66] From this test we can therefore make the following deductions: that in any given state jurisdiction there can be no more than a single authority and no more than a single set of laws; that statehood follows the lifespan of the state and it dissolves as soon as the state ceases to exist; and finally that the current notion of sovereignty itself precludes international legal norms from infringing upon the sovereignty of each and every individual member of the international community.[67]

All these notions are now being put to the test, as they are gradually losing ground before the advent of computer-networked warfare, which seems to be defying them with relative ease. A potential answer to this predicament could lie in a new sovereignty paradigm, according to which sovereignty would likely spring from a contract each and every state has drawn, not only with its own people, but also with the rest of the international community.[68] The legal norms on international state responsibility could be at the center of the actual development of such a new paradigm. This would not be an entirely new theory of statehood, as it was first introduced in the U.S. Constitution, which does not delegate full sovereignty to the federal government by reserving certain powers only for the people. This notion of states that are not vested with full sovereignty has never become popular outside the United States, as the international constitutional order has evolved along the lines of the traditional European statehood paradigm, which considers this type of sovereignty as simply unthinkable. The first chink in the armor of absolute state sovereignty was the process of European integration, which started in the 1950s and led to the 1991 Treaty of Maastricht and the establishment of the European Union.[69] The Treaty of Maastricht has effectively limited the freedom of action of state parties to it by taking over specific elements of their sovereignty and creating a supranational legal institution with the purpose of overseeing certain areas of state activity that would normally fall under the exclusive jurisdiction of a state's government.[70] A second sign of change appeared during the 1990s when "humanitarian intervention" became the means through which the international community began to challenge the tendency of some of its members to commit gross human rights violations.[71]

This is exactly the point where the rules on state responsibility become relevant and could be instrumental to future legal reform, as sovereignty involves certain obligations not only toward a state's own people but also toward the rest of the international community. As a consequence, there may be instances during which if a state commits certain actions in violation of the aforementioned obligations, it should forfeit its sovereignty and be lawfully open to outside intervention.[72] Such actions could comprise widespread acts of violence, both within and outside a state's own territory; the sponsoring of nonstate actors of aggression, or simply refusing to take the necessary steps in order to prevent such actors from operating from within its borders; being engaged directly or indirectly in the proliferation of any controlled substance, technology, or weaponry in contravention of its bilateral or multilateral international obligations; committing genocide, ethnic cleansing, or any form of religious persecution; being engaged in acts of slavery, human trafficking, or experimentation; and finally, the starvation of a given population.

Any major shift in the traditional state sovereignty paradigm, especially one that takes place along the above advocated lines, could easily be abused, hence creating even more crisis situations than the ones it might actually try to resolve. On the other hand, such a shift could just as easily form the basis for developing a new international strategic doctrine, which would be specifically tailored and thus better suited to successfully cope with the security challenges brought about by the advent of cyberwarfare, which appears to be questioning the most important aspects of currently prevailing international legal norms, especially those relating to the use of force. The purpose of such a new paradigm, preferably in combination with the rules of state responsibility and the norm that is known as the "duty to prevent,"[73] would be to create a new international legal obligation, according to which the members of the international community will have to resort to preventive action, which might also be of a military nature, whenever a state (or states, as the case may be) violates the responsibility it has with regard to protecting life and liberty and to promote basic human rights. However, it is important to keep in mind that a key feature of the aforementioned responsibility, and a major difference from the security constraints of the era of the nation-state, is that this is not simply about respecting the rights of one's own population; it is also, and primarily so, about treating with respect the rights of other states.

In the end, if we are to stand up successfully to this enormous challenge we seem to be facing, we would have to establish a new international legal paradigm, which would be specifically designed for regulating all the aforementioned issues and could therefore minimize the risks that accompany them. Still, success may not be possible unless we can strike the right balance between acceptable practices, effective action, law, strategy, and the protection of our civil and constitutional rights. It is important to realize that we are in fact beyond the boundaries of traditional conventional legal thinking. The issues highlighted in this work—most notably, the speed and clandestine tactics of twenty-first-century global networked terrorism; the slippery and thin line between private, criminal, and state-sponsored aggression; the proliferation of sensitive technology and materials; the transnational and highly strategic nature of the threat at hand; the difficulty of tracing, identifying, and eventually targeting global networked terrorists; the unprecedented scale and effects of the damage that might be caused by modern terrorist attacks; and above all the inability of our existing defenses to adapt to the threat we face—all point toward a need to reform existing rules on the use of force. This work, which could easily serve as a paradigm for more specific inroads to the various aspects of global networked terrorist activities, has attempted to show that once the means of applying force have so escaped the traditional boundaries of state monopoly, the legal and strategic thinking that is based on the types of violence that are available exclusively to the state is completely and utterly obsolete. The advent of the market state and of global networked terrorism has in fact pushed us into a field beyond traditional law.

NOTES

1. C. H. Morgan, *Cyber Attacks and Computer Intrusion Investigations* (Colorado Springs, CO: Air Force Office of Special Investigations, 2001), 5.

2. See P. Bobbitt, *Terror and Consent: The Wars of the Twenty First Century* (London: Penguin, 2009), 40–41. See also M. Burgess, "A Brief History of Terrorism," Center for Defense Information, July 2, 2003, http://www.cdi.org/.

3. See, generally, P. Bobbitt, *The Shield of Achilles: War, Peace and the Course of History* (London: Penguin, 2002), 229 et seq. See also Bobbitt, *Terror and Consent*, 27 et seq.

4. See A. K. Cronin, "Rethinking Sovereignty: American Strategy in the Age of Terrorism," *Survival* 44, no. 2 (2002): 135; Steven Simon and Daniel Benjamin, "The Terror," *Survival* 43, no. 4 (2001): 5–87; and Steven Simon and Daniel Benjamin, "America and the New Terrorism," *Survival* 42, no. 1 (2000): 59.

5. Ibid.

6. See Brian Michael Jenkins, "The Future Course of International Terrorism," *Futurist*, July–August 1987.

7. See Brian Michael Jenkins, "Terrorism: Current and Long Term Threats," statement to the Senate Armed Services Subcommittee on Emerging Threats, November 15, 2001, http://www.rand.org/.

8. During the 1970s civilian casualties from terrorist activity were less than a hundred. In the 1980s this figure went up in the range of several hundred, with terrorist activity becoming more frequent. In the 1990s there was an additional increase of about 20 percent in civilian deaths, while in the first decade of the twenty-first century civilian deaths from terrorism reached a figure of several thousands. Based on existing data, there is no evidence to support that this ratio of magnitude increase per decade will not continue. As a consequence, there is a good chance we may have to face the possibility of coping with incidents that may cause tens of thousands of casualties. For details, see MIPT Terrorism Knowledge Base, "TKB Incident Analysis Wizard," accessed November 22, 2006, http://www.tkb.org/.; and Brian Michael Jenkins, "Combating Global War on Terrorism," in *Countering Terrorism and WMD: Creating a Global Counter-Terrorist Network*, ed. P. Katona, M. B. Intriligator, and J. P. Sullivan, 181–98 (New York: Routledge, 2006), 182.

9. See, generally, L. Napoleoni, *Terror Incorporated: Tracing the Money behind Global Terrorism* (New York: Penguin, 2003), 214 et seq.

10. As Bobbitt has correctly pointed out, Al-Qaeda took off with regard to the actual scale of its activities from the moment that Osama Bin Laden won the support of a wealthy and powerful entrepreneur called Mohammed Atta, who agreed to support and more importantly fund its activities. For details, see Bobbitt, *Terror and Consent*, 50.

11. Once we understand the globalized, networked nature of twenty-first-century warfare, it is much easier to appreciate how it was possible for multiple and rather complex and demanding terrorist attacks, such as the ones at London and Madrid and the almost successful one at Miami, to be launched at practically the same time. See P. N. Neumann, "Europe's Jihadist Dilemma," *Survival* 48, no. 2 (2006): 77.

12. See John Arquilla, David Ronfeldt, and Michele Zanini, "Networks, Netwar, and Information-Age Terrorism," in *Countering the New Terrorism*, by Ian O. Lesser et al., 39–84 (Santa Monica, CA: Rand, 1999), 45–46; and B. Berkowitz, *The New Face of War: How War Will Be Fought in the 21st Century* (New York: Free Press, 2003), 15 et seq.

13. See C. Hegland, "Global Jihad," *National Journal* 36 (2004): 1400–401; and Bobbitt, *Terror and Consent*, 53.

14. See Joseph S. Nye Jr., "Cyber Power," Massachusetts Institute of Technology, Accessed August 28, 2015, http://web.mit.edu/; Joseph S. Nye Jr., "How to Counter Terrorism's Online Generation," *Financial Times*, October 13, 2005, 19; and David Talbot, "Terror's Server: Fraud, Gruesome Propaganda, Terror Planning; The Net Enables It All; The Online Industry Can Help Fix It," *Technology Review* 108, no. 2 (2005): 48.

15. See R. F. Worth, "Iraqi Insurgents Put the Web in Their Arsenal," *International Herald Tribune*, March 12, 2005, I.

16. See James K. Campbell, "Excerpts from Research Study 'Weapons of Mass Destruction and Terrorism: Proliferation by Non State Actors,'" *Terrorism and Political Violence* 9, no. 2 (1997): 25.

17. To realize the magnitude of the problem and the risks involved we only need to consider that currently at least twelve states that are allegedly connected with various terrorist groups are heavily involved in pursuing their own WMD programs, involving potential nuclear, biological, radiological, explosive, or cyberwarfare capabilities. For details, see Worth, "Iraqi Insurgents," I.

18. See W. Shawcross, *Allies: The US, Britain, Europe and the War in Iraq* (New York: Public Affairs, 2005), 262.

19. See D. Angillotti, *Corso di Diritto Internationale I* (Padua, Italy: CEDAM, 1955), 385; W. Wengler, *Volkerrecht I* (Berlin: Springer, 1964), 499; G. I. Tunkin, *Teoria Mezhdunarodnogo Prava* (Moscow: Mezdhuranodye Otnoshenia, 1970), 470; E. J. de Arechaga, "International Responsibility," in *Manual of Public International Law* (London: Macmillan, 1968), 533; B. Conforti, *Diritto Internazionale* (Milan: Editoriale Scientifica, 1995), 332; R. Wolfrum, "Internationally Wrongful Acts," in *Encyclopedia of Public International Law* (Amsterdam: North Holland, 1995), 1398; P. M. Dupuy, *Droit International Public* (Paris: Precis Dalloz, 1998), 414; I. Brownlie, *Principles of Public International Law* (Oxford, UK: Clarendon, 1998), 435; J. Crawford, *The International Law Commission's Articles on State Responsibility* (Cambridge: Cambridge University Press, 2002), 77, 78–79; and ILC UN GAOR 56th Sess. Supp. No. 10, 43, "Draft Articles on Responsibility of States for Internationally Wrongful Acts," in Report of the International Law Commission on the Work of Its Fifty Third Session, UN Doc. A/56/10 (2001), article 8 commentary, para. 7, http://www.un.org/law/ilc.

20. See Phosphates in Morocco (Preliminary Objections), [1938] PCIJ Series A/B no. 74, paras. 10, 28; Corfu Channel Case (merits), [1949] ICJ Reports 4, paras. 142, 149; ICJ Case on Military and Paramilitary Activities in and against Nicaragua (merits), ICJ Reports (1986) 14, paras. 142, 149, 283, 292 (hereafter ICJ Nicaragua Case); ICJ Gabcikovo-Nagymaros Project (Hungary v. Slovakia), [1997] ICJ Reports 7, paras. 38, 47; Interpretation of Peace Treaties with Bulgaria, Hungary and Romania (Second Phase), [1950] ICJ Reports paras. 221, 228; RIAA XV (1901) at 395, 399, 401, 404, 407, 408, 409; RIAA II (1925) at 615, 641; RIAA XIV (1953) at 159, 163; and RIAA XX (1990) at 217.

21. See Michael N. Schmitt, ed., *Tallinn Manual on the International Law Applicable to Cyberwarfare* (Cambridge: Cambridge University Press, 2013), 30–31.

22. See ICJ Accordance with International Law of the Unilateral Declaration of Independence in Respect of Kosovo (Advisory Opinion), ICJ Reports (2010) 403, para. 84., http://www.icj-cij.org/; and PCIJ The Case of the S.S. Lotus (France v. Turkey), 1927 PCIJ (ser. A) no. 10 (September 7) at 18, http://www.worldcourts.com/.

23. See ILC UN GAOR 56th Sess. Supp. No. 10, 43, "Draft Articles," article 8 commentary, para. 7.

24. See Angillotti, *Corso di Diritto*, 385; H. Kelsen, *Principles of International Law* (New York: Holt, Rinehart and Winston, 1966), 22; and H. Lauterpacht, *Oppenheim's International Law I* (London: Longmans, 1955), 353–54.

25. See ICJ Barcelona Traction Light and Power Company Limited (Second Phase), [1970] ICJ Reports 3, paras. 32–33; ICJ East Timor, [1995] ICJ Reports 90, para. 29; ICJ Advisory Opinion on the Legality of the Threat or Use of Nuclear Weapons, [1996] ICJ Reports 226, para. 83; ICJ Application of the Convention on the Prevention and Punishment of the Crime of Genocide (Preliminary Objections), [1996] ICJ Reports 505, paras. 31–32; and ICJ Advisory

Opinion on the Legal Consequences of the Construction of a Wall in the Occupied Palestinian Territory, [2004] ICJ Reports 131, paras. 3–4.

26. See ILC UN GAOR 56th Sess. Supp. No. 10, 43, "Draft Articles," article 8 commentary, para. 7.

27. See ICJ United States Diplomatic and Consular Staff in Tehran, [1980] ICJ Reports 3, para. 56; ICJ Nicaragua Case, paras. 117–18, 226; and ICJ Gabcikovo-Nagymaros Project, para. 78.

28. See ICJ Corfu Channel Case (merits), [1949] ICJ Reports 4, paras. 22–23.

29. See ICJ United States Diplomatic and Consular Staff in Tehran, [1980] ICJ Reports 3, paras. 63–67.

30. See ICJ Germans Settlers in Poland, [1923] PCIJ Series B 6, para. 22.

31. See I. Brownlie, *System of the Law of Nations: State Responsibility (Part I)* (Oxford, UK: Clarendon, 1983); D. D. Caron, "The Basics of Responsibility: Attribution and Other Trans-Substance Rules," in *The Iran-United States Claims Tribunal: Its Contribution to the Law of State Responsibility*, ed. R. Lillich and D. Magraw (Irvington on Hudson, NY: Transnational, 1998); Crawford, *International Law Commission's Articles*, 91; "Moses Case," in Moore, International Arbitrations, III, 3127–29 (1871); Claims of Italian Nationals Resident in Peru, RIAA XV, 395, 399, 401, 404, 407–11; Finnish Ship-owners, RIAA III, 1479, 1501; UN League of Nations Conference for the Codification of International Law, Bases of Discussion for the Conference Drawn up by the Preparatory Committee III: Responsibility of States for Damage Caused in their Territory to the Person or Property of Foreigners (Doc. C.75 M.69 1929 V.) 25, 41, 52; and ILC UN GAOR 56th Sess. Supp. No. 10, 43, "Draft Articles," article 8 commentary, para. 7.

32. See Salvador Commercial Company Case, (1902) RIAA XV 455, 477 (1902); Chattin Case (1927) RIAA IV 282, 285–86; and Dispute concerning the Interpretation of Article 79 of the Treaty of Peace (1955) RIAA XIII 389, 438.

33. See ILC UN GAOR 56th Sess. Supp. No. 10, 43, "Draft Articles," articles 4, 5, 7–8.

34. See RIAA The Zafiro Case, [1925] RIAA VI 160; RIAA Stephens Case, [1927] RIAA IV 265–67; and RIAA Lehigh Valley Railroad Company and Others (Sabotage Cases: Black Tom and Kings Land Incidents), [1930] RIAA VIII 84, [1939] RIAA VIII 225, 458.

35. See ICJ Nicaragua Case, para. 115; ICJ Case concerning Application of the Convention of the Prevention and Punishment of the Crime of Genocide: Bosnia and Herzegovina v. Serbia and Montenegro (judgment), ICJ Reports (2007), paras. 399–401. http://www.icj-cij.org/; ICJ Tadic Case (judgment of the Appeals Chamber), IT-94-1 (1999) 4, para. 145. http://www.icty. org/; and ILC UN GAOR 56th Sess. Supp. No. 10, 43, "Draft Articles," article 8 commentary, para. 7.

36. Ibid.

37. See ICJ Case concerning United States Diplomatic and Consular Staff in Tehran (judgment), ICJ Reports (1980) 3, para. 74, http://www.icj-cij.org/; and ICJ Tadic Case (judgment of the Appeals Chamber), IT-94-1 (1999) 4, para. 145, http://www.icty.org/.

38. See note 29; and Schmitt, *Tallinn Manual*, 32.

39. See notes 26 and 27.

40. See ILC UN GAOR 56th Sess. Supp. No. 10, 43, "Draft Articles," article 11, and commentary to article 11.

41. See Schmitt, *Tallinn Manual*, 33.

42. See ILC UN GAOR 56th Sess. Supp. No. 10, 43, "Draft Articles," articles 22, 49–53. Also, for details on countermeasures and cyberwarfare activities, see, generally, Schmitt, *Tallinn Manual*, 36 et seq.

43. See Oscar Schachter, *International Law in Theory and Practice: General Course in Public International Law*, Collected Courses of the Hague Academy of International Law 178 (Leiden, Netherlands: Martinus Nijhoff, 1982), 168; Yoram Dinstein, *War, Aggression and Self-Defense* (Cambridge: Cambridge University Press, 2001), 192; Ian Brownlie, *International Law and the Use of Force by States* (Oxford, UK: Clarendon, 1963), 304–6; I. Brownlie, *The Rule of Law in International Affairs: International Law at the Fifteenth Anniversary of the UN* (London: Martinus Nijhoff, 1998), 205–6; and ILC Report of the International Law Commission, 32nd Session, [1980] II (2) ILC Ybk 1, 53–54.

44. See ILC UN GAOR 56th Sess. Supp. No. 10, 43, "Draft Articles," articles 52 (1), 52 (2).

45. Ibid., article 50.

46. See ICJ Oil Platforms Case: Iran v. United States, judgment (2003) ICJ 161 (November 6), paras. 12–13 (separate opinion of Judge Simma).

47. See ILC UN GAOR 56th Sess. Supp. No. 10, 43, "Draft Articles," article 49 (3).

48. See Schmitt, *Tallinn Manual*, 37.

49. See RIAA Responsibility of Germany for Damage Caused in the Portuguese Colonies in the South Africa (Naulilaa Arbitration) (Portugal v. Germany), July 31, 1928, 2 RIAA 1011 at 1028.

50. See ICJ Gabcikovo-Nagymaros Project, para. 85.

51. See ILC UN GAOR 56th Sess. Supp. No. 10, 43, "Draft Articles," article 48.

52. Ibid., article 25 and commentary to article 25; see also Schmitt, *Tallinn Manual*, 38; and ICJ Gabcikovo-Nagymaros Project, para. 55.

53. See ILC UN GAOR 56th Sess. Supp. No. 10, 43, "Draft Articles," article 34.

54. See PCIJ Case concerning the Factory at Chorzow (Jurisdiction), [1927] PCIJ Series A9 at 21.

55. See ibid., Series A17 at 47.

56. ILC UN GAOR 56th Sess. Supp. No. 10, 43, "Draft Articles," articles 35, 36.

57. Ibid., articles 31 (2), 37. See also S. Roseme, "State Responsibility and International Crimes: Further Reflections on Article 19 of the Draft Articles on State Responsibility," *New York University Journal of International Law and Politics* 30, nos. 1–2 (1997–1998): 145, 164.

58. ILC UN GAOR 56th Sess. Supp. No. 10, 43, "Draft Articles," article 35. See also Crawford, *International Law Commission's Articles*, 212.

59. See Dinstein, *War, Aggression*, 99; Versailles Treaty of Peace with Germany, Peace Treaties Series II (1919) 1265, 1934; and Philip Quincy Wright, "The Outlawry of War and the Law of War," *American Journal of International Law* 47, no. 3 (1953): 365, 372.

60. See ICJ Nicaragua Case, paras. 142–43 and 146–49; and ICJ Advisory Opinion on the Legal Consequences of the Construction of a Wall in the Occupied Palestinian Territory, [2004] ICJ Reports 131, para. 145.

61. See Hague Convention IV Respecting the Laws and Customs of War on Land, 1907 Hague Conventions 100, 103; and Protocol Additional to the Geneva Conventions of August 12, 1949, Relating to the Protection of Victims of International Armed Conflicts (Protocol I), [1977] UNJY 95 at 132. See R. F. Worth, "Iraqi Insurgents Put the Web in Their Arsenal," *International Herald Tribune*, 12 March 2005, I. Also, see P. Bobbitt, *Terror and Consent: The Wars of the 21st Century* (London: Penguin Books, 2009) 452.

62. See Worth, "Iraqi Insurgents," I; and Bobbitt, *Terror and Consent*, 452.

63. Bobbitt, *Terror and Consent*, 710.

64. See UNTS "Geneva Convention Relative to the Treatment of Prisoners of War," August 12, 1949, United Nations Treaty Series 75, no. 972 (1950), articles 2, 3, and 4, pp. 137–38. See also, generally, D. Rumsfeld, "Status of Taliban and Al-Qaeda," memorandum for Chairman of the Joint Chiefs of Staff, January 19, 2002, http://www.defenselink.mil/.

65. See Bobbitt, *Terror and Consent*, 456.

66. See Dan Philpott, "Sovereignty," in *Stanford Encyclopedia of Philosophy*, ed. E. N. Zalta (2003), http://plato.stanford.edu/.

67. See Bobbitt, *Terror and Consent*, 465.

68. The establishment of such a new paradigm would not be something previously unheard of in the historical evolution of the international legal order, and it could easily take shape along the lines of what Bobbitt defines as the idea of "transparent sovereignty." The overall concept is based on the American constitutional theory of "limited government," which is enshrined in the text of the U.S. Constitution and which provides that the people possess certain unalienable rights that cannot be delegated to the government. For details, see, generally, Bobbitt, *Terror and Consent*, 466–70. See also Philip Bobbitt, *Constitutional Fate: Theory of the Constitution* (New York: Oxford University Press, 1982), 108 et seq; and N. McCormick, "Beyond the Sovereign State," Chorley Lecture 21, London School of Economics, *Modern Law Review*, June 3, 1992, http://www.modernlawreview.co.uk/.

69. See Bobbitt, *Terror and Consent*, 40–41; and Burgess, "Brief History of Terrorism."

70. See, generally, James Kitfield, "Anti-Terror Alliance," *Government Executive* 33, no. 2 (2001): 51.

71. Humanitarian intervention took place on quite a few occasions, such as the cases of Iraq and Kuwait; the breakup of the Former Federal Republic of Yugoslavia; in Somalia; in Rwanda; in Haiti; in Sierra Leone; in Cambodia; in Liberia; and in East Timor. In most of these cases, the interventions took place without the consent of the government that happened to be on the receiving end of it and were also finally endorsed by the UN Security Council and other regional international organizations, even though under normal conditions they would be deemed unthinkable under the traditional concept of full state sovereignty. See, generally, UN Security Council Resolution 1244, June 10, 1999 (4011th meeting); UN Security Council Resolution 1483, May 22, 2003 (4761st meeting); UN Security Council Resolution 1511, October 16, 2003 (4844th meeting); UN Security Council Resolution 1546, June 8, 2004 (4987th meeting); Mahmoud Hmoud, "The Use of Force against Iraq: Occupation and Security Council Resolution 1483," *Cornell International Law Journal* 36, no. 3 (2004): 448; D. J. Scheffer, "Agora: Future Implications of the Iraq Conflict," *American Journal of International Law* 97 (2003): 844–47; and W. Michael Reisman, "Sovereignty and Human Rights in Contemporary International Law," *American Journal of International Law* 84, no. 4 (1990): 872.

72. See Reisman, "Sovereignty and Human Rights," 872.

73. See L. Feinstein and A. M. Slaughter, "A Duty to Prevent," *Foreign Affairs* 83, no. 1 (2004): 136–50; G. Evans and M. Sahnoun, "The Responsibility to Protect," *Foreign Affairs* 81, no. 6 (2002): 99–110; generally, K. Annan, "Secretary General's Address to the General Assembly," United Nations, New York, September 23, 2003, http://www.un.org/; UN Secretary General's High-Level Panel on Threats, Challenges, and Change, A More Secure World: Our Shared Responsibility, UN Doc. A/59/565, December 2004, http://www.un.org/; UN General Assembly, "2005 World Summit Outcome," UN Doc. A/Res/60/I, September 16, 2005, 30, http://www.un.org/; and, generally, G. Evans and Mohamed Sahnoun, and International Commission on Intervention and State Sovereignty, *The Responsibility to Protect* (Ottawa: International Development Research Centre, 2001), http://www.iciss.ca/.

Chapter Three

In Harm's Way

Harmonizing Security and Human Rights in the Internet Age

Roy Balleste

Another necessary precaution relates to the time, when it is proper to undertake war, which depends upon a due calculation, whether there are resources and strength sufficient to support or just pretensions. This is conformable to what was said by Augustus, that no war should be undertaken, but where the hopes of advantage could be shown to overbalance the apprehensions of ruin.
—Hugo Grotius[1]

THE SOCIAL CONTRACT

Cybersecurity has become militarized. It is now a matter of winning. The key lies in the strategy that will defeat the enemy. What should be the cost, if any, of this perceived strategy? This is the theme that takes me to the beginning of this analysis. I was a member of the U.S. Navy. The experience that lasted four years taught me two important lessons. It taught me above all else the importance of humility. It also taught me about the protection of one's country, a responsibility that we may equate with patriotism. One of the first requirements of joining the U.S. Navy is a literal contract of service that requires the willingness to die for one's country. Regarding this requirement, there are no doubts in the mind of the individual joining the navy. The military life demands sacrifice and total commitment. This is at the heart of the concept of *national security*. Thus, a sailor becomes a member of the armed forces bound by duty to die, if necessary, for the security of the nation. This outlook is accepted without question, and a potential war becomes that fight for freedom. This is at the heart of the Declaration of Independence of those thirteen colonies that long ago sought out a new future, away from those old European empires. From these colonies, a new movement for independence awoke ideals that would resonate into the future. The U.S. Declaration of Independence notes that all men "are endowed by their Creator with certain inalienable rights, that among these are life, liberty, and the pursuit of happiness." These ideas I would later advocate within the ambit of the Internet.

Before the harmonization of cybersecurity and human rights can be achieved, any accepted proposal for power, surveillance, and control requires the protection of social values and those human relations that stimulate the participation of the local and global communities in governance.[2] This governance is instilled by the standards that permeate the association of individuals while making their societies more than an artificial construct. For example, this association, or *social contract*, was at the heart of the ideals found in the U.S. Declaration of Independence. One of the greatest exponents of the social contract, Jean-Jacques Rousseau, explained that this contract draws its lawfulness from the "legitimate rule of administration."[3] Rousseau noted that "man is born free; and everywhere he is in chains."[4] He recognized that the oppression forced upon individuals is unnatural and that to question oppression is a valid proposition.[5] But a voluntary surrender to a higher power by an individual to become part of a greater group of individuals means that by uniting for mutual benefit, and forming a society, these individuals' freedoms are also reinforced by their agreement, or contract.[6] It follows that a good government, in turn, is reflected by the existence of that *social contract*.[7] Legal experts Sarah Joseph, Jenny Schultz, and Melissa Castan explain that this social contract requires a light-touch approach by government in the lives of citizens, only intervening when necessary. An intervention could not interfere with the liberties inalienable in all humanity. Based on their analysis, we can reason that cybersecurity, being an activity of governments (with the assistance of the private-business sector), would require mainly a policy of little or no interference. The notion of the social contract is one that is at the core of all democratic governments but one that has been difficult to reconcile with the Internet. If citizens are to give up some of their freedoms, then in return, their elected officials must represent and fight for their common interests. At least, that is the way it is supposed to work. This is not always the case, and for this reason individuals' rights are lost in political and financial dealings that usually favor a few. In nondemocratic societies, it is worst, where the individual has little voice or exists as a nonentity vulnerable to the whims of a few. The social contract could then be described by a set of values that when considered together, increases the potential for a dignified life. For this reason, both the social contract and cybersecurity may coexist if certain steps are considered and followed.

There is no doubt that the protection of private communications is in danger. This is the first sign of the erosion of human rights and freedoms. The assurance that Internet users can continue to enjoy the Internet is also in jeopardy. Should any cybersecurity initiative take into account whether a nation-state filters out content that it deems counter to its concept of national security or morality? What about surveillance? What is really necessary? What is too much? Who will decide? As the years have progressed, the evolution of the Internet and the World Wide Web reminds users that behind every new technology lurks someone's desire to exploit it. The struggle has centered particularly on security measures and the bad actors hiding in the "shadows" of cyberspace. A mechanism has become necessary to reconcile the use of the Internet and the need to keep its stability and security. There is no question that Internet users continue to be abused by online threats in the form of phishing, viruses, worms, malware, spyware, hacking, hate speech, and identity theft. These are real threats that should not be ignored and require the attention of all users.

A social contract must aspire to promote public order. Legal scholars Myers McDougal, Harold Lasswell, and Lung-chu Chen reason that a public order, one that provides the greatest access to all things cherished by humanity, would be centered in eight values: wealth, power, enlightenment, skill, well-being, affection, respect, and rectitude.[8] These values, when examined closely, provide an effective strategy to reconcile cybersecurity with those things cherished by humanity, such as life, liberty, and the pursuit of happiness. Accordingly, it is fitting to consider the Internet's security in terms of the eight values in the global society. These values not merely help us dissect the problem but also provide the beginning of the solution.

THE TRIDENT EFFECT: HARMONIZING CYBERSECURITY

During my time in the navy, I was also inescapably a participant of solemn ceremonies. It was here that I heard for the first time the U.S. Navy hymn: "Eternal Father strong to save. . . . Oh, hear us when we cry to Thee, For those in peril on the sea!"[9] Not only is it inspirational, but also it is a reminder of the fragility of human life. Our mortality is omnipresent and unavoidable. It is also a reminder that we are all one race: the human race. In the expanse of the high seas, our voice is lost beyond the unending horizons where borders have no meaning. With the advent of the Internet, new security threats have emerged for all nations, perhaps more so in nations that display high technological resources such as the United States of America. It is contradictory to see how easy and with how much energy human beings harm one another. Despite long-ago struggles, humanity today holds great potential. But this potential is in jeopardy, because needless surveillance, cyber attacks, and the weaponization of the Internet have become exponentially disastrous. This tripart minefield of upsetting actions is what I call the *trident effect*.

Historian George Grote noted that the mythology of Greece acknowledged the great Poseidon (Ποσειδῶν), one of the twelve gods of Olympus and master of the oceans.[10] The story of Poseidon is interesting because, as potentate of the seas, he used a trident to agitate the oceans or could intercede *for those in peril on the sea*.[11] It could be said that in his hand rested good and evil, war and peace, and love and hate. The story of Poseidon may be mythological, but his dual nature is very much part of the realm of cyberspace. The prevalence of global communications and the rise of connectivity have demonstrated its importance to the world. The Internet is so vast and complex that it defies real-world definitions based on territory. The Internet has blurred the line between cyberspace and real space. Along with its potential to enhance social and economic interactions, it has become a public phenomenon. It has offered a new forum for knowledge sharing and discussion.

I have noted before that when considering the unlimited distances of outer space and its cosmological construct, the Internet may also seem to be without beginning or end.[12] Yet, any constraints directed at it from the physical world, including the desire by governments to balkanize it, have only proven detrimental to its intended purpose after the decision of commercialization in 1994. True, it began as a project to protect communications during the Cold War. Those great souls that participated in its design placed the Internet on the world stage, and once it was commercialized, it was transformed into something new, far beyond their opinions and vision. While millions of dollars have passed through endless transactions online, and information has connected the world, unscrupulous individuals and misguided government officials have turned the Internet into a battlefield where the words "security," "hackers," and "terrorists" have become a gray blur. This is the new world of *cyber* or networked technologies.[13]

For sure, cybersecurity, including the management of economic resources for a public order, requires an assessment of the value of *wealth* as it applies to the availability of technology and its accessibility around the world. While we may look at the Internet as an agent of development, we must first consider the capacity of the global community to share technological resources. For this reason, McDougal, Lasswell, and Chen would suggest that controlling *wealth* means the opposite; all technological resources should be available without restriction to benefit the world community.[14] Ensuring wealth requires the acknowledgment that meeting the needs of the world community promotes the necessary tools for a global community's enjoyment of the resources produced and distributed in the Internet.[15] These resources have the capacity to enlighten all users of the Internet.

Why then do we perceive a depressing feeling in the air and a sensation that the future will be unnecessarily conflictive? Perhaps it is due to damaging influences of the same old corrupted activities that have plagued humanity for millennia. Should militarization be understood as the most efficient model to counter threats in the Internet? While seeking the answer to this question, we must remember that the fundamental problem with which we have been concerned relates to how we can harmonize human rights with cybersecurity. This is the key at the center of the challenge: looking back at the much simpler days before the Internet and, while pondering how to recapture the control that existed before its commercialization of 1994, apply it to a much more complex present reality.

The Internet has become a source of new challenges for scholars around the world because it defies traditional governance standards. These challenges are not necessarily negative if by dealing with them we improve human civilization. Yet, a process conducive to improvement requires a plan of cyber risk reduction with the capacity to increase well-being around the world. The value of *well-being* is not an ideal based on naïve illusions. It is directly tied to the use of the Internet and what that activity may entail: democracy, greater skills, and a greater awareness of humanity's place within our world society. McDougal, Lasswell, and Chen would also note that well-being requires the protection of the individual in that society. [16] Thus, the use of the Internet must be strengthened hand in hand with the continued improvement of human dignity.

ON POWER AND RECTITUDE

The origins of cyberspace describe the achievements of the U.S. government and, above all, the ideas and ideals of those original creators of that great technology. The considerations involved in cybersecurity reveal part of that historical process of human claims along with its conflictive nature, and the quest for a universally accepted system of secure governance. The process of claims and decisions observed over the years serves to emphasize a common interest of all stakeholders and sheds light on the necessity to maintain a stable and secure Internet. There is no doubt that threats exist and that security measures are needed to maintain a secure and stable Internet. On the other hand, all measures must be proportional. An apodictic assessment of history traverses the guiding light of Dr. Jon Postel. He understood the meaning of power as a given consent to perform duties in trust for the enhancement of the social contract. [17] In this manner, the human value of *power* functions through governments and businesses providing authority with stewardship on behalf of all Internet users. While there is no debate that governmental decisions have been seen for hundreds of years as a recognition of national sovereignty, the process of finding a "common ground" for the development of appropriate cybersecurity standards continues to be challenging for all stakeholders involved in the process but more so for governments. A true cyber-risk-reduction initiative requires the participation of all stakeholders, including individuals. For this reason, governments must not isolate themselves and instead must act in good faith and openly share in the duties and rights that build and develop civilizations. These steps would be compatible with a constitutive process harmonized with the dignity of the human person. Human rights are always seen as controversial when policy is developed for the Internet and when governments are to be held accountable for the implementation of those policies. During the first five years of the Internet Governance Forum (IGF), the overall theme of human rights was not addressed as one of the main areas, although it was considered in relation to other subjects, or discussed in workshops or dynamic coalitions. This trend would change during the second mandate of the IGF. It is difficult to grasp why human rights have become such a difficult concept to consolidate with the policy development process of the work performed by the Internet Corporation for Assigned Names and Numbers (ICANN). While there is an advisory committee on security, one for technical matters, one for government advice, and one for root operations, there is none for human rights. Perhaps this shortcoming will also be rectified in the future by those brave souls that will manage the Internet in trust for humanity. When ICANN's policy work is analyzed from the point of view of human rights, privacy rises to the top as a major source of concern and debate. Perhaps it is because, from the start, cybersecurity was tied directly to the Advanced Research Projects Agency Network (ARPANET) and its military roots. In other words, national sovereignty concerns cannot be ignored. Cybersecurity should be seen as a recognized arrangement that serves the global community and contributes to the recognition of all individuals as persons, with the right to enjoy a safe life. Governmental power also requires authority and control to be effectively recognized as law.[18] Consequently, both authority and control have also been a part of corrupted governments and the acquiescence of some in the business sector. The present reality recognizes that cybersecurity has become a matter of winning one fight after another. Again, the question should be, at what cost?

In 2008 I commented on a law review article about a hypothetical scenario as shown in the award-winning 1990s television series *Babylon 5*, in which Earth's legitimate world government was removed by a coup d'etat.[19] In this allegory, the corrupt government that followed quickly declared martial law supposedly for the security of the citizens. In reality, this government utilized the circumstances of "a state of emergency" for all that has been recognized as wrong with corruption: enforced disappearances, censorship, preventing the dissemination of information at key political moments, arbitrary arrests, harassment, and intimidation. When we look closer at our present reality, we discover that in many cases these type of stories transcend general hypocrisy and directly address problems that we can perceive in our present world society. The recognition of these problems is always too painful to discuss. Indeed, what I noted with the fictional story of *Babylon 5*, legal scholars Paul Joseph and Sharon Carton analyzed with equally relevant stories of *Star Trek*, while also considering whether these shows "had anything to teach us about our present reality and the directions which our society should or should not take."[20] The answer to their question was a resounding *yes*. A legal system, Joseph and Carton reasoned, was in essence a reflection of human culture. Indeed, the ultimate goal has never changed. Our exercise to deploy cybersecurity measures requires that human dignity and control of technology be at the center of the discussion. This also means that it is the nation-state that ultimately must prove its legitimacy as the good steward and protector of the Internet.

Another allegory closer to the subject of cybersecurity is the story of Andrew E. Wiggin, the main character of the *New York Times* best-seller novel *Ender's Game*, by American author Orson Scott Card. This fascinating story includes military strategy in a world where humanity binds together to fight the Formics, an invading insectisoid alien race. However, the most haunting elements of the story revolve around the ethics of conducting warfare. Thus, Wiggin reflects on the reasons behind preemptive strikes, wars of aggression, and the impending destruction of the enemy's entire race. While security is an imperative, Wiggin notices that the cost of winning may be too high in cases where military operations are undermined by erroneous assumptions. He notices that including ethics while conducting a war is necessary for a meaningful victory.

A technologically literate civilization recognizes its place in history, while accepting the reality that the future will be better, largely because of the participatory process that promotes progress. Perhaps war is ingrained in humanity and the consequences of war are all near, lurking as a constant threat. On the other hand, humanity's efforts and pursuing of a true cybersecurity initiative should progress toward something greater. This is the true ideal that supports an effective plan for cyber risk reduction. This risk reduction begins and ends with the protection of all human beings and all the rights that a dignified life entails. For example, to prepare for the World Conference on International Telecommunications of 2012, the United Nations International Telecommunication Union (ITU) issued several "Background Briefs" to address various challenges. Brief 6 provided a grim look at the state of cybersecurity around the world.[21] It noted an increase in the number of cyber attacks and the level of their sophistication. The brief noted the following:

- at least seventy million different pieces of malware in circulation world-wide; and
- at least 70 percent of e-mails were spam.

While considering these statistics, it seems that all actions taken to reduce risks rely on the premise that we expect governments to take action while conducting their affairs as the equalizers of fairness. Sometimes, warnings about security threats and risks feel more like attempts by governments to assert their control over the Internet. It is hard to ignore the detrimental practices around the world that threaten to undermine the ability of the Internet to aid humanity. Restrictions of content, arbitrary filtering, illegitimate criminalization, cyber attacks, and the *weaponization* of the Internet stand to weaken the values inherent in a free society. These activities are not science fiction or mere hypotheticals. The Internet, and its security, must be studied from the prism of international human rights standards. The 2011 report submitted to the United Nations Human Rights Council by Frank La Rue, special rapporteur, identified the Internet as a medium for the exercise of freedom of expression.[22] However, the rapporteur explained that arbitrary criminalization to sanction free expression created a "chilling effect," leading to human rights violations.[23] La Rue also noted the blocking of specific websites, filtering technologies, "timed blocking" to prevent access during political moments, restrictions on the dissemination of content, and arbitrary arrests, all perpetrated by governments. These actions, ironically, have made cybersecurity a somewhat suspect endeavor, especially when not tempered by considerations of human rights.

One final, and relevant, observation to be made about La Rue's report involves intermediaries. As he explained, the Internet transmits information largely depending on "intermediaries," in essence, private corporations providing services, such as Internet service providers (ISPs), search engines, and blogging services. By putting unnecessary pressure on them, and by attempting to increase their legal liability, La Rue cautioned governments not to place businesses in line to be complicit in human rights violations. Even more relevant to cybersecurity, La Rue made two additional relevant observations:

- *Internet as a weapon:* "When a cyber attack, such as Distributed Denial of Service (DDoS) attacks, can be attributed to [a government], it clearly constitutes inter alia a violation of its obligation to respect the right to freedom of opinion and expression."
- *Surveillance*: "A number of [governments] are also introducing laws or modifying existing laws to increase their power to monitor Internet users' activities and content of communication without providing sufficient guarantees against abuse."[24]

The *skill* value, also necessary for a public order, would promote the utilization of technological know-how for the development of our global civilization. La Rue's concerns highlight that these technological skills, on occasion, are utilized to hamper human rights. While governments may be eager to track down usage online, U.S. citizens, for example, see their privacy challenged online. This was the conclusion of the 2014 report of the Pew Research Center. Mary Madden, senior researcher for the Pew Research Center's Internet Project, summarized the findings and highlighted some interesting observations. Madden noted that most American adults doubted their online privacy regarding personal information. The report noted that Americans continued to value "their space, their 'stuff,' their solitude, and, importantly, their rights."[25] More alarming, and also noted in the report, is that Americans lack confidence to control their personal information. In particular, most were concerned by how the private sector collected and utilized their data, and even about the government's monitoring of phone calls and Internet communications.

ON WAR: THE SHIELD OF CYBER RISK REDUCTION

It would be impossible to disregard the great significance of knowledge and the values inherent in the participation and contributions of the private sector and academia. This sense of cooperation is reflected in the value of *rectitude*, found within a global community, that promotes the cultivation of human dignity, while tolerating opposing views.[26] Authority is legitimate when its actions include a human rights dimension. Thus, the world community must take into account that the number one entity responsible for the protection of human rights is the nation-state.[27] It is governments, as stewards of the process of decision making, that must guard the social contract necessary for the secure life of the human person.

Recently, members of the military have been concentrating their discussions on "cyberwar" and, by indirect consequence, eclipsing the positive aspects of the Internet. The constant warnings about identity theft, attacks on government websites, and other crimes seem to never end. The word *terrorism* is widely utilized by governments and constantly repeated by the media. While some may call this fearmongering, or exaggerations, there is in fact a true reason to be concerned about cyber attacks. Actions to reduce risk rely on the premise that we expect governments to behave in good faith. A proper plan to reduce risks online depends on governments and the private sector implementing measures in the Internet not as a weapon to be wielded like a trident but rather as a shield to protect the benefits owed to humanity.

For this reason, the value of *enlightenment* serves as reminder that cybersecurity is directly related to the dissemination of information and the steps that must be taken to promote education in the cyber-risk-reduction process.[28] This can be the center of balance, as information also becomes a source of power. Indeed, even today, the promotion of openness and accessibility to information depends not only on technology but also on the actions of all participants in the management of the Internet. This is particularly applicable to governments and those in the business sector that continue to regulate, supply, and manage the tools of cybersecurity.

The Internet has been credited with contributing to scientific research, the connectivity of communications, and the closeness of humanity. Unfortunately, this technology must also be seen from the perspective of security and censorship, in the context of both national security and abuse of power. While governments could reject any management process that attempts to dilute their power and privilege, increasing perception of the more immediate economic and informational value of the Internet has prompted demands for radical changes in its management to increase access to the wealth and power of this limitless electronic frontier.

Accordingly, the services that users enjoy today were built upon the knowledge of the creators of the Internet. Enlightenment thus refers to the early records of the creators of the Internet; these creators demonstrated their skill and ability to share knowledge delineated in technical documents. The technical coordination of key aspects of the Internet's infrastructure created a historical precedent for the appropriate management of the Internet and its technical mission. Above all, while new technologies continue to create new challenges, all stakeholders must not allow the wrong solutions to hinder the protection of human rights.[29] Human rights will forever be a legal obligation and, as such, must be placed in the future agenda of cybersecurity initiatives.

CYBERSECURITY WITHIN THE GLOBAL CONTEXT

On October 10, 2012, I had the honor of participating, at the invitation of the U.S. Air Force Research Institute, in the second cyberpower conference at the Maxwell's Officer Training School. I had the opportunity to work with military and civilian experts to consider the challenges brought about by cyber attacks. The conference, Cyber Power: The Quest Toward a Common Ground, served as the catalysts for serious discussion in search of "ways to organize a unified response to cyber attacks."[30] One of the challenges so far involves individuals or groups, acting independently or as government proxies, maintaining a clear advantage in cyberspace.[31] It is a gloomy but real state of affairs when we encounter that the Internet has been transformed into another battlefield. One approach to counter the problem in the United States has been the recommendation to create a new military branch, the "cyber force," designating cyberspace as a new global battlefield for cyber warriors.[32] It is a matter of concern and a depressing reality to know that cyber-warfare has found its way into the Internet. The recent willingness of some governments to utilize emerging computer technologies for military purposes has threatened the true nature of the Internet. In return, the entire world's infrastructure has become vulnerable.

An approach to potential cyberwars, and one rooted in anticipatory measures, demonstrates that there are reasons to be concerned. For example, when the Stuxnet computer worm was discovered, it was eventually equated to artillery fire in a battlefield, and even possibly some kind of covert action.[33] On the other hand, why even make those comparisons? While the international community may lack an all-encompassing international strategy on cybersecurity, there can be no doubt that guideposts already exist to determine what should be the proper response in these cases. If an argument is going to be made that some cyber attacks rise to the level of armed conflict that necessitate an action recognized under article 51 of the Charter of the United Nations, then it must be clearly delineated by a recognized international standard. This argument also means that a secure and stable Internet is dependent on the need for international peace and security. Before any government resorts to the formula contained in chapter 7 of the United Nations Charter, in particular article 51, the assessment must consider if the actions in question constituted a real attack and to whom this attack will be attributed.[34] Most likely the bad actors behind the cyber attacks would be difficult to identify due to their stealthier nature and worldwide scope. Before considering the use of force, article 51 states that

> nothing in the present Charter shall impair the inherent right of individual or collective self-defense if an armed attack occurs against a Member of the United Nations, until the Security Council has taken measures necessary to maintain international peace and security. Measures taken by Members in the exercise of this right of self-defense shall be immediately reported to the Security Council and shall not in any way affect the authority and responsibility of the Security Council under the present Charter to take at any time such action as it deems necessary in order to maintain or restore international peace and security.

In fact, it has been suggested that the Internet, by default, has shaped a "non-obvious warfare," in which the identity of attackers and their actions are completely ambiguous.[35] This ambiguity and uncertainty continue to make the victimized nations hesitant about initiating a military response.[36] Any response is tempered by the *attribution* element, in which the targeted nation must identify with certainty the perpetrator of the cybercrime or cyber attacks.[37] But should we also consider the behavior of those nations that by their lack of action indirectly participate in the rogue activities perpetrated within their borders? This is not difficult to answer when considering, above all, that we should strive for an achievable peace in cyberspace. The world is not as chaotic as sometimes portrayed, although it makes for great stories on television. This is why any measure of anticipatory self-defense should also be considered suspect within the context of attribution. Doomsday scenarios should not be the cornerstone of a cyber risk analysis. Rather, difficult scenarios should be utilized to improve the identification of the attackers (or enemies) and policies that deal with real and measurable threats. This is not to say that nation-states should stand still when facing threats in cyberspace. To the contrary, the real test is how they will face those dangers while recognizing the borderless nature of the Internet and while protecting the open flow of information. A case in point is that nothing is gained by predicting Armageddon over threats in the Internet. The threats that may be encountered in cyberspace are of growing concern, not just for governments, but also for all users. While we all agree that these cyber criminals need to be stopped, it is not enough to address cybersecurity with criminal law principles. There is a danger of parochialism that could turn these laws only for the benefit of a few elites. Sometimes cybersecurity threats are utilized by governments who want to assert their control over the Internet without regard to the end user. The security of the Internet has to be more than the acquisition of power. A well-conceived plan needs to demonstrate that it would not betray the public trust.

THE NORTH AMERICAN EXAMPLE

The North American region has moved forward with a plan to protect the entire territory against threats in cyberspace. The U.S. Department of Homeland Security (DHS) and Public Safety Canada (PSC) decided to engage in a coordinated regional process to enhance the resiliency of their cyber infrastructure. Was this a good idea? It would depend on whether the plan created was designed to target security risks and threats, while keeping cooperation, risk reduction, and inclusion of all stakeholders. The Cybersecurity Action Plan is intended "to enhance the cybersecurity of our nations through increased integration of PS' and DHS' respective national cybersecurity activities and improved collaboration with the private sector."[38] This plan is important, because the Internet knows no borders, and the United States and Canada have a responsibility to "prevent, respond to, and recover from cyber disruptions and to make cyberspace safer for all citizens across the region." To understand and assess the success of this regional plan, it is necessary to consider that Canada and the United States have both concentrated efforts in preparing and combating threats and have sought out ways to reduce risks via their own individual plans. But this also means that there is a clear understanding of what cybersecurity should be in relation to both societies. While cybersecurity may relate to the defense of individual networks and their data, today it goes beyond that limited mandate and extends into new top-level domains and the overall preservation of online freedoms.[39] The North American region may face, on the other hand, potential threats from other foreign military services and their "proxy forces."[40] This is a revelation and an outrage, to realize that one of the biggest threats to the Internet comes from some unscrupulous governments. This also places at the forefront the use by governments of Computer Emergency Readiness Teams. The constant attacks that the United States may face to its military complex are ironically strategically valuable. For the attribution problem becomes less of a problem when a nation faces "multiple events" and studies them with the appropriate intelligence measures.[41] One potential solution is reflected, for example, by the efforts of the U.S. Computer Emergency Readiness Team (US-CERT), which involves the participation of public and private sector entities, such as "critical infrastructure owners and operators, academia, federal agencies, Information Sharing and Analysis Centers (ISAC), state and local partners, and domestic and international organizations."[42]

The government-funded US-CERT, operating from the Carnegie Mellon University, is one of many efforts around the world taken to look for best practices, technologies, and trained individuals to respond to cyber attacks.[43] Canada has followed a similar approach toward the protection of its citizens with the Public Safety Canadian Cyber Incident Response Centre (CCIRC), guided by the Cybersecurity Strategy of 2010.[44] This well-drafted strategy is designed to deal with cyberthreats and reduce risks. It follows three main objectives:

1. securing infrastructure and strengthening resiliency of governments systems;
2. creating a partnership including the federal, provincial, and territorial governments; and
3. educating and securing Canadians online.[45]

Public Safety Canada notes that CCIRC is, above all, a computer security incident response team for national coordination, designated to prepare and act in case of any incident that puts in danger the nation and its citizens. At its core is a diligent group of trained and experienced technicians that do not work in isolation, and their activities are organized with other relevant partners within the nation and abroad.

I am reminded of the early words referencing the Internet by the U.S. Supreme Court when it described it as a "unique medium . . . located in no particular geographical location but available to anyone, anywhere in the world, with access to" it.[46] It is because of this reality that regional plans are an excellent idea. In fact, it has been suggested that "information can be both a weapon and a target."[47] The efforts from Canada and the United States are now merged into a unified regional effort called the "Cybersecurity Action Plan between Public Safety Canada and the Department of Homeland Security."[48] Taking into consideration their shared border, this action plan delineates "the objectives articulated by President Obama and Prime Minister Harper in the February 2011 declaration, *Beyond the Border: A Vision for Perimeter Security and Economic Competitiveness.*" The plan outlined goals for improved collaboration with the private sector with public awareness activities, to be conducted in accordance with the June 2012 "Statement of Privacy Principles by the United States and Canada." This plan was designed with three comprehensive objectives:

1. It placed at center stage "Enhanced Cyber Incident Management" for real-time collaboration, information sharing, standardized processes, and sharing technical information.
2. It engaged the private sector by collaborating in the development of briefing materials.
3. It created public awareness.

The management of the Internet demands a careful and judicious protection of information from both unauthorized access and modification.[49] Because nations, organizations, corporations, and individuals are participants in the security aspects of the Internet, each becomes a part of the process and a reaffirmation of its legitimacy. Thus, the regional level of cyber risk reduction can be achieved in North America, although, it requires as a precondition the necessity of a special "stake" that qualifies the participants to share in a positive and stable management of the Internet. This is the key for the protection of freedom of expression. While this right may be "restricted" under certain circumstances, interference with it would only be legitimate under certain limited conditions. This is required first and foremost on the part of nation-states, which at the moment all too often engage in deliberate manipulation of threats to satisfy their own agendas. It is also a responsibility of the private sector, which possesses large amounts of data on Internet users and should protect it. There is no doubt that with new technologies we will find new difficulties. In turn, these difficulties should not be turned into controls that ultimately hinder human rights.

An examination of history shows that technology has played a crucial role in the success of human development. The implementation of a cyber-risk-reduction plan would be compatible with that history and with the Charter of the United Nations, which states as one of its ends in the preamble, "to unite our strength to maintain international peace and security." This is not to say that a UN agency has to run the Internet or its security, but certainly parallels exist to the cooperation that nations offer one another via treaties. The Internet has become engrained in the life of the world community. While the Internet has changed our history forever, it has presented challenges to our fundamental freedoms and overall human dignity.[50] Taking the example of the North American region, the coordinated regional process headed by the DHS and PSC are enhanced by the efforts of a plan implemented to target security risks and threats, while keeping cooperation, risk reduction, and inclusion of all stakeholders.[51] While the Internet provides many peaceful uses for global communications, its borderless nature demands that nations establish a regional plan, "with a worldwide approach to prevent, respond to, and recover from cyber attacks."[52] Any unilateral control of the Internet is incompatible with the present realities of a global society, where the Internet's array of global communications systems must benefit all of humanity— despite some governments' agenda to restrict its use. This is the biggest flaw in the present security system. Individuals require freedom and democracy in order to lead dignified lives, but governments exists only to ensure the common good for all individuals.[53] The human being, therefore, is at the center of the story.

REBALANCING THE WORLD

Various challenges around the world remind us that human rights are not a hypothetical but rather become threatened during times of conflict. They are standards that protect the human race because they are inviolable. For this reason, it is inescapable to reason that technology in our society is fixed to standards that must serve the goals of the global community, recognizing that all individuals are persons with the right to be part of an effective process of governance and free from coercion.[54] The fifteenth-century legal scholar Hugo Grotius suggested that law infused by humanity created a direct connection to the individuals' *well-being*, while alluding to a distinctive prerequisite of stewardship of governments in trust for all human beings.[55] Grotius wrote about the law that was the same among all nations and that was innate in every individual. He explained that the law extended over nations that were "scrupulously just."[56]

Possibly, and somewhat surprising, is the realization of the vanishing concept of the supremacy of the nation-state as the only existing subject within Internet governance. The stature of the individual human being as a participant in international human rights law demonstrates in part that evolution. The other one is the Internet. Indeed, individuals and businesses have become objects of international law, with legal stature to invoke the responsibility of nation-states in matters of human rights.[57]

In early February 2011, two nation-states faced political turmoil that threatened to spread to other bordering nations. The leader of Tunisia was forced out, and violent protests cried for the removal of President Hosni Mubarak in Egypt.[58] Certainly, it would be inaccurate to conclude that the Internet was the single cause of the political and social upheaval associated with these events. However, it is hard to forget that Tunis hosted a major Internet-governance event (the second phase of the World Summit on the Information Society) and that Egypt hosted the fourth meeting of the Internet Governance Forum. Again, to conclude that these meetings were the cause of these political and social upheavals would be an overstatement. Still, we have to wonder. Access to the Internet has had influence during political upheavals, and the social media impact cannot be dismissed or ignored.[59]

The clear lesson to be learned from both nations is that declaring states of emergency for political reasons while blocking the Internet had a direct and contrary effect to that intended by the authoritarian government, or for that matter, for any government that abuses its power. The lack of access to information, when blocked under a nation's direct mandate or by tampering with its functionality, becomes a fundamental violation of international human rights law. From this point onward, the world community must carefully examine all events, so that it is recognized as a challenge to successfully protect humanity.

The value of *respect* compels stakeholders to see themselves increasingly as full participants able to make claims in their own names.[60] Thus, respect demands that all governments give all other stakeholders the avenue to discover participation—a goal intrinsically related to the governance of the Internet. Respect, like power, requires greater recognition of participation in the decision-making process. It is the level of recognition, respect, and democratic protection that has formed the basis for the development of a successful process of governance. This is the key for the protection of freedom of expression. While this freedom may be "lessened" under certain circumstances, it may be legitimately constrained only under limited conditions enumerated in article 4 of the International Covenant on Civil and Political Rights (ICCPR). The ICCPR is the most important international human rights law treaty in existence and one that has been adopted by most governments in the world. The treaty's influence has been directly tied to the Universal Declaration of Human Rights, recognized widely as a customary international law applicable to the world.

The required protection of human rights are all too often ignored by governments that engage in deliberate manipulation of threats to satisfy their own agendas. But these rights should also be a responsibility for businesses that possess large amounts of data on Internet users and work closely, many times as proxy for governments. Any initiative focused on national defense exclusively only considers the negative aspects of the Internet, while failing to resolve the greater challenge. While it is much easier to just focus on security and militarization (although both are necessary), the ultimate goal should be the inclusiveness of additional actors such as nongovernmental organizations, transnational business entities, and individuals. Thus, Internet users cannot assume that governments, unlike other participants of the process, must be given wider latitude as if they never did anything wrong.

For example, a state of emergency during times of conflict always becomes a potential ground for abuses. The line between security and violation of human rights is very tenuous. Fear and misinformation are the weapons of the oppressor. The ICCPR directly opposes human rights becoming a collateral damage. The ICCPR allows nations to derogate from certain human rights guarantees, but this *derogation*, in essence, allows a government to suspend partially the functioning of the treaty within its borders. For example, in declaring a state of emergency, ICCPR articles 4 and 40 continue to bind governments to maintain their obligations toward citizens. Every time a government ignores the limits laid down by international human rights law, the worst violations of human rights have occurred to the detriment of innocent individuals. The Internet provides individuals, organizations, and businesses with freedom of expression, collaboration, and political participation.

The legislative drafting history of the ICCPR, also known as the *Travaux Preparatoires*, notes in the deliberations explanations regarding article 4.[61] Article 4 allows for derogation of some of the rights protected only in times of national emergency that threatens the existence of a nation. The *Travaux Preparatoires* revealed a desire by the treaty drafters to prohibit all derogations without any exceptions at all times. This was modified to allow some small exceptions. The experts on the subject of the ICCPR, the UN Human Rights Committee, has stated in their "General Comment No. 29 State of Emergency (Article 4)" that derogation is only permitted under exceptional circumstances and only briefly.[62] It is likely that many cybersecurity emergencies would not be exempt from this high threshold. Above all, the ICCPR's legislative history shows that governments that joined the treaty lacked the unilateral power to decide when and how they were to exercise the emergency powers found in that clause within the treaty.[63]

Could we say that some governments have chosen to exercise emergency powers in an abusive manner? In other words, can we say that governments will be good trustees of the Internet? The United Nations Universal Declaration of Human Rights is the additional point of departure for an assessment of a cyber-risk plan. Article 1 states that "all human beings are born free and equal in dignity and rights." A cyber-risk plan should also rely on various positive human rights guarantees that, in one way or another, apply directly to the issue of access and, even more, to the issue of control over the management of the Internet. The ICCPR proclaimed in its preamble that these human rights were "derived from the inherent dignity of the human person." The ICCPR, article 2, requires that governments ensure for "all individuals within their territories and subject to their jurisdiction" the accorded protection of their human rights. For this reason, cybersecurity must also consider individual freedoms. Human rights are more than just guarantees of individual freedom to access information; these guarantees may also strengthen any new chosen plan of cybersecurity. The UN Human Rights Committee explained in their General Comment 3 the importance of knowledge of rights by individuals and the obligations of administrative and judicial authorities.[64] The ICCPR enshrines the protection of the right to hold opinions without interference and the right to freedom of expression.[65] General Comment 10 emphasizes the obligation of nations to protect the right to freedom of expression, which includes freedom to "impart information and ideas of all kinds," and the freedom to seek and receive them regardless of the frontiers explored and medium utilized.[66] The enlightenment of the world community has been enshrined by human rights defenders for some time now. Indeed, as explained in *Kivenmaa v. Finland* (412/1990), "the right for an individual to express his political opinions, including obviously his opinions on the question of human rights, forms part of the freedom of expression guaranteed by article 19" of the ICCPR.[67] The case of *Gauthier v. Canada* (633/1995) determined that the right to access information protects actions such as seeking and receiving information.[68] Other guarantees are noted in article 13 of the International Covenant on Economic, Social and Cultural Rights, which remind of the obligation of governments to recognize everyone's rights to education;[69] while the International Convention on the Elimination of All Forms of Racial Discrimination requires states to adopt immediate and effective measures in the fields of teaching, education, culture, and information.[70] As a final point, the Convention on the Elimination of All Forms of Discrimination against Women urges governments to protect equal rights for women in the field of education,[71] and the Convention on the Rights of the Child requires states to agree that the education of children shall be directed to the development of respect for human rights and fundamental freedoms.[72] These are the contemporary challenges to human rights protections online.

A government's restrictions and obstruction of expression would only be legitimate if it clearly outlines the conditions whereby human rights can be restricted under extraordinary circumstances and within an extremely limited timetable. There may arise a moment in time where a cyber attack rises to such level of necessity. However, these occasions should be considered exceptional. The challenge to be faced is how to prevent cyberpower from harming our global community while protecting democratic values and human rights. Of course, democratic values must be applied between nations and within nations. There is no doubt that there are no easy answers. In the end, the greater responsibility falls on governments. For this reason, "the legitimacy of a government [is judged] by whether it lives up to the international standards of convenience."[73] Human rights are sacrosanct. Convenience should not be sacrificed by perceived efficiency or overzealous security. They are not hypothetical concepts that need to be reassessed or reconsidered by the private sector or governments. Indeed, the sine qua non of online freedom is tied to an open and accessible Internet.

FINAL THOUGHTS

Cybersecurity demands a further step, requiring a unique approach in governance. It is here that human rights standards fill the gap, by guiding the participant to find that justice and fairness is considered not only appropriate but also divine.[74] Fear and misinformation are extremely powerful tools that can cause devastating results. I have noted before that the management of the Internet does not belong in the ambit of the well-behaved hegemon. Instead, a cybersecurity policy requires the analysis of *affection*, the final value noted here to highlight a needed positive approach toward others and the Internet community.[75] While it may seem a lofty goal, this value is most visible within the multidimensional public policy discussions at ICANN meetings, specifically when policy decisions follow a bottom-up process that shapes the exchange of information and promotes cooperation among all stakeholders. Here, freedom of expression is vital for the promotion of the capabilities necessary to govern effectively while shaping the sharing of values.[76] While Internet-related issues will continue to be plagued by self-centered interests related to territorial borders and national power, we must recognize that the Internet needs to be secured while protecting full respect for the human need to hold opinions, hear them, and share information and ideas without interference or fear, regardless of frontiers. Affection requires the avoidance of regimes that would allow global restrictions on freedom of expression online and any governmental or corporate involvement in the suppression of human rights. Indeed, the importance of intensive communication, good faith, and honest dealings within the multistakeholder process has the potential to play a key role in the resolution of security challenges.

The outline of the eight values presented in this chapter should be seen as the standard for the appraisal of past practices and the development of new standards. Ideas with the complexity and structure of an appropriate cybersecurity process herald the reality of a civilization seeking out greater understanding of the human person and greater rights, understanding that all other matters are peripheral. In order to approach the challenges of cybersecurity and find a pragmatic solution, we must first be confident in the protection of human dignity. For this reason, all stakeholders must promote the protection of human life, online and off line.

There is no doubt that human rights are more than hypothetical constructs. The values previously presented have now run headlong into the realities and needs of today's Internet. Will security and human rights be harmonized in the Internet age? If we fail in this endeavor we will suffer a true tragedy. This tragedy will be not one of resources but one of information, wisdom, and civilization. Internet users have learned that governments, unlike other participants of the process, have taken for themselves wider latitude. Giving up everything for security is simply the incorrect cause of action. Humanity cannot lose itself in that kind of quest. To follow that path is to forget that there is more that unites us than divides us. Dishonesty related to threats in the real world or exaggerating threats that exist in cyberspace potentially offer indirect results when pandered at the national and international level, becoming a catalyst for the weakening of human rights. We should not forget that those rights are innate to all humans. We should not lose our values and the traits that make us great but instead remember our humanity and become better now and in the future.

NOTES

1. Hugo Grotius, *The Rights of War and Peace, including the Law of Nature and of Nations* (New York: Cosimo, 2007), 284.

2. Harold D. Lasswell and Myers S. McDougal, *Jurisprudence for a Free Society* (New Haven, CT: Yale University Press,1992), 1,245.

3. Jean-Jacques Rousseau, *On the Social Contract* (Mineola, NY: Dover, 2003), 1.

4. Ibid.

5. Ibid., 3–4.

6. Ibid., 8–9.

7. This paragraph is based on the book by Sarah Joseph, Jenny Schultz, and Melissa Castan, *The International Covenant on Civil and Political Rights: Cases, Materials, and Commentary*, 2nd ed. (Oxford: Oxford University Press, 2005), 5, para. 1.05 (explaining the idea behind the social contract).

8. Myers S. McDougal, Harold D. Lasswell, and Lung-chu Chen, eds., *Human Rights and the World Public Order: The Basic Policies of an International Law of Human Dignity* (New Haven, CT: 1980), 154–55.

9. The navy hymn is based on the writings by William Whiting of England. "Eternal Father, Strong to Save," Center for Church Music, accessed September 2, 2015, http://songsandhymns.org/. See Royal Naval Association, "Frequently Asked Questions," accessed August 29, 2015, http://www.royal-naval-association.co.uk/; and America's Navy, "Eternal Father: The Navy Hymn," last updated August 17, 2009, http://www.navy.mil/.

10. George Grote, *History of Greece* (Boston: Elibron Classics, 2004), 3, 11, 56, 194.

11. Kathleen Sears, *Mythology 101: From Gods and Goddesses to Monsters and Mortals; Your Guide to Ancient Mythology* (Avon, MA: Adams, 2014), 73, 78, 101.

12. Joanna Kulesza and Roy Balleste, "Signs and Portents in Cyberspace: The Rise of Jus Internet as a New Order in International Law," *Fordham Intellectual Property, Media, and Entertainment Law Journal* 23 (2013): 1311–49.

13. Chris Demchak, "Resilience, Disruption, and a 'Cyber Westphalia': Options for National Security in a Cybered Conflict World," in *Securing Cyberspace: A New Domain for National Security*, ed. Nicholas Burns and Jonathan Price (Washington, DC: Aspen Institute, 2012), 63.

14. McDougal, Lasswell, and Chen, *Human Rights*, 394.

15. Myers S. McDougal, Harold D. Lasswell, and James C. Miller, *The Interpretation of Agreements and World Public Order: Principles of Content and Procedure* (New Haven, CT: Yale University Press, 1967), 3.

16. McDougal, Lasswell, and Chen, *Human Rights*, 390.

17. Jon Postel, "Domain Name System Structure and Delegation," Information Sciences Institute, March 1994, https://www.ietf.org/.

18. Lasswell and McDougal, *Jurisprudence*, 400.

19. Roy Balleste, "The Earth Alliance Constitution: International Human Rights Law and Babylon," *Florida Coastal Law Review* 10, no. 1 (2008): 33–66. *Babylon 5* is a registered trademark of PTN Consortium and Warner Bros. Television. *Babylon 5* is the creation of American writer J. Michael Straczynski. See Paul Joseph and Sharon Carton, "The Law of the Federation: Images of Law, Lawyers, and the Legal System in 'Star Trek: The Next Generation,'" *University of Toledo Law Review* 24 (1992): 43–85.

20. See Joseph and Carton, "Law of the Federation"; and Balleste, "Earth Alliance Constitution."

21. "Cybersecurity," World Conference on International Telecommunications (WCIT) 2012, Background Brief 6, accessed September 2, 2015, http://www.itu.int/.

22. See UN Frank La Rue Report of the Special Rapporteur on the Promotion and Protection of the Right to Freedom of Opinion and Expression, para. 60, Human Rights Council, Seventeenth Session, A/HRC/17/27, May 16, 2011.

23. This chapter section is based on La Rue's report, specifically of paragraphs 28–30, 33, 38–44, 52, and 55.

24. UN Frank La Rue Report, paras. 52, 55.

25. Mary Madden, "Public Perceptions of Privacy and Security in the Post-Snowden Era," Pew Research Internet Project, November 12, 2014, http://www.pewinternet.org/.

26. W. Michael Reisman, "Development and Nation-Building: A Framework for Policy-Oriented Inquiry," *Maine Law Review* 60, no. 2 (2008): 313.

27. Walter Kälin and Jörg Künzli, *The Law of International Human Rights Protection* (Oxford: Oxford University Press, 2009), 78.

28. Reisman, "Development and Nation-Building," 312.

29. Wolfgang Benedek, "Internet Governance and Human Rights," in *Internet Governance and the Information Society: Global Perspectives and European Dimensions*, ed. Wolfgang Benedek, Veronika Bauer, and Matthias C. Kettemann (Utrecht, Netherlands: Eleven International, 2008), 47.

30. The Air Force Research Institute conducted a conference to consider strengthening the unified response to cyber incidents. Air University public affairs staff, Air University, Maxwell Air Force Base, Alabama, October 19, 2012 .

31. Demchak, "Resilience, Disruption," 60.

32. Natasha Solce, "The Battlefield of Cyberspace: The Inevitable New Military Branch—The Cyber Force," *Albany Law Journal of Science and Technology* 18, no. 1 (2008): 295, 296.

33. Scott J. Shackelford and Richard B. Andres, "State Responsibility for Cyber Attacks: Competing Standards for a Growing Problem," *Georgetown Journal of International Law* 42, no. 4 (2011): 973.

34. Paul Rozenweig, *Cyber Warfare: How Conflicts in Cyberspace Are Challenging America and Changing the World* (Santa Barbara, CA: Praeger, 2013), 51.

35. Martin C. Libicki, "The Specter of Non-Obvious Warfare," *Strategic Studies Quarterly* 6, no. 3 (2012): 88–101.

36. Ibid., 89.

37. E. M. Mudrinich, "Cyber 3.0: The Department of Defense Strategy for Operating in Cyberspace and the Attribution Problem," *Air Force Law Review* 68 (2012): 204–5.

38. Public Safety Canada and Department of Homeland Security, "Cybersecurity Action Plan between Public Safety Canada and the Department of Homeland Security," 2012, last updated March 4, 2014, http://www.publicsafety.gc.ca/, 2–3.

39. James A. Lewis, "Harnessing Leviathan: Internet Governance and Cybersecurity," in *Securing Cyberspace: A New Domain for National Security*, ed. Nicholas Burns and Jonathan Price (Washington, DC: Aspen Institute, 2012), 113.

40. Ibid., 117.

41. Ibid., 118.

42. "About Us," U.S. Computer Emergency Readiness Team (US-CERT), accessed September 2, 2015, https://www.us-cert.gov/.

43. Greg Shannon, "CERT Research Report," Software Engineering Institute, Carnegie Mellon University, 2010, accessed August 29, 2015, https://resources.sei.cmu.edu/, 2.

44. Public Safety Canada, "Canadian Cyber Incident Response Centre (CCIRC)," last updated December 12, 2014, http://www.publicsafety.gc.ca/.

45. Public Safety Canada, "Cyber Security: A Shared Responsibility," 2010, last updated March 4, 2014, http://www.publicsafety.gc.ca/cyber.

46. Reno v. ACLU, 521 US 844, 850–51 (1997).

47. Deborah A. Liptak, "Information Warfare and Cybersecurity," in *Web of Deceit: Misinformation and Manipulation in the Age of Social Media*, ed. Anne P. Mintz (Medford, NJ: CyberAge Books, 2012).

48. Public Safety Canada and Department of Homeland Security, "Cybersecurity Action Plan," 2.

49. Liptak, "Information Warfare," 84.

50. Maud de Boer-Buquicchio, foreword, in *Media Matters in the Cultural Contradictions of the "Information Society": Towards a Human-Rights-Based Governance*, by Divina Frau-Meigs (Strasbourg, France: Council of Europe Publishing, 2011), 5.

51. Public Safety Canada and Department of Homeland Security, "Cybersecurity Action Plan," 2–3.

52. W. J. Lynn, "Remarks on the Department of Defense Cyber Strategy" (speech), National Defense University, Washington, DC, July 14, 2011, http://www.defense.gov/.

53. Pope John XXIII, *Pacem in Terris* (Peace on Earth) (Boston: Daughters of St. Paul, 1963), para. 24.

54. McDougal, Lasswell, and Chen, *Human Rights*, 383–84.

55. See Hugo Grotius, *The Freedom of the Seas; or, The Right Which Belongs to the Dutch to Take Part in the East Indian Trade*, ed. James Brown Scott (New York: Oxford University Press, 1916), 5, 53.

56. Ibid.

57. See James Crawford, "The System of International Responsibility," in *The Law of International Responsibility*, ed. James Crawford, Alain Pellet, Simon Olleson, and Kate Parlett (Oxford: Oxford University Press, 2010), 5–7.

58. "Egypt: Mubarak Sacks Cabinet and Defends Security Role," *BBC News*, January 29, 2011, http://www.bbc.co.uk/. See also Soumaya Ghannoushi, "Tunisians Must Dismantle the Monster Ben Ali Built," *Guardian*, January 18, 2011, http://www.guardian.co.uk/.

59. For example, see Tanya Talaga, "How Social Media Is Fuelling Ukraine's Protests," *Star.com*, March 4, 2015, http://www.thestar.com/.

60. Reisman, "Development and Nation-Building," 313.

61. Marc J. Bossuyt, *Guide to the "travaux Préparatoires" of the International Covenant on Civil and Political Rights* (Boston: Martinus Nijhoff, 1987), 81–102 (detailing the legislative history of article 4).

62. UN Human Rights Commission [CCPR], General Comment No. 29, State of Emergency, article 4, para. 2, UN Doc. CCPR/C/21/Rev.1/Add 11 (August 31, 2001).

63. Ibid.

64. UN CCPR General Comment No. 03: Implementation at the National Level, article 2, Thirteenth session, July 29, 1981.

65. International Covenant on Economic, Social and Cultural Rights, GA res. 2200A (XXI), article 19 (1) and (2).

66. UN CCPR General Comment No. 10: Freedom of Expression, article 19, Nineteenth session, June 29, 1983.

67. Kivenmaa v. Finland, Human Rights Committee, Communication No. 412/1990, CCPR/C/50/D/412/1990, March 31, 1994. See also Joseph, Schultz, and Castan, *International Covenant on Civil and Political Rights*, 519–20.

68. Joseph, Schultz, and Castan, *International Covenant on Civil and Political Rights*, 519–20. See also Gauthier v. Canada, Human Rights Committee, Communication no. 633 (1995), CCPR/C/65/D/633 (1995), April 7, 1999.

69. International Covenant on Economic, Social and Cultural Rights, GA res. 2200A (XXI).

70. International Convention on the Elimination of All Forms of Racial Discrimination, article 7, G.A. res. 2106 (XX), Annex, 20 U.N. GAOR Supp. No. 14 at 47, U.N. Doc. A/6014 (1966), 660 U.N.T.S. 195, entered into force January 4, 1969.

71. Convention on the Elimination of All Forms of Discrimination against Women, article 10, December 18, 1979, 1249 U.N.T.S. 13; 19 I.L.M. 33 (1980).

72. Convention on the Rights of the Child, article 29(b), November 20, 1989, 1577 U.N.T.S. 3; 28 I.L.M. 1456 (1989).

73. Lung-chu Chen, "In Affectionate Memory of Professor Myres McDougal: Champion for an International Law of Human Dignity," *Yale Law Journal* 108, no. 5 (1999): 956.

74. Alexander Orakhelashvili, "Natural Law and Justice," in *Max Planck Encyclopedia of Public International Law* (New York: Oxford University Press, 2007), para. 33.

75. Reisman, "Development and Nation-Building," 313.

76. McDougal, Lasswell, and Chen, *Human Rights and the World Public Order*, 156.

Chapter Four

Privacy versus Security

Identifying the Challenges in a Global Information Society

Rolf H. Weber and Dominic N. Staiger

TENSIONS BETWEEN PRIVACY AND SECURITY

Since the medieval times, all forms of governments have walked the fine line between maintaining public order whilst upholding the privacy rights of its citizens. Although privacy as a freestanding legal concept has only arisen over the past decades, the right to freedom from arbitrary interference by governments has long been an accepted principle in society. For example, property of a citizen could only be searched and seized in England under an appropriate writ.[1] Furthermore, constitutions such as the U.S. Constitution contain express clauses in this regard.[2] Privacy in one's actions, resonating strongly with the requirement of anonymity, allows people to be courageous in expressing their opinion and advocating fundamental rights. Thus from a social perspective, the right to privacy is central to a working democracy.[3] Despite these advantages, a balance must be maintained as otherwise privacy rights will also be abused for illegitimate purposes. The limits of privacy become apparent when the rights of one individual interfere with the rights of another. It is therefore in the hands of the legislator to decide to what extent privacy infringements are necessary in specific circumstances and to implement clear structures for privacy protection.

The envisaged measures must be checked against international agreements and fundamental legal concepts enshrined in state constitutions as otherwise government power could grow in an unlimited fashion through the creation of new laws. The main question in most privacy cases is not whether the government's objective in collecting or intercepting data is legitimate but whether the way in which the measures occur is proportionate to the risk to be prevented. In order for a state to infringe on the privacy rights of its citizens, first a constitutionally valid law must be in place permitting the desired action. Second, the measure to be taken must be proportionate to the harm to be prevented and the infringement that would occur. Third, the measure must be suitable in the best possible manner to achieve the desired objective of the government action.[4] The last two points are commonly known as the necessity test and the strict scrutiny review.[5]

The growth in new technologies has enabled ease of access to various forms of personal information. Related privacy concerns are only going to grow over the next decades with the increase of interconnectedness of various devices (Internet of Things) as well as the rise in processing capabilities. Any personal movement and characteristics are easily ascertainable through various sources. It is therefore essential to develop a framework that will bridge the gap between technical capabilities and privacy laws as they stand today. Of particular importance in this regard are the internationally binding legal instruments as well as the constitutional protections that either specifically or indirectly contain an individual privacy-protection right.

CURRENT PRIVACY-PROTECTION FRAMEWORKS

International Agreements

Article 12 of the Universal Declaration of Human Rights (UDHR), passed by the United Nations in 1948, provides for the protection of privacy. Furthermore, the 1966 International Covenant on Civil and Political Rights (ICCPR) contains the same protection in article 17. However, at the time these laws were passed, technology had not yet evolved to the degree it has today. In particular the scope of potential privacy infringements was still negligible. Over the years various guidelines have been published by international organizations such as the UN, but only the ICCPR is legally binding on state legislators.[6] The Human Rights Committee interpreted the ICCPR to ban any public interest justification for the infringement of human rights and fundamental democratic tenets.[7] Furthermore, the European Court of Human Rights has clarified the application of human rights to individual cases arising in relation to European member state laws.

In 2006, the Convention on Cybercrime of the Council of Europe entered into force with aims of addressing cybercrime issues that have arisen over the last decade. However, as the terminology of the convention is based on the 1990s technology, it cannot cater for all online criminal conduct present today. Furthermore, not all states that signed the convention have ratified it because of its incompatibility with national constitutions such as limitations on freedom of speech.

Constitutional Privacy Protection

Currently, various constitutional privacy-protection concepts exist around the world or are derived from constitutional court judgments. For example, the Philippine Supreme Court has established that the compulsory issuance of an ID would violate a citizen's privacy rights.[8] A similar conclusion was previously reached by the constitutional court of Hungary.[9] Furthermore, the U.S. Constitution contains in its Fourth Amendment a right against unreasonable search and seizures that is the main basis for the U.S. privacy protection. Most European countries also have similar constitutional protections that ensure the self-determination of their citizens. In particular the German Federal Constitutional Court accepted a right to computer confidentiality and integrity.[10]

Selected State Laws

In addition to constitutional protections, various countries have implemented their own data-protection and privacy laws that sometimes cover all types of data or only a specific business sector. During the course of carrying out their tasks, government agencies accumulate various forms of data. This information is in most instances placed under some degree of protection by privacy legislation such as the U.S. Privacy Act,[11] the EU Data Protection Directive, or privacy laws of the EU member states. Recent controversies over various data-protection issues have shown that these laws differ in key aspects regarding their scope and applicability. In Europe, data protection is currently regulated through the EU Data Protection Directive, which sets out the minimum standard to be enforced by the EU member states through their national data-protection laws.[12] The United States is entirely different in this regard as the federal versus state distinction places limitations on the federal government's ability to regulate all aspects of privacy and data protection. On the constitutional level there is only a protection against the unreasonable search and seizure of information that is somewhat limited in situations in which private information such as a social security number or the address of a person are supplied by a public agency to a third party or used by it. It is therefore essential to first apply the U.S. Privacy Act and then identify whether other state laws protect the information in a given circumstance.

Potentially situations arise where a request for information is made to a state agency by an individual concerning another person. In order to assess whether the information should be disclosed, all facts of the case need to be closely evaluated and balanced against each other. For example, a court in

Michigan declined to require a social service to disclose the location of children to their father as he was not able to show "compelling circumstances affecting the health or safety" of his children.[13] Thus on balance privacy should be maintained unless there are convincing reasons for a disclosure. The Dutch Intelligence and Security Services Act (2002) requires the intelligence agencies to first check open sources before resorting to more invasive measures in obtaining intelligence data on an individual.

PRIVACY VERSUS SECURITY

Data Collection and Use

The growth in technological developments has seen governments expand their data collection across all service areas, such as registrations for cars, residency, taxation, financial information, marital status, electricity, and water use. With such a vast array of data, the agencies can predict usage and service requirements as well as optimize their service deployment. In doing so they must find ways to protect the privacy of the individuals from whom they collect the data. This applies in particular as the information must be compulsorily supplied by the citizens and the procedure is governed by public law. Thus, a disclosure of the collected data may be required under a freedom of information request that forms part of the administrative law of many countries. Safeguards and clear structures are necessary to prevent disclosure of previously not-collected information, and objection rights must be granted to any individual affected. Furthermore, combining the collected data sets from various sources by public agencies should only be allowed subject to consent by the individual whose data is stored in these systems. In combination with other data sets, the information can be used for a wide array of purposes, allowing the identification of an individual's behavior and characteristics.

New regulation is required to limit the type and amount of data public agencies are allowed to request and retain. Additionally, the use of this data must be restricted to only those tasks necessary for the performance of the agency's function. As public entities are increasingly carrying out functions of private enterprises, the blurring of the type of data usage can be avoided through such restrictions in order to ultimately retain its public use definition.

Today globalization allows everyone access to a seemingly unlimited amount of data from any location in the world. Despite technological advances and the growth in available data, control mechanisms have not been able to keep up with the previously known security standards. In an analog world, it was easy to physically prevent access to data. Cloud computing and other technologies now enable on-demand access to data from anywhere. Thus security features must not only be universal in their worldwide application but also operate 24-7. Striking the balance between access limitation and ease of access is one of the dominant challenges faced by enterprises implementing privacy-protection frameworks. [14]

Access to Public Service Data

Who has access and when to public data is generally regulated by freedom of information laws. Particular challenges for these laws are the situations in which a private individual wants access to data stored by a public service authority relating to another individual. In such a case the individual seeking the information must generally demonstrate that his or her interest in receiving the information outweighs the privacy implications to the individual whose data is stored. Importantly not even the first amendment grants the press a right to access information that is not available to the general public. [15] Furthermore, this also applies to property of the government to which to some extent the data stored on government servers belong. [16] Thus there is no freestanding right under the First Amendment to access records or information within the government's possession. [17]

In *Whalen v. Roe*, [18] the U.S. Supreme Court reiterated that there are essentially two types of privacy interests that are constitutionally protected: "One is the individual interest in avoiding disclosure of personal matters, and another is the interest in independence in making certain kinds of important decisions." The right to informational privacy, however, "is not absolute; rather, it is a conditional right which may be infringed upon a showing of proper governmental interest." [19]

The requirements in order to allow disclosure are subject to much debate and opposing judgments. Courts have held that when the government releases information, it must be of a highly personal nature before constitutional privacy rights will attach. In its judgment in *Eagle v. Morgan*, the U.S. Court of Appeal highlighted that "to violate [a person's] constitutional right of privacy, the information disclosed must be either a shocking degradation or an egregious humiliation." [20]

Constitutional privacy protection only extends to "the most intimate aspects of human affairs," and a person's "legitimate expectation of privacy" bears on the constitutional analysis. [21] In this context, for example, "mandatory disclosure of an individual's Social Security Number (SSN) to the Department of Motor Vehicles does not threaten the sanctity of individual privacy so as to require constitutional protection," and constitutional privacy rights apply only to more personal matters such as marriage, procreation, and family. [22] Despite the varying judgments, the issue of privacy remains a contested one. Each individual case has different facets potentially resulting in decisions based on the weighing of the privacy impact.

In Europe public authorities are bound by national as well as EU laws on data processing. The EU has limited the processing and collection of personal data through various directives.[23] However, recently the EU Data Retention Directive was found to violate EU law and was invalidated by the European Court of Justice (ECJ).[24]

Big Data Archives

Big Data is the new promising technology that will enable enormous efficiency gains as it allows companies to move quickly from data to knowledge and to action. However, challenges to privacy protection also arise from Big Data technologies enabling the processing of vast amount of data and deriving individual and group behavioral patterns from the data.[25]

The Obama administration has taken a very open stance to government data. It has effectively made a vast amount of government data available on its website http://www.data.gov/. Its aim in doing so is to strengthen democracy and improve the life of its citizens by driving economic opportunity. With Executive Order 13642, the president established a new approach to open data in 2013 by requiring all federal agencies to consider openness and machine readability as a default for all their information. Additionally, the agencies are required to appropriately guard privacy that can be achieved through various privacy-enhancing technologies discussed in the section titled "Privacy-Enhancing Technologies" below.

During the Second World War, the United States relied on confidential government data to ascertain areas in which Japanese Americans lived in order to detain them in camps for the duration of the war. Today such measures could go far beyond what was possible in the 1940s. Big Data allows the government to select virtually any variable it likes and determine to which citizens it applies.

Already in 1980 the OECD pointed out in its Guidelines on the Protection of Privacy and Transborder Flows of Personal Data in paragraph 9 that once the data stored no longer serves a purpose, the lack of interest may result in negligent treatment of such data and pose a threat to privacy. Deleting unused data therefore is an important pillar of privacy protection. Often the argument is made that the data can be anonymized, thus a collection of all DNA data should not be prevented as the risk is low. Only the actual personalization of the data should be subject to close regulation and oversight. What such an argument fails to address is the fact that once such vast amounts of data are collected, invariably the risk to unauthorized access grows as the security measures required must also keep up with the amount of data stored. Furthermore, if a party steals such information, it will not be governed by any form of regulation. Thus, only collecting the DNA when this is warranted in the individual case appears to be the most risk-averse and prudent solution.[26]

Smart Metering

Smart metering is another method of further infringing on personal privacy by exactly identifying the electricity use of an individual. Data is collected by a so-called smart meter that constantly communicates the electricity use to the electricity supplier. With this information, individual behavior patterns can be identified. By accumulating the data with other smart-meter data across a country, entire power-usage predictions can be carried out. However, despite the advantages of having the data to increase efficiency in the electricity grid, serious privacy as well as health concerns arise with these devices. For example, these meters have been used in some U.S. states where people have started to complain of health issues resulting from the electromagnetic smog the devices are creating. Additionally, opposition has formed against the constant surveillance of one's power use. As electricity supply is a state monopoly, the user has no right to object to the installation of such a device as long as there are no laws in place allowing the individual to opt out of the new meter use.[27] In Europe some state data-protection laws currently prevent the compulsory installation of such privacy-infringing devices, which is why the meters have not yet been installed on a big scale.

Identification

Identity Cards

Increasing the level of technology included in identity cards is creating serious privacy issues. For example, all EU member states as well as other countries wanting to participate in the U.S. Visa Waiver Program have implemented biometric passports. These include fingerprint as well as other personal-characteristic information. Tests have shown that the data can be read out of the chip on the passport without requiring sophisticated hacking knowledge.

New identity cards will in the future include so-called RFID chips that won't even require contact to the card as the information stored can be read through a wireless system. Thus, a reading device could access all identification cards within a certain space without knowledge of their owners.[28] Biometrics are also being tested for credit cards and will soon spread across many business sectors, increasing the need for regulatory action.[29]

Some countries such as Estonia embrace the opportunities new technologies provide. In Estonia, online voting with a digital ID is already reality. Additionally, most public services can be accessed online. Other countries such as India have a very skeptical view toward such new technologies.

These differences are based in their culture as well as the size of the country and its development level. Estonia is relatively small, thus making the implementation of fundamental system changes easier. Additionally, it only recently joined the EU and the Euro zone. Previously there was no other financial framework in place as, for example, the check system in the United States and the UK. Thus the implementation of a new system was easier to achieve as there was no need to convince the population that the new system is better than the old. Other countries struggle with the hurdle of their already preexisting frameworks that are mostly outdated.

Further application of such technology for online identification, access to public databases, and voting create enormous privacy risks.[30] These are regulatory as well as technical in nature. On the one side the legislator must clearly specify how, when, and for what purpose this data can be used and by whom. On the other side, technical safeguards must be made mandatory in order to prevent abuse of the information stored on the identification cards.

Iris Scanning in Schools

In 2006, New Jersey tested as part of a new security study in public schools an iris-scanning system (the iris is the colored part of the human eye). This technology allows a nearly 100 percent fail-proof identification of every individual who wants to gain access to a public school. As a first step, the irises of the children and parents have to be scanned. This information is stored on a server and compared to the iris scan at the front gate whenever an individual wants to gain access. If the data matches, the person is granted access to the school grounds. In the future such a system will prevent strangers from accessing schools, thus minimizing the risks for the children and employees of the school. Furthermore, costs are reduced as less security guards are required. As the technology is cloud ready,[31] it presents great privacy risks based on the uniqueness of an iris, which allows the fail-proof identification of any person. Without proper legislation ensuring certain protection measures and security standards, abuse of such valuable data is likely.

In the UK the Protection of Freedoms Act 2012, chapter 2, requires schools and colleges to obtain consent of one parent of a child under eighteen years for acquiring and processing the child's biometric information and gives the child rights to stop the processing of their biometric information regardless of any parental consent. It also states that if any parent of the child objects to the processing of biometric information, it must be discontinued.

In addition to iris scanning, vein-pattern recognition has also evolved as an identification tool whereby the veins of individuals are scanned and used to determine their identity.[32] The technology is contactless as the veins are scanned through the use of light of which the wave length differs depending on the tissue it is reflected from.

DNA Matching

Today, DNA collection from crime scenes and its matching to known offenders is a very standard procedure. However, it remains important to delineate the boundaries of such biometric data collection. In particular, its risk for abuse is to be taken into account in any collection scenario.[33] In the United States, the gathering of DNA samples can be conducted without the person's consent where the person is convicted of certain grave offenses, arrested, or facing charges under a federal statute.[34] Compulsory DNA collection laws have been upheld by various judgments.[35] Once the DNA information is collected, it is stored in the National DNA Index System (NDIS) to which the investigating authorities can send a disclosure request when they have obtained DNA in connection with an offense.[36]

Despite various procedural safeguards, the risk in having such a database lies in the DNA that is collected under a so-called "voluntary" request for a sample.[37] If a person gives such a sample freely, it is also stored in the system and can be used for later identification. Currently the use is limited to identification of individuals in relation to a crime. However, in the future, new uses of such a big DNA database could be envisioned for research and demographic variables (i.e., race, gender, etc.).

Other countries such as the UK also maintain DNA databases. The secretary of state in the UK is required by law to make arrangements for a "National DNA Database Strategy Board" to oversee the operation of a DNA database.[38] Before the passing of the Protection of Freedoms Act in 2012, the UK extensively stored DNA information even of innocent people and children. After the passing of the law, over 7.5 million DNA samples had to be destroyed and approximately 1.5 million DNA records deleted from the system as their retention was not warranted anymore under the stricter law. It is estimated that around 10 percent of the UK's population is on the database putting it well ahead of all other EU countries.[39]

In 2005, the German law on DNA collection was reformed and its scope significantly expanded. It now also allows storing DNA, even for nonserious crimes, if it can be expected that they will be repeated, thereby interpreting them to sum up to a major offense. Random tests in Germany have shown that 42 percent of the data had to be deleted following the inquiry as the stored DNA information did not even comply with the lax German law.[40]

The mentioned examples demonstrate the need for strong oversight and enforcement as otherwise DNA collecting is abused. Furthermore, it has been shown that an increase of DNA information does not necessarily lead to an increase in convictions. As the subjects of an investigation are in most instances known, taking their DNA after the offense has been committed does not present particular problems. The DNA collected at crime scenes can always be stored. Thus the police have effective tools at their disposal to ascertain whether a person committed an offense or was present at a scene. There is no need to retain DNA of innocent people just for the purpose of potentially identifying them as criminals at a later date. Their DNA can still be collected when a situation arises, and the collection is then warranted on the facts of the new case.

Surveillance

Drones

Currently drones fall under the definition of unmanned airplanes included in the 1944 Convention on International Civil Aviation, which gives the regulatory power to enact legislation pertaining to civil aviation to the individual states.[41] In Europe, article 8 of the European Convention on Human Rights (ECHR) as well as article 17 of the International Covenant on Civil and Political Rights set boundaries for privacy infringements through drones. Recent case law suggests that the article 8 ECHR protection requires a state not only to abstain from interfering but also to take positive steps in adopting measures to secure respect for private life.[42]

Generally the public does not have access to areas out of their sight. Drones enable the state to gain access or at least view these previously unknown areas. The U.S. case of *California v. Ciraolo* established, in regard to a warrantless search challenge brought by a person convicted of planting marijuana in his backyard, that if it can be seen from the air without additional equipment such as an infrared camera, this would not qualify as a search for purposes of the Fourth Amendment protection.[43]

A distinction must be drawn between recording a person through a security camera and taking a photograph.[44] Of particular importance is thereby the potential storage of the information collected. If the data is only needed for maneuvering or carrying out the drone's purpose and is not permanently stored anywhere, the slight privacy infringement may be justified. However, when all sensory data including film and sound is stored on a database, this would likely violate an individual's privacy rights. Such an infringement must be balanced against other legitimate public interests in determining whether the infringement was justified and proportional.

CCTV

The use of closed-circuit television (CCTV) cameras has significantly increased in recent years resulting in constant infringements of individual privacy rights.[45] The UK was one of the first countries to implement widespread CCTV. However, today every major city around the world has some form of CCTV surveillance. It provides a fast, cost-efficient, and automated method of identifying people as well as behavioral-pattern recognition and risk detection. Currently software is being developed that will allow analyzing people's movement and behavior. This data can be used to conduct an automated risk assessment and automatic flagging of suspicious individuals.[46] On the downside, an excited person being caught by a camera could potentially also be flagged to an officer who then has to determine the threat level the person potentially presents.

Generally considered private matters would be evaluated by an individual sitting on a computer. Encryption in order to anonymize the data is also not a viable option for reducing the privacy infringement of stored CCTV recordings as decryption is still possible at any time.[47] Any publication of such stored footage will infringe upon an individual's privacy in a very serious fashion. The ECHR has pointed out that such a disclosure would go beyond the mere passerby or security observation that can be foreseen by the individual concerned and thus would be in violation of article 8 of the convention.[48] In contrast, in *Perry v. United Kingdom* the court held that when the data is not recorded no human rights violation takes place.[49]

Many countries have now issued guidelines on CCTV. For example, Italy has issued guidelines on video surveillance requiring actual, specific risks or the suppression of concrete dangers in order to warrant video surveillance.[50] The UK CCTV Code of Practice takes a more lenient approach by classifying the different needs such as for monitoring, detecting, recognizing, and identifying a certain individual or circumstance. Depending on the category, a varying form of recording devices must be used whereby in all cases the privacy infringement is to be kept to a minimum.[51] In the United States, the prevailing view is that individuals do not have a reasonable expectation of privacy in a public space, thus recording by CCTV is allowed.[52]

Number Plate Recognition

The increased use of cameras on various locations enables the police and other public authorities to carry out scans for certain number plates. When a car, for example, drives by such a camera system on the highway, the number plate is identified and matched against a database. If it turns up with a positive match, then the photo taken will be stored and the police informed. In 2008, such a system was implemented in Germany and challenged before the constitutional court. The court in its judgment found the law to violate a person's right to self-determination (a right included in the German constitution).[53] Central to the reasoning was the fact that this data in combination with other information would enable the identification and tracking of any person. Furthermore, the use of the data was not limited to specific situations, and the law did not define whether also information concerning passengers could be collected. Thus, the privacy infringements were not proportionate to any legitimate objective. However, the court left it open to the legislator to limit the scope of the number-plate-recognition law in order to bring it in line with its requirements.

Google street view is a service that enables every Internet user to view any street and building that has been recorded by the Google camera car. The privacy infringement becomes apparent when a government uses the data collected to find properties that are not on the public registry. This has, for example, led to the detection of tax evasion of previously undeclared property.[54]

Passenger Name Record

Currently all EU countries use a so-called passenger name record (PNR) system to identify their airline passengers. These databases include all personal (i.e., credit card details, meal options, etc.) data, which is entered upon booking by the passenger. The purpose for collection at this point is purely commercial, to offer the service.[55] Under the current agreements with the EU, the United States has access to the data of the airlines. The EU has also long wanted to benefit from this data. Therefore, currently the EU commission has proposed a new EU PNR. The implementing law would allow tracking all passengers in real time as well as retrospective flight and other pattern analysis by EU authorities.

In order to carry out such processing, the technical capabilities with regard to storage must be developed and regulated. As the data is collected for commercial purposes, only such measures stand in contrast to the purpose limitation principles enshrined in EU data-protection laws.[56] A further concern is the proposed retention period of up to five years for such data, which does not seem warranted in light of the goal to make air travel safe. As a safety measure, the anonymization of the data is required after thirty days, which, however, does not prevent the repersonalization at a later point. Through the reversibility of the anonymization, the value of the data is retained.[57] A further growing concern is the ability of the executive branch to access this data by way of subpoenas or other legal instruments. As the data is purely commercial, handing over such data should only be warranted in an individual case and determined on a case-by-case basis. The risk of unwanted disclosure also grows the longer the data is stored.

Internet Surveillance

Internet surveillance is one of the most discussed topics in today's online world. Recent revelations by Edward Snowden have shown just how far governments are going to access information. For example, the well-known case of *Smith v. Maryland* addressed the issue of collecting caller numbers through a pen registry.[58] The court determined that once a phone number was dialed and transferred to the operator, it effectively lost any reasonable expectation of privacy and therefore could be collected without a warrant by law enforcement officers. Thus the judgment was based on the notion of publicizing information rather than on weighing the public interest favoring disclosure.[59]

Public authorities have a legitimate interest in accessing data and communication streams for crime prevention and investigation. Telecommunication and Internet service providers are required to assist the authorities according to various laws under which orders can be issued. As retaining and accessing the information is costly, U.S. telecommunication companies sought compensation for their cooperation.[60] In 1994, the U.S. congress was forced to approve five hundred million U.S. dollars to compensate telephone companies for their costs of upgrading their systems in order to be compliant with FBI requirements. If this money would not have been granted, the companies would have retained their objection to a new surveillance law, the Communications Assistance for Law Enforcement Act (CALEA), which was necessary to cater for the technological developments in the nineties. In 2005, a further adjustment was carried out by expanding its scope to include also voice-over IP (VoIP) communications via the Internet. The terror attack in 2001 has seen an unprecedented expansion of surveillance powers through the U.S. Patriot Act[61] granting nearly unlimited access to government agencies through a complex system of national security letters and secret court subpoenas.[62]

Of great concern for privacy is the White House's stance on surveillance by simply ignoring the Department of Justice's (DoJ) refusal to sign off on the reauthorization of the President's Surveillance Program (PSP), which includes warrantless wiretapping and other forms of expansive surveillance. Legally an approval by the DoJ is required, but after its refusal the White House simply continued the program without the required authorization.

The foundations for a functioning surveillance framework are accountability, strict oversight, and enforcement procedures. Furthermore, the results of these measures must be regularly analyzed to determine whether the privacy infringements they create are still proportional to their impact on law enforcement and crime prevention. Currently, many legal professionals question if this balance is maintained considering the broad-scale surveillance and data collection without any noticeable results on crime statistics.

In its effort to counter terrorism, the U.S. government monitors all traffic to and from federal agency websites. A banner warns users that their traffic is monitored, and consequently, there is no reasonable expectation of privacy that would protect such communication.[63] Rerouting and anonymization tools can prevent or at least make it harder to track a user. The most commonly used system is TOR (The Onion Routing), which anonymizes the routing of the data sent and received. Its aim is to prevent a party from identifying the receiver or sender of the transferred data.[64] However, the U.S.

government has already tried to gain access to the TOR system and has expressed its view that the system was aiding terrorism and thus should not be used. New malware sites allow the government to install programs that enable them to identify the user even when he or she is using a TOR system. Such measures were previously only used in specific instances but seem to have become common practice in the FBI's daily dealings.[65] Any user accessing the TOR website is closely monitored by the U.S. surveillance agencies.

Spyware is the new tool of choice for surveillance agencies around the world.[66] It allows unnoticed access to most personal computers. The information that can be gained from such malware is highly valuable as a large amount of personal and private information is stored and communicated through personal computers. Because of the malware's potential to damage a computer system and open back doors for other parties beside the surveillance agencies, its use should be strictly limited to identified targets as is currently the case in Switzerland.[67]

Amidst the surveillance issues, Europe has recently placed strong limits on the availability of data for government agencies. In April 2014, the European Court held that the directive regulating the storage of user identification data is contrary to EU privacy laws as its objective and scope are too broad. The EU member states must now determine how they will implement a framework that will be least privacy invasive whilst still ensuring that the investigating authorities have the required data to combat criminal activity.[68]

In the EU as well as in Switzerland, the common method to obtain information on an individual is through a court order that allows interception of communication and identification of an individual's communication. For example, the UK Regulatory Investigatory Powers Act (RIPA) 2000 regulates targeted surveillance by requiring a warrant to be issued by the home secretary before private communication can be intercepted.

Network and Provider Shutdown

A government generally has only limited powers to shut down an Internet service provider or file hoster. Countries with no freedom-of-speech protection or corrupt governments frequently limit Internet access, shut it down completely, or ban certain websites. In the Western world the main reason for blocking a website has recently emerged in regard to privacy infringements by the movie portal kino.to. The highest Austrian court determined that blocking the website upon request of the rights owners of the movies available on the portal was justified.[69]

Open-Source Data Collection

Open-source collection of information has long been used for various grounds. On first glance the collection of data for security purposes appears not to infringe privacy rights as the data is available to the public at large.[70] Despite this seemingly simple argument, new technology is now able to ascertain a lot more information through open-source data by way of analytical processes, the results of which can have real-life repercussions. Therefore any such data use must be closely analyzed in order to determine the exact privacy risks that are created. For example, the sourced data might not be up to date, might be faulty, or might be wrongly interpreted in light of limited information.

Based on research carried out by the U.S. Congressional Research Service, 90 percent of intelligence data comes from open sources.[71] These include sources from which information can "lawfully be obtained by request, purchase or observation."[72] In particular, social-networking sites and video channels are a valuable source for identifying the private context in which individuals operate.

The risk lies in the data's interpretation, which might create a completely misplaced impression when randomly collected online by the agencies. A second aspect to the collection and use of open-source information is whether such conduct is ethical. Wrong or incomplete information can seriously harm an innocent person, thus safeguards must be put in place to validate the information.[73] Furthermore, the person affected should be given some form of recourse and information in order to disprove the validity of the data on which a decision was reached.[74]

Social media has blurred the clear distinction among different types of information that is targeted at various audiences. For example, privacy settings on social media sites should allow a user to determine who is allowed to see what content. In practice, the use and access to a user's data is far greater than expected. Standard social-media site settings allow others to access certain information that cannot be blocked. This data could easily be collected by anyone including governmental agencies.

The fear of terroristic threats remains high in society. In order to combat such threats, the USA Patriot Act was passed to expand the surveillance powers of federal government agencies.[75] However, it seems as if the trust that was placed on the agencies to utilize this power for the good of society was abused. In particular, the revelations of Edward Snowden have proven the vast amount of data-collection and privacy infringements of U.S. citizens as well as people abroad.[76]

Profiling

Steps have been initiated on the international level to address the issue of profiling carried out by state actors utilizing new technologies such as Big Data.[77] In September 2013, the Thirty-Fifth International Conference of Data Protection and Privacy Commissioners called upon all parties using profiling to adhere to a set list of boundaries formulated at the meeting.[78] These broad principles are the cornerstone for the enactment of state legislation. They incorporate central concepts requiring information to the public on the nature and extent of profiling. This will allow affected persons to implement systems in order to minimize their exposure.[79]

Furthermore, mobile devices allow the constant tracking of its users, which is why a resolution against tracking has been passed in order to reduce such surveillance.[80] It includes a purpose limitation provision and information policies that aim at reducing the impact.

VeriChip

Fingerprint scanners and other related technologies that were very safe a decade ago can be easily fooled today. In order to ensure the security of certain data or restricted areas, human implantable microchips are a solution. This technology was used by the Mexican attorney general's office to ensure that only a handful of selected people gained access to highly confidential case files on running investigations. Every member of the team received an implanted chip into the arm with an imbedded code allowing access to various restricted areas.

The risk of this technology lies in its forceful application by governments. For example, a law could be passed requiring every newborn to receive such a chip, which enables the easy identification and tracking of a person. The individual in question would lose his or her privacy completely. Those that object to the implant could be barred from receiving any public service, or once the technology is established as a standard identification tool, objectors could be excluded from the private markets entirely.

PRIVACY PROTECTION THROUGH REGULATORY AND TECHNICAL SAFEGUARDS

Privacy-Enhancing Technologies

Privacy-enhancing technologies (PET) are on the forefront of technological measures reducing privacy risks. They can be grouped into four main categories, encompassing encryption tools, policy tools, filtering tools, and anonymity tools. PET improve a user's privacy control and remove unnecessary personal identifiers from data sent. For an individual, private-user encryption software provides a good, cheap measure for protecting communication. However, encryption also requires that the other party to whom the communication is sent uses the same encryption system. New policy tools are currently being developed, such as the framework suggested by W3C that encompasses automated decision making once privacy settings are applied to the browser's privacy policy. If the requested site does not meet the privacy standard set by the user, the site will automatically be blocked from accessing the user's information. Masking IP addresses with specific tools will also decrease the likelihood of tracking as the tracking software must be able to identify the IP address to track a user.

This technique has so far been the prevailing system. However, recently new technology has evolved that does not require an IP address anymore. It simply uses the unique characteristics of a browser to identify a user. As every browser has slightly different frameworks when installed, it can be uniquely identified. Therefore, as the tracking capabilities are evolving, so must the privacy-protection tools.

Data Protection Regulation

The EU has taken steps to strengthen its data protection in light of the growing number of new technologies. The Data Protection Regulation,[81] once in force, aims at resolving some of these issues created through the transborder flow of personal data and the jurisdictional issues. However, as the legislative process is a long one, the regulation will not cater and address all the issues that have been raised by new technologies. Essentially the law will still in some parts be inadequate in meeting the requirements of the IT market. On one side, better data protection is required from various actors in the IT business, but on the other side no practical solutions are provided that would allow the enforcement of such measures. In particular, the international nature of data processing has not been accounted for in the law. Conflicts between various jurisdictions can arise, putting companies between a rock and a hard place. Future regulation must invariably take account of the international nature of privacy and data protection.

OUTLOOK

The legal frameworks in the EU and around the world are constantly being adjusted to the growing number of challenges created by technologies. However, in practice the measures taken are only reactive and do not foreshadow and cater for potential future developments. Furthermore, the focus of the regulation is more directed to the private sector and its conduct in regard to personal data.

Nevertheless, it will remain essential for the protection of fundamental human rights to also address the concerns in regard to public access, collection, and use of data as a lot of the information a government acquires about its citizens is not voluntarily disclosed but required by law. Public agencies can at any time request information from enterprises that initially collected such data for totally different purposes than the one the state agency requesting the data had in mind. Clear rules on how to deal with such requests are necessary in particular in light of the pressure governments can place on enterprises. This is the forefront of privacy protection, and as such the enterprises should be given the necessary tools in the form of laws in order to respond and object to requests that are clearly excessive or infringe the privacy of an individual in an unreasonable fashion.

In addition to the state measures, the extraterritoriality of the information that a government wants to acquire poses further issues. For example, the U.S. FBI required Google to disclose data that was stored in Ireland and never transferred to the United States. Such a request would under normal criminal law require the U.S. authorities to submit a formal request to the Irish state, which would then decide whether to issue a warrant for the collection of such data. However, in that case, the FBI threatened sanction in the United States if Google would not copy and hand over the information stored abroad.

The issue is therefore more of a practical nature, making the conclusion of an international agreement desirable. Maintaining the current frameworks will invariably lead to additional pressure on the industries involved. Without an international agreement, the EU will likely increase its data-protection requirements, making business for U.S. companies in the EU much harder. Particular circumstances can be envisioned in which the disclosure of EU data carries European criminal sanctions and nondisclosure carries U.S. criminal sanctions. Such a conflict is not in the interest of either the EU or the United States as the risks created for business can significantly influence economic growth.

NOTES

1. Entick v. Carrington, 19 State Trials 1029 (1765).
2. Olmstead v. United States, 277 U.S. 438, 478 (1928) (Brandeis, J dissenting). The majority found that the wiretapping did not involve "tangible" things and thus did not afford the constitutional protection. This case has later been overruled. See also Samuel D. Warren and Louis Dembitz Brandeis, "The Right to Privacy," *Harvard Law Review* 4, no. 5 (December 15, 1890): 193–220.
3. Rolf H. Weber and Ulrike I. Heinrich, *Anonymization*, Springer Briefs in Cybersecurity (London: Springer, 2012), 3.
4. Krone Verlag GmbH and Co. KG v. Austria, judgment, February 26, 2002, No. 34315/96, section 34.
5. Weber and Heinrich, *Anonymization*, 50.

6. Ibid., 25.

7. Human Rights Committee, International Covenant on Civil and Political Rights, 102nd session, September 12, 2011, CCPR-C-GC/34, no. 23.

8. Ople v. Torres, G.R. No. 127685, July 23, 1998.

9. No. 15-AB of April 13, 1991, Constitution chapter 12, article 59.

10. ECJ judgment of February 27, 2008, 1 BvR 370/07; 1 BvR 595/07.

11. Privacy Act of 1974, 5 U.S.C. § 552a, http://www.gpo.gov/.

12. Directive 95/46/EC of the European Parliament and of the Council of October 24, 1995, on the Protection of Individuals with Regard to the Processing of Personal Data and on the Free Movement of Such Data, http://eur-lex.europa.eu/.

13. Roger Deplanche v. Joseph A. Califano, Secretary of Health, Education and Welfare, individually and in his official capacity as secretary, 549 F.Supp. 685.

14. Alexandra Rengel, *Privacy in the 21st Century*, Studies in Intercultural Human Rights (Leiden, Netherlands: Martinus Nijhoff, 2013), 42.

15. Houchins v. KQED, Inc., 438 U.S. 1, 98 S. Ct. 2588, 57 L. Ed. 2d 553 (1978); Nixon v. Warner Communications, Inc., 435 U.S. 589, 98 S. Ct. 1306, 55 L. Ed. 2d 570 (1978).

16. JB Pictures, Inc., v. Department of Defense, 86 F.3d 236 (D.C. Cir. 1996).

17. Ritchie v. Coldwater Community Schools, 947 F. Supp. 2d 791 (W.D. Mich. 2013).

18. Whalen v. Roe, 429 U.S. at 598–99, 97 S.Ct. 869, 51 L.Ed.2d 64 (1977).

19. Doe v. Attorney General of U.S., 941 F.2d at 796.

20. Eagle v. Morgan, 88 F.3d at 625 C.A.8 (Ark.) (1996).

21. Ibid.

22. Stoianoff v. Commissioner of Motor Vehicles, 107 F.Supp.2d 439 (S.D.N.Y. 2000).

23. Directive 2006/24/EC of the European Parliament and of the Council of March 15, 2006, on the Retention of Data Generated or Processed in Connection with the Provision of Publicly Available Electronic Communications Services or of Public Communications Networks and Amending Directive 2002/58/EC, http://eur-lex.europa.eu/; 25.01.2012. COM(2012) 10. See also Proposal for a Directive of the European Parliament and of the Council on the Protection of Individuals with Regard to the Processing of Personal Data by Competent Authorities for the Purposes of Prevention, Investigation, Detection or Prosecution of Criminal Offences or the Execution of Criminal Penalties, and the Free Movement of Such Data, http://eur-lex.europa.eu/.

24. ECJ judgment in joint cases C-293/12 and C-594/12 Digital Rights Ireland and Seitlinger and Others, http://curia.europa.eu/.

25. "Big Data: Seizing Opportunities, Preserving Values," Executive Office of the President, May 2014, http://www.whitehouse.gov/.

26. Judith Rauhofer, "Round and Round the Garden? Big Data, Small Government and the Balance of Power in the Information Age," in *Proceedings of the 17th International Legal Informatics Symposium (IRIS) 2014*, ed. E. Schweighofer, F. Krummer, and W. Hötzendorfer (Vienna: OCG, 2014), 607, 611.

27. Juliane Schiemenz, "US-Bürger wehren sich gegen Stromzähler: Widerstand im Wohnwagen," *Spiegel Online*, May 8, 2014, http://www.spiegel.de/.

28. David Lyon, "National ID's in a Global World: Surveillance, Security, and Citizenship," *Case Western Reserve Journal of International Law* 42, no. 3 (2010): 607.

29. David Banisar and Simon Davies, "Privacy and Human Rights: An International Survey of Privacy Laws and Practice," Global Internet Liberty Campaign, Privacy International, accessed August 28, 2015, http://www.gilc.org/.

30. Statewatch, "Statewatch Briefing: ID Cards in the EU; Current State of Play," accessed August 29, 2015, http://statewatch.org/.

31. Laurie Sullivan, "Iris Scanning for New Jersey Grade School," *Information Week*, January 23, 2006, http://www.informationweek.com/.

32. Find Biometrics, "Vein Recognition," accessed August 30, 2015, http://www.findbiometrics.com/.

33. Melissa Gymrek, Amy L. McGuire, David Golan, Eran Halperin, and Yaniv Erlich, "Identifying Personal Genomes by Surname Inference," *Science* 339, no. 6117 (2013): 321–24.

34. 42 U.S. Code § 14135a.

35. U.S. v. Kincade, 379 F.3d 813, 818–19 (9th Cir. 2004).

36. "DNA: Federal DNA Database Unit (FDDU)," FBI, accessed September 3, 2015, http://www.fbi.gov/.

37. Bonnie L. Taylor, "Storing DNA Samples of Non-Convicted Persons and the Debate over DNA Database Expansion," *Thomas M. Cooley Law Review* 20, no. 3 (2003): 511.

38. Protection of Freedoms Act 2012, chapter 1, section 24.

39. GeneWatch UK, "The UK Police National DNA Database," accessed August 28, 2015, http://www.genewatch.org/.

40. Susanne Schultz, "'Stop the DNA Collection Frenzy!' Expansion of Germany's DNA Database," Forensic Genetics Policy Initiative, accessed September 3, 2015, http://dnapolicyinitiative.org/.

41. Convention on International Civil Aviation, Document 7300, http://www.icao.int/.

42. ECHR Von Hannover v. Germany, June 24, 2004, Case-Nr. 59320/00, http://hudoc.echr.coe.int/.

43. California v. Ciraolo, 476 U.S. 207 (1986).

44. ECHR Herbecq and the association Ligue des droits de l'homme v. Belgium, January 14, 1998, Case-Nr. 32200/96 and 32201/96.

45. Mathias Vermeulen and Rocco Bellanova, "European 'Smart' Surveillance: What's at Stake for Data Protection, Privacy and Non-discrimination?" *Security and Human Rights* 23, no. 4 (2013): 297–311.

46. European Commission, DG Enterprise and Industry, Towards a More Secure Society and Increased Industrial Competitiveness: Security Research Projects under the 7th Framework Programme for Research, Security, European Commission, Brussels (2009), 6.

47. Article 29 Data Protection Working Party, Opinion 4/2004 on the Processing of Personal Data by Means of Video Surveillance, Brussels, 15.

48. Peck v. the United Kingdom, 36 EHRR 41 (2003).

49. Perry v. United Kingdom, [2003] ECHR 375, (2004) 39 EHRR 3, § 38.

50. Fanny Coudert, "When Video Cameras Watch and Screen: Privacy Implications of Pattern Recognition Technologies," *Computer Law and Security Review* 26, no. 4 (2010): 382.

51. Information Commissioner's Office, "In the Picture: A Data Protection Code of Practice for Surveillance Cameras and Personal Information," 2008, http://ico.org.uk/.

52. Katz v. United States, 389 U.S. 347 (1967).

53. Bundesverfassungsgericht (1 BvR 2074/05), unreported March 11, 2008.

54. "Finanzämter fahnden per Street View nach Tricksern," WinFuture, accessed September 3, 2015, http://winfuture.de/

55. European Commission, Communication from the Commission on the Global Approach to Transfers of Passenger Name Record Data to Third Countries, European Commission, Brussels (2010), 3.

56. Article 29 Working Party, European Data Protection Authorities Clarify Principle of Purpose Limitation, Brussels, April 8, 2013, http://ec.europa.eu/.

57. Article 9.2 EU PRN proposal.

58. Smith v. Maryland, 442 U.S. 735 (1979).

59. Rolf H. Weber and Dominic N. Staiger, "Bridging the Gap between Individual Privacy and Public Security," *Groningen Journal of International Law* 2, no. 2 (2014): 14–32.

60. 18 U.S.C. § 2518(4) provides for compensation to the private entity.

61. Uniting and Strengthening America by Providing Appropriate Tools Required to Intercept and Obstruct Terrorism (USA Patriot Act) Act of 2001, http://www.gpo.gov/.

62. Rolf H. Weber and Dominic N. Staiger, "Spannungsfelder von Datenschutz und Datenüberwachung in der Schweiz und in den USA," *Jusletter IT* 9 (May 15, 2014), http://richterzeitung.weblaw.ch/.

63. U.S. Department of Homeland Security, National Cyber Division, U.S. Computer Emergency Readiness Team, "Privacy Impact Assessment: Einstein Program; Collecting, Analyzing, and Sharing Computer Security Information across the Federal Civilian Government," September 2004, http://www.dhs.gov/.

64. "Inception," Tor, accessed September 3, 2015, http://www.torproject.org/.

65. Kevin Poulson, "Visit the Wrong Website, and the FBI Could End Up in Your Computer," *Wired*, August 5, 2014, http://www.wired.com/.

66. Federal Business Opportunities, "Malware, Solicitation Number: RFQ1307A," February 3, 2014, https://www.fbo.gov/.

67. Weber and Staiger, "Spannungsfelder."

68. ECJ judgment in joint cases C-293/12 and C-594/12, press statement 54/14, Luxemburg, April 8, 2014, http://curia.europa.eu/.

69. OGH 24.6.2014 4 Ob 71/14s.

70. Line C. Pouchard, Jonathan M. Dobson, and Joseph P. Trien, "A Framework for the Systematic Collection of Open Source Intelligence," Association for the Advancement of Artificial Intelligence, 2009, accessed August 28, 2015, http://www.aaai.org/.

71. Richard A. Best and Alfred Cumming, "Open Source Intelligence (OSINT): Issues for Congress," Congressional Research Service, December 5, 2007, http://www.au.af.mil/.

72. National Open Source Enterprise, Intelligence Community Directive 301, July 2006.

73. Dana Boyd, "Privacy and Publicity in the Context of Big Data," WWW2010, April 29, 2010, http://www.danah.org/.

74. Ben Hayes, "Spying on a See Through World: The 'Open Source' Intelligence Industry," *Statewatch Bulletin* 20, no. 1 (2010), http://database.statewatch.org/.

75. Uniting and Strengthening America (USA Patriot Act).

76. Weber and Staiger, "Spannungsfelder."

77. Big Data usually includes data sets with sizes beyond the ability of commonly used software tools to capture, curate, manage, and process the data within a tolerable elapsed time. See Chris Snijders, Uwe Matzat, and Ulf-Dietrich Reips, "'Big Data': Big Gaps of Knowledge in the Field of Internet," *International Journal of Internet Science* 7, no. 1 (2012): 1–5, http://www.ijis.net/.

78. The conference was held on September 23–26, 2013, in Warsaw. WorldLII, "Resolution on Profiling," Thirty-Fifth International Conference of Data Protection and Privacy Commissioners Resolutions and Declarations 3, September 26, 2013, http://www.worldlii.org/.

79. Weber and Staiger, "Bridging the Gap."

80. WorldLII, "Resolution on Web Tracking and Privacy," Thirty-Fifth International Conference of Data Protection and Privacy Commissioners Resolutions and Declarations 9, September 26, 2013, http://www.worldlii.org/.

81. EU Parliament, Proposal for a Regulation of the European Parliament and of the Council on the Protection of Individuals with Regard to the Processing of Personal Data and on the Free Movement of Such Data (General Data Protection Regulation) (2012).

Chapter Five

Freedom of Expression, Human Rights Standards, and Private Online Censorship

Monica Horten

THE PROBLEM WITH COPYRIGHT AND FREEDOM OF EXPRESSION ONLINE

States are bound under international conventions to guarantee human rights, including the right to freedom of expression, and they also have the sovereign right to determine what content is acceptable within their own jurisdiction. However, when it comes to electronic communications networks, private actors are increasingly being asked to act on behalf of states in implementing content restrictions. These private actors are not bound by these international conventions, but they do fall under the jurisdiction of the state.[1] Their position therefore could become pivotal with regard to freedom of expression online. This chapter therefore addresses the question of how to interpret the duty of states with regard to private actors, in the context of content restrictions and the right to freedom of expression. This chapter considers this question with regard to liberal democracies such as the member states of the European Union, where demands for restrictions on access to content are creating some difficult policy challenges. In a human rights context, does it matter whether the private actor is applying content restrictions in response to a government request or if it is doing so of its own accord?[2]

Human rights law is intended to protect against interference with free speech. Under the European Convention on Human Rights (ECHR), the right to freedom of expression states "without interference from a public authority." Governments who are signatories to international human rights conventions, notably those who have signed the ECHR, have a duty to guarantee the right to freedom of expression and to protect against such interference. From a human rights perspective, the Internet is the communications medium of choice for the exercise of democratic citizenship and free speech.[3] It is also a communications system that facilitates every aspect of life. All kinds of people rely on the Internet as a tool for essential everyday activities—banking, shopping, education, work, social life, and paying taxes. It encompasses both public and private speech, ranging from the most trivial interjection to the highest forms of intellectual thought. The underlying network technologies that run the Internet are therefore essential enablers of free speech; however, they present policy challenges in the form of ongoing developments, taking the Internet from a neutral platform to one that has a sophisticated, built-in intelligence. Notably, those underlying technologies contain powerful functionality, such as blocking and filtering, to restrict users' activity.[4] It is this restrictive functionality that is the subject of this chapter.

The chapter discusses the ways in which this restrictive functionality could engage free speech rights. This does not mean that any speech goes. Nor does it mean that governments cannot impose restrictions. It does mean that governments wanting to impose restrictions must first of all test them for compliance with human rights law. The restrictive possibilities within the technology are being translated into policy actions such as blocking injunctions and takedown notices, content-filtering implementations, and graduated response or disconnection measures. These measures tend to be taken in response to certain specific concerns that include, but are not exclusive to, copyright enforcement, the need for counterterrorism measures, and demands for parental controls. The issue for policy making is to understand the ways in which such engagement is created and whether a law or policy addressed to private actors is likely to meet the human rights compliance requirements.

This chapter uses inductive analysis of case law and regulatory and technical studies to consider the ways in which the underlying network technology creates interference with free speech rights. It investigates the duties of states with regard to private actors, and drawing on expert legal opinion, including United Nations guidelines for business and human rights, it considers how those duties might be interpreted in the Internet context. The chapter will use copyright enforcement as a specific example of the policy demands and responses.

TECHNOLOGY AND POLICY CHALLENGES

The capacity of broadband providers to act on the traffic that transmits their networks has dramatically increased to an extent that could not have been foreseen when the Internet was born in the early 1990s.[5] They are able to automatically monitor user activity and deter or prevent transmissions, and have at their disposal a range of functions to render websites inaccessible.[6] These functions include the ability to put in place an automated block as well as to intercept the users' traffic when they try to view specific content, or alter the access speed to make it difficult for users to get certain types of content.[7] This vast and sophisticated blocking capability has placed the broadband providers at the center of the political debate about Internet content and what should and should not be permitted. They have become a target for many third parties who have desires to prevent or stop content and are seeking the means to do so.

Applying Lawrence Lessig's ideas of "code is law," what is happening is that norms and markets are being disrupted to such an extent that the affected stakeholder interests are clamoring to policy makers for legal changes to amend the "code" of the network.[8] For example, norms of acceptable behavior are changing as a result of a series of technology developments. The camera in the mobile phone, and the platforms such as Instagram, have generated a new norm where people take photographs and publish them not just to friends and family but also to the world. Those images could be embarrassing or invasive of privacy. Social media platforms provide a new mechanism that transfers a quiet grudge spoken to a friend into a published comment that is potentially defamatory.[9] The potential for abuse in terms of breach of privacy and defamation led to a judicial procedure for content takedown being built in to the 2013 Defamation Act.[10]

The potential of any of these new norms to be used for the purposes of terrorist activities has led to calls from national security agencies for blocking and filtering of content. For example, "We need a new deal between democratic governments and the technology companies in the area of protecting our citizens. It should be a deal rooted in the democratic values we share. That means addressing some uncomfortable truths."[11]

Moreover, market disruption has occurred in relation to copyright, where distribution of creative works online and the alleged piracy has led to political demands for a variety of blocking options.[12] Hence governments have been receiving demands from groups of stakeholders seeking Internet restrictions to address policy goals such as parental controls over children's access to content, stalking, harassment, and copyright enforcement. All of these demands present a policy challenge. States are seeking the cooperation of broadband providers to take action that may conflict with their duty to protect free speech rights.

Central to policy measures proposed in this context is the obligation being placed onto the broadband providers to take action. Broadband providers are the gateways to the Internet, and they fall within the jurisdiction of nation-states, so they can be governed by law, contrary to the popular perception of the Internet as an ungoverned space.[13] In terms of Lessig's "code is law," the law that can change the "code" governing the disruptive behaviors is that which governs the broadband provider's networks. Hence, there is pressure on the providers to change the code in order to control the behaviors. Restriction on access to or distribution of content by blocking and filtering features frequently in these demands.

Broadband providers could either be asked to block access to the network or to block specific content that resides on the network. The blocks can be carried out such that either an entire website or an individual web page is unavailable to all users. There are different techniques to implement blocking, with varying levels of effectiveness and side effects. One technique is using the IP address, which is the string of numbers that identifies any device connected to the Internet. The IP address system enables data to be sent around the network by any route and arrive safely at the correct destination, because all IP addresses are unique. The data is divided into little packets that carry the IP address on them. It's similar to putting an address on an envelope to go in the post. The block works by the network provider modifying its routers to send the packets to a nonexistent route. IP address blocking brings the risk that legitimate content residing in the same location may also be blocked (overblocking), as happened when a block on a football streaming site also blocked the Radio Times.[14]

Another blocking technique is to target the content by means of the universal resource locator (URL); effectively, this is the address of the website, web page or pages, or the individual item such as an image. This method operates by checking the individual URLs against a database of blocked items and either dropping it, so that user gets an error page, or sending a warning page back to the user. URL blocking is more targeted than is IP address blocking, but the risk is that erroneous classification or an overbroad implementation, for example, using the URL of a whole website or platform, results in overblocking. This happened in the case of *Yildirim v. Turkey*, where the Turkish government sought to block a website that had allegedly insulted the memory of Atatürk, the father of the Turkish state. The offending content was only on one particular website, but the entire platform of Google Sites (http://sites.google.com/) was blocked.[15] As a consequence, the applicant's website was blocked along with the offending content.

A third technique is to block the domain name system (DNS) so it is no longer possible for a website to be found.[16] The DNS is the system that keeps a record of where the content for a web domain or website is physically located on the infrastructure. This is why a domain can be registered in one country with the content on servers in another. DNS is essential for the Internet to operate. DNS blocking is done by "rewriting" the answers given by the system in response to a request by the user to view a website. The rewrite tells the system to send a message that the site does not exist. Alternatively, it may tell the system to go to an alternative web page, which may contain a warning or government message. Some experts use the analogy that it's as if the system is telling a lie, and they express concern about the way that DNS blocking manipulates a system that is a core element of the functioning of the Internet—without DNS, there would be no Internet.[17]

DNS blocking should not be confused with domain seizure. This is where the domain is taken off line at the request of the authorities and the website disappears because there is no means of finding it. This was the case with the domain seizures by the U.S. Immigration and Customs Enforcement (ICE) in 2010.[18] Both DNS blocking and domain seizures carry a risk of overblocking because a domain may have several subdomains and it may well be that some of those subdomains are operating legitimate services.[19] For example, in 2008 a British businessman operating legitimate holiday travel services to Cuba found that his domains had been taken down by order of the U.S. Treasury, rendering his websites unavailable and having the effect of shutting down his business.[20]

To implement any kind of blocking system, a list or database of sites and pages needs to be compiled and maintained. The database will be classified into categories that define the blocking criteria. In some countries, such as Russia, the list is compiled centrally by the state.[21] There are four registries that are maintained by the telecoms regulatory authority Roskomnadzor. The data for the lists is supplied by other government agencies. The broadband providers are obligated to check the lists and implement the blocks within twenty-four hours. In Britain, the broadband providers obtain a single limited list of URLs to block from a third party, the Internet Watch Foundation, for the purpose of addressing child pornography. However, there is a separate system for parental controls that operates quite different. In this case, each of the network providers operate their own bespoke blocking system, including determination of blocking criteria and database compilation. In the parental controls filtering, there is no shared list, and each of the network providers has to identify for themselves the content to be blocked and compile their own list. The blocking criteria vary from one provider to another: BT has seventeen categories, and Virgin has eight. They do not share data between them, and in fact, the blocklist compilation is outsourced to third-party security specialists.[22]

The actual sites to be blocked are typically found using keyword analysis. This analysis may be as simple as looking at the URL. If it contains a banned keyword, then it will be blocked, irrespective of whether its actual content is legitimate. It may be that the banned keyword is picked up in the web page or site content. However, with the notable exception of the Chinese state, few have the resources to conduct a detailed analysis of web content. Hence, there is a risk of false categorization resulting in overbroad blocking.[23] The possibility for abuse of powers to block legitimate content also exists. Erroneous classification can easily happen when inserting sites into the blocklist, as when a serious article in the *Guardian* about a school for lesbian and gay students was caught up in a keyword filter for a parental controls system.[24] In these circumstances, especially where there are multiple blocklists created by competing private actors, it is impossible for users to know what is being blocked and on what basis it is being done. In Britain, the providers do not share data about sites that have been erroneously blocked, and the blocking action is not foreseeable by website owner or user, nor is it notified to them.

A network-level blocking system requires Internet service providers to systematically examine all of a user's communications traffic in order to identify the pages in the blocklist and cease the transmission.[25] This is done using a content-filtering system combined with another technology known as Deep Packet Inspection (DPI).[26] A filtering system will identify the content requested by users and will check each request against the database. The filtering can be implemented on the network routers, where all requests for pages on the blocklist will be intercepted and dropped or diverted. Alternatively, it can be done at the level of the individual subscriber, in which case, the filtering system will hold a database of the websites and services that that individual is permitted to see and will screen against it. Every page that the user tries to access will be checked before access is permitted.

Deep Packet Inspection is the technology that examines the data packets for particular characteristics. DPI is often explained using a metaphor of the post office: it's a bit like the post office examining the mail and opening the envelopes and then deciding whether to permit it to continue on the basis of what it finds. This is a bit simplistic, but it broadly reflects the principle on which DPI operates. It looks at the header information—analogous to the address and other information on the envelope—and it can look deeper into the content.[27] If a DPI system finds, for example, traffic destined for a website that is meant to be blocked, it can simply drop—and effectively block—that traffic.[28] According to an Ofcom report on site blocking, this kind of blocking is technically "trivial," but it carries the caveat that there must be careful consideration of the blocking criteria, and any failure on that part risks false positives or the erroneous overblocking of legitimate traffic.[29] Ofcom further warns that the use of Deep Packet Inspection may raise privacy concerns.[30] The systems implemented by the British broadband providers to implement filtering for parental controls use such a combination of DPI with URL, IP address, or DNS blocking.[31]

INTERFERENCE AND HUMAN RIGHTS LAW

Given this analysis of the technology, it would suggest that content filtering and network-level blocking go hand in hand with surveillance practices, such as monitoring and interception.[32] The overall outcome can result in negative consequences for legitimate content such as overblocking.[33] It is these two factors that raise the human rights issues. Filtering and blocking practices that render web content invisible or inaccessible, or cause it to disappear entirely, targeting users' ability to access or distribute content, combined with the risk of overblocking, immediately create an engagement with the right to freedom of expression. Overblocking can happen due to technical error; it can also happen when the block is not sufficiently specific or the content has been erroneously classified. The surveillance practices raise obvious concerns regarding the right to privacy as a corollary right. In this context, it becomes evident that there is an inconsistency between the capabilities of the network providers and what the law permits.[34]

Human rights law in relation to freedom of expression is predicated on the notion of noninterference by the state. Article 10 of the ECHR states that freedom of expression must be guaranteed "without interference by public authority."[35] Article 10, a two-way right to access and to distribute information, is an important one when considering freedom of expression on the Internet because individuals have the ability to upload content, and in that context they can publish or distribute it, as well as passively access content to gain knowledge. A necessary corollary to the right to freedom of expression is ECHR article 8, the right to privacy,[36] because it protects not only the right to a private life but also a right to private correspondence, without interference from the state.

Legal scholars underscore that international norms with regard to freedom of expression are fully applicable to the Internet.[37] The European Court of Human Rights (ECtHR) has underlined the importance of the Internet in enhancing people's access to news and in generally facilitating the dissemination of knowledge, based on its capacity to store and communicate vast amounts of information and its ease of access. The ECtHR confirmed that the right to freedom of expression applies not just to the content itself but also to the means of transmission of data over the network and to the means of its reception.[38] That would seem to confirm its applicability to the use of broadband networks and to the broadband access connection. It's interesting that the ECtHR said that article 10 rights also apply to putting in place the means for others to receive and impart information.[39] In this specific instance, it was referring to a file-sharing network, but it could arguably be a catchall for Internet platforms, such as YouTube, that facilitate free speech in their role as intermediaries.[40] Hence, the users' rights of Internet access can be important in the context of freedom of expression, as well as the network and the technology platform.

The ECtHR furthermore stated that article 10 rights apply to everyone, and there is "no distinction for profit-making."[41] This was a reminder that the right to freedom of expression applies to someone "speaking" in the context of running a business, as well as to individuals posting their personal thoughts onto Facebook or Twitter. In particular, it applies to news media and journalists.

Finally, article 10 applies "regardless of frontiers."[42] Restrictive measures can create cross-border effects such as overblocking and upstream filtering. In 2008, the Pakistan authorities ordered a block on YouTube that resulted in the video-streaming site being inaccessible worldwide—a global case of overblocking. It was found to be due to routing errors in implementing the block, and it illustrates how blocking may have much wider effects than intended.[43] Upstream filtering is where a network provider is filtering content according to rules in one jurisdiction and providing services for citizens in another. Those citizens in the second jurisdiction may find themselves unable to view content that is legitimate in their country but not in the one whose filtering rules are being applied. In other words, "upstream filtering" by private actors could entail a violation of the rights of the "downstream" citizens. States may have a duty of due diligence in this regard, which under international law, implies that they should do all that they reasonably can to avoid or minimize harm across national borders.[44]

The central issue for policy makers is the notion of "interference" and notably to establish what constitutes "interference" in the Internet space. The ECHR was drafted at a period in time just after World War II, when it was assumed that the interferer would be the state. The nature of the interference was assumed to be physical, such as visits from the secret police or the burning of books in the streets, as happened in Germany in 1933. It was not foreseen that interference would come from commercial entities, nor that it could happen automatically on such a vast scale as to take out thousands of works at a time. The situation we face today is that the network providers are private actors who work in conjunction with states and other private interests to apply automated restrictions. The question concerns the duty of the state to introduce some form of accountability for the actions of those private actors.

Given our analysis of the technology, it would seem that the use by network providers of blocking and filtering systems to restrict Internet content does constitute interference for the purpose of ECHR article 10.[45] The interference is created through monitoring of content access as well as by interception and diversion, overblocking, abuse of trust, and false categorization. Disconnection of Internet access or slowing of traffic speech can also represent a form of interference.

This view is borne out by legal opinion. For example, the former British public prosecutor, Lord Macdonald, stated that "the power to have content removed from the Internet represents, on its face, a serious interference with the rights of others."[46] Lord Macdonald added that even if the network provider believed the content were criminally pornographic, the company would have to be absolutely certain that it had the remit to remove that content.

The ECtHR has said that "any restriction imposed on access to content necessarily interferes with the right to receive and impart information."[47] This means that whenever blocking or filtering measures are considered, the right to freedom of expression is engaged and the measures must be evaluated against human rights law.

It begs the question as to whether without interference in the Internet era means no blocking at all, or whether there are circumstances when blocking might be justified. In this matter, the ECtHR has provided helpful guidance, Firstly, it says that access to the network is a necessary element for individuals to exercise their right to freedom of expression: "Blocking access to the Internet, or parts of the Internet, for whole populations or segments of the public can never be justified, including in the interests of justice, public order or national security." [48] In the case of *Yildirim v. Turkey*, where the applicant was unable to access his own website, which contained legitimate content, and the site was rendered invisible to the wider public, the ECtHR stated that this did constitute interference and was a breach of article 10, with a reminder that any blocking should be prescribed by law, pursue a legitimate aim, and is necessary in a democratic society.[49]

The ECtHR has said that any restrictive measures must be clearly and tightly defined, including the method of blocking. The scope of any restricting order must be sufficiently clear that it is obvious what kind of content is likely to be blocked and whether any particular types of content or publishers are being targeted; the geographical area to which they apply must be defined; and a time limit should be given. There should be a clear process for implementation and a notification to those whose content is affected, and a possibility of appeal or judicial review.[50] Any "indiscriminate blocking measure which interferes with lawful content, sites or platforms as a collateral effect of a measure aimed at illegal content or an illegal site or platform" would not be legal, and "blocking orders imposed on sites and platforms which remain valid indefinitely or for long periods are tantamount to inadmissible forms of prior restraint, in other words, to pure censorship."[51]

Filtering of traffic on the network may also constitute interference. The European Court of Justice (ECJ) said that a filtering system engages the right to freedom of expression because it may not be able to accurately distinguish between lawful and unlawful content.[52] It would also engage the right to privacy since it would have to systematically examine all content and identify the IP addresses of the individual users.

The right to privacy is a necessary corollary to freedom of expression because it guarantees confidentiality of communications, notably that the state will not intercept private correspondence. The large-scale monitoring of individual behavior and of their communications has been condemned by European data-protection experts, who argue that these rights should not be surrendered "through neglect."[53]

In that regard, EU law does not permit an injunction ordering a network provider to filter all traffic "indiscriminately, to all its customers, as a preventative measure, exclusively at its expense, and for an unlimited period."[54] Effectively, this means that anything involving continuous monitoring of all content for an unlimited period of time would comprise a general obligation to monitor and would be illegal under EU law. This does not preclude filtering measures being ordered, but there are strict legal criteria that should be met. The ECJ has stated that filtering measures must be necessary and proportionate, they should be targeted, and the determination of the filtering criteria or the content to be filtered should be ordered by a court or a body independent of political influence and should be subject to judicial oversight. In addition, the ECJ claims such measures should not impose excessive costs on the broadband providers.[55]

In other words, article 10 is a qualified right, which means that states may circumscribe it, but only when it is prescribed by law, pursuing a legitimate aim and necessary in a democratic society.[56] The state must be pursuing a policy aim that clearly justifies the need to implement restrictions and must provide that justification.[57] Legal experts point out that the requirement for narrow and targeted measures is especially important where the justification for the restriction concerns public order, national security, or public morals: restrictive measures can be easily abused to protect the interests of the government rather than to protect citizens' rights, and they may be co-opted to serve a favored set of stakeholder interests and avoid consideration of the human rights balance.[58]

Hence, the policy makers' role is to balance the different sets of interests when confronted with content-blocking demands. They should establish a fair balance between freedom of expression and the competing interests involved.[59] In Britain, they must complete a Human Rights Memorandum for any new law, and civil servants are urged to undertake this as an integral element of the policy-making process and not as a last-minute exercise.

The kinds of dilemmas that policy makers face in finding the right balance are illustrated by the case of the so-called Internet Freedom provision.[60] This provision is a reminder in EU telecoms law—the law that addresses broadband service provision—that national measures to restrict the Internet must be subject to a prior, fair, and impartial hearing. The Internet Freedom provision was inserted after a political argument over specific copyright measures, known as graduated response, demanded by the entertainment industries for enforcement purposes. Graduated response was conceived as a system of warnings to an Internet user regarding alleged copyright infringement followed by disconnection or "cutting off" Internet access.[61] The identification of the users was carried out via surveillance of peer-to-peer file-sharing networks. This process was exemplified in the French Creation and Internet Law, although the system created by it has subsequently been disbanded.[62] In some implementations, notably the U.S. "six strikes" Copyright Alert System,[63] and the UK's Digital Economy Act,[64] there is also a possibility to slow down or take some other restrictive action with regard to the user's connection, making it impossible for them to download content. A graduated response system therefore relies on the broadband provider to impose the disconnection or slowing-down Internet traffic. Disconnection engages free speech rights. It further engages the right to privacy because of the requirement to identify the individual subscriber. Identification was presumed to be feasible via the IP address, although this has proved to be problematic in practice because the IP address relates to the connection, which is not necessarily the same as the individual. Nevertheless, the engagement of these rights is underscored by a report of the Joint Parliamentary Committee on Human Rights, which said that "it is generally accepted that measures taken to limit individual access to internet services by the State will engage Articles 8 and 10 ECHR."[65] If imposed as a sanction, disconnection would affect not only any unlawful downloading of copyrighted content but also lawful activities such as work, education, and banking.[66]

In formulating the Internet Freedom provision, the European Parliament was concerned about two elements: First, the possibility of disconnections being ordered on the basis of a privately operated, administrative procedure, bypassing the courts. Moreover, such a private process would have a presumption of guilt built in, contrary to the principle of presumption of innocence that is built into European law.[67] On that basis, ECHR article 6, the right to due process, was invoked, and the European Parliament considered that disconnection should be carried out only following a prior, fair, and impartial hearing.[68] Second, the European Parliament could foresee other types of Internet restrictions, such as network-level blocking and filtering. It was on that basis that the language of "national measures" was chosen, with the intention of addressing a range of other possibilities.[69] In ensuing reviews of intellectual property rights, the European Commission has been careful to state that all fundamental rights must be respected, including the right to a private life, freedom of expression, and an effective remedy.[70]

It is now generally considered that, in copyright enforcement cases, policy makers and courts should balance the right to freedom of expression against the right to property. Copyright is a private right and would usually be addressed under civil law.[71] It is generally argued that copyright is a property right under the ECHR protocol 1, article 1, which mandates the "peaceful enjoyment of possessions."[72] The European Union Charter of Fundamental Rights adds a right to intellectual property, as a subset of the more general right to property, in article 17.2.[73] According to a British Parliamentary committee, policy makers must strike this balance with care. Governments may consider the right to property in the context of a general public interest, but when it comes to the right to freedom of expression, the require-

ment to show that the proposed interference is prescribed by law and necessary in a democratic society to meet a legitimate aim is a higher level of legal
test.[74] Noting that the right to privacy is a corollary to freedom of expression,
European case law says that courts should balance the right to privacy
against the right to intellectual property, taking into account the principle of
proportionality.[75]

General filtering of Internet content on broadband networks for the purpose of copyright enforcement was ruled out by the ECJ in the case of
Scarlet Extended.[76] As a consequence, copyright holders have turned to
blocking injunctions under article 8.3 of the EU copyright directive.[77] This
correlates to article 11 of the intellectual property right enforcement directive
articles 12–15 of the e-commerce directive, and section 97a of the UK's
Copyright, Designs and Patents Act.[78] The entertainment industry's political
lobbyists would like to see a fast-track injunction codified in law, such that a
blocking order could be obtained within a short space of time—days or even
hours. This was the intention behind the provisional measures in the now-
defunct Anti-Counterfeiting Trade Agreement and also section 102 of the
also now-defunct Stop Online Piracy Act in the United States.[79] However,
injunctions are made in consideration of human rights law. In the UK, injunctions will be implemented by some network providers using the same
technology that is in place for content-filtering measures as outlined above.
They therefore entail a form of interference with the user's communications
and engage articles 8 and 10 rights.[80] Hence, the UK courts have found that
content-blocking injunctions may be ordered, but they must be narrow in
scope and specific to the aim.[81]

STATES AND PRIVATE ACTORS

By constraining injunctions in this way, states may fulfill their duty to guarantee the rights to freedom of expression, as established by the European
Convention on Human Rights. In this context, that duty can be interpreted to
mean that states are obligated to guarantee noninterference with Internet
content as well as with Internet access. However, when policy makers are
faced with demands for blocking legislation, they will need to understand
how this obligation applies when the restrictions are imposed by law on
broadband providers who are private actors.

Guidance is provided by the United Nations, which has drafted some
general principles for business and human rights. The essential principle is
that states must protect against human rights abuses by third parties in their
jurisdiction and that they should set out an expectation that businesses operating within their jurisdiction will respect human rights.[82] The broadband
providers are regulated under telecoms policy, and in the European Union,

they are legally considered to be "mere conduits." That means they carry content but do not have any interest in it, and member state governments are expressly forbidden from giving them any general obligation to monitor content.[83] The mere conduit provision would seem de facto to have the effect of protecting freedom of expression, whether or not that was its intended purpose, but if that status is altered, then it will pose issues for policy makers. The notion of "general monitoring" is another important legal distinction. EU law says that telecoms providers may not be given a "general obligation to monitor."[84] Blocking and filtering systems will fall foul of any net neutrality law, and notably the proposed law in the EU would mean that measures undertaken by the broadband providers without statutory backing would be illegal.[85]

If making laws to restrict the Internet, policy makers have to weigh up the rights of the intermediary to conduct business, enshrined under the EU Charter of Fundamental Rights along with freedom of expression and any other rights, such as copyright.[86] They have to find the most appropriate balance between the conflicting rights and the interests involved. Within this context, there are tensions between the freedom of expression rights of the individual Internet user and the rights of others (where others could be children in this context, or they could be copyright holders).[87] Hence, when a government is considering restrictive measures, for example, to protect copyright, it must balance that policy objective against both of these fundamental rights, and it has a duty to justify its reasons for interfering with them.[88] What's important is that the legal tests for interfering with freedom of expression—necessity, proportionality, and legitimate aim—are of a higher order than the public interest test for protecting copyright.

The United Nations guidelines state that businesses should respect human rights and avoid adverse human rights impacts.[89] Blocking and filtering measures may result in a de facto requirement for broadband providers to exercise a quasi-legal judgment in multiple cases. As private organizations, they are not generally set up or competent to act as content censors, and noting the risk of overblocking outlined above, such a decision-making requirement would create uncertainty for the business, potentially exposing them to liabilities under civil law, as well as possible violations of the rights of users.[90]

States should enforce laws aimed at guarantees for human rights, support businesses on how to respect human rights, and encourage businesses to communicate how they address human rights impacts.[91] This would suggest a requirement for regulatory safeguards. States will be under an obligation to ensure that restrictive measures such as blocking and filtering are not implemented in an arbitrary or overbroad manner.[92] There should be a rigorous justification process, evaluating the proposed blocking measures against a legitimate aim and ensuring that they are necessary to achieve that aim and proportionate to it. This means they must be the minimum needed to achieve the aim.[93] Citizens should be clearly informed of the policy justification.[94]

Both citizens and Internet service providers should be in a position to know whether their actions are legal or not. This means that they should be informed of the blocking criteria and know what to do if they either encounter blocked content or find that their own content is blocked.[95] States should take appropriate steps to prevent and deal with any abuses, through legislation and other policy instruments.[96] Decisions on the blocking criteria and the specific content to be blocked should be overseen by a judicial process or by an administrative body that is independent of any stakeholder interests in the blocking measures.[97] There should be independent processes to handle complaints, challenges, or appeals. These processes may be administrative or judicial, as long as they are in compliance with ECHR article 6. The entire process should be subject to judicial review.

From the perspective of policy makers, putting the matter in the hands of an administrative body may look like an attractive option, but a case in Spain illustrates how an administrative body may not meet the compliance requirements for due process under ECHR article 6. The issue arose when the Spanish government wanted to pass a law to have websites blocked for copyright enforcement purposes.[98] In Spain, freedom of expression is constitutionally guaranteed. Article 20 of the Spanish Constitution states that "seizure of publications, recordings, or other means of information may only be adopted by a judicial decision."[99] The government had proposed that a purely administrative body could order the shutting down of websites, but the constitution was invoked and it was determined that the blocking order had to be authorized by the judicial authorities.[100] This view was confirmed in a report by the public prosecutor at the request of the Ministry of Justice.[101]

There is another temptation for policy makers to opt for a privately run process, operated by the broadband providers together with the relevant stakeholder interests. This is sometimes euphemistically referred to as "voluntary measures" or "co-operative efforts."[102] However, the Spanish experience shows that voluntary agreements in this context are extremely difficult to broker.[103] The broadband providers are unsurprisingly resistant to any such agreement, and the rights holders are unwilling to compromise. In Spain, negotiations began in 2007, and by 2009, they had reached no conclusion, so the government introduced legislation. A similar attempt by the European Commission to broker a "voluntary" agreement at the European level also broke down.[104] After heated arguments between the rights holders and the telecoms industry groups, the commission decided that it was no longer viable to continue, concluding that "fundamental differences of opinion remain on most of the topics."[105] The commission acknowledged the difficulties in reaching a consensus.

Aside from the difficulties in reaching a deal, these voluntary agreements are problematic in other ways. Arguably, they are an attempt by the state to shift responsibility for a policy action onto the private sector, where the broadband providers would consent to take the demanded actions without the backing of legislation. As they are nonlegislative agreements, they rely on industry stakeholder goodwill. In this regard, voluntary agreements would seem to run counter to the United Nations guidelines, which suggest that states should exercise oversight and provide guidance "when contracting with businesses to provide services that may impact on human rights."[106] A voluntary agreement reliant on goodwill is not subject to judicial oversight. Arguably, too, they create a policy dynamic where industry is able to set the terms for that goodwill and may rely on interpersonal relationships in order to function. It's arguable that this dependency mitigates in favor of a "state-promoted private ordering" with nondisclosure and nontransparent regulation, "insulated from public scrutiny and that can be tailored, by virtue of that insulation, to serve corporate interests at the public's expense."[107]

However, if a voluntary agreement is put in place, the UN guidelines call for private actors, to avoid causing adverse impacts to freedom of expression, and seek to mitigate them if they occur. They also call for businesses to communicate externally on their policies with regard to freedom of expression and restrictive measures.[108] This could be interpreted to mean that broadband providers must communicate details of their blocking criteria and blocklists to Internet users and content providers, and they must take clear steps to avoid overblocking and to protect against abuse by employees or contractors. The state would remain under a duty to ensure that those obligations were met, which implies regulatory supervision as minimum level of compliance.

BALANCING INTERFERENCE AND STATE DUTIES

It would seem, therefore, that both voluntary and statutory measures for restricting the Internet carry a requirement for regulatory oversight. In particular, safeguards are needed against error and misuse. These safeguards would take the form of judicial or regulatory oversight, including compliance with due process under ECHR article 6, combined with requirements placed on private actors to inform the public such that citizens can reasonably foresee the consequences of their actions. This would enable the measures to fall in line with the guiding principles adopted by the United Nations for business and human rights.

The form that these safeguards would take does not yet have a model; however, individual Internet users would need to know the circumstances under which their content could be blocked. By inference, Internet users would also need to be informed which websites, services, and applications were being blocked. If this kind of information was available, they would be able to take informed decisions when uploading their own content—whether for private use or for public distribution. They would also be able to know whether or not downloading of content was legitimate.

These safeguards are critical because Internet restrictions may cause interference not only with the ability to access content but also with the ability to publish or distribute it. The interference is created by the network infrastructure technology, which by means of surveillance, monitoring, and interception, makes it possible to bar requests and hide content from view—not actually destroying it but as good as doing so from the user's or publisher's perspective. The balance of rights turns on the level of interference. Content restrictions lack the dramatic impact of piles of burning books, but in terms of their potential effect on censorship on a wide scale, the harm they could generate is much deeper. Leaving them in the hands of private actors without adequate safeguards would seem to entail inherent risks to freedom of expression. It is for that reason that governments, pressed with demands to block or filter Internet content, have special duties with regard to private actors.

NOTES

1. Rundle and Birding 2008, 74–77, 84.
2. Ibid., 77.
3. Council of Europe 2009, 2; Conseil Constitutionnel 2009; EDPS 2014; ECHR, Yildirim v. Turkey, Application No. 3111/10, December 18, 2012, final March 18, 2013, section 54.
4. Tom Wheeler, Federal Communications Commission (FCC) chairman, speaking at the FCC meeting on February 26, 2015 (watched by the author via webcast).
5. Mueller, Kuehn, and Santoso 2012, 349.
6. See Peha and Mateus 2014 (discussion of monitoring and detection of peer-to-peer file sharing of copyrighted material).
7. Ofcom 2011.
8. Lessig 1999, 121–32.
9. House of Lords, House of Commons 2011, S.92–107; McNair-Wilson 2011.
10. Defamation Act 2013, clause 13 order to remove statement or cease distribution.
11. Hannigan 2014.
12. See Horten (2013) for a discussion of the entertainment industry lobbying.
13. For a discussion of network providers and how they may be controlled by governments, see Goldsmith and Wu (2006), 68–84.
14. Cookson 2013.
15. *Yildirim*, sections 12–14.
16. This account is drawn from Ofcom (2011), 28–37; and Cartier International v. British Sky Broadcasting, October 17, 2014, no. HC14C01382, High Court of Justice, judgment, section 25.
17. Emert 2011.
18. Ibid.; Ofcom 2011, 23–24; U.S. Department of Immigration and Customs Enforcement (ICE) 2010.
19. Ofcom 2011, 34.
20. Liptak 2008.

21. Weaver and Clover 2012; Tselikov 2014, 10.

22. *Cartier International*, sections 45, 48–49, 62.

23. Zittrain and Palfrey 2008, 38–43.

24. This was a tweet from a *Guardian* reader, on January 16, 2015, of which the author holds a copy. It is cited because it illustrates how overblocking can happen. There is not yet any case law on this point.

25. Stalla-Bourdillon 2013, section 4.

26. Bendrath and Mueller 2011, 1145–46; Ofcom 2011, 29, 39.

27. Stalla-Bourdillon, Papadakia, and Chown 2014. This paper provides a detailed explanation of DPI. See also TTA (2012); this is the technical specification for DPI drafted under the auspices of the International Telecommunications Union.

28. See TTA (2012).

29. Ofcom 2011, 39.

30. Ibid., 50.

31. *Cartier International*, sections 38–51.

32. Zittrain and Palfrey 2008, 50.

33. Stalla-Bourdillon 2013, section 4.

34. Mueller, Kuehn, and Santoso 2012, 349.

35. ECHR article 10:

1. Everyone has the right to freedom of expression. This right shall include freedom to hold opinions and to receive and impart information and ideas without interference by public authority and regardless of frontiers. This article shall not prevent States from requiring the licensing of broadcasting, television or cinema enterprises.

2. The exercise of these freedoms, since it carries with it duties and responsibilities, may be subject to such formalities, conditions, restrictions or penalties as are prescribed by law and are necessary in a democratic society, in the interests of national security, territorial integrity or public safety, for the prevention of disorder or crime, for the protection of health or morals, for the protection of the reputation or rights of others, for preventing the disclosure of information received in confidence, or for maintaining the authority and impartiality of the judiciary.

36. ECHR article 8:

1. Everyone has the right to respect for his private and family life, his home and his correspondence.

2. There shall be no interference by a public authority with the exercise of this right except such as is in accordance with the law and is necessary in a democratic society in the interests of national security, public safety or the economic well-being of the country, for the prevention of disorder or crime, for the protection of health or morals, or for the protection of the rights and freedoms of others.

37. Barron 2010, 312.

38. ECHR Neij and Sunde Kolmisoppi against Sweden in the European Court of Human Rights Application no. 40397/12 (2013), p. 9. This was an appeal made by two operators of the Pirate Bay to the European Court of Human Rights in 2013. In this instance, the court also upheld the decision of the Swedish court; however, it is interesting that it confirmed the engagement of the right to freedom of expression.

39. Ibid.

40. Schroeder 2013, 67.

41. ECHR Neij and Sunde Kolmisoppi, p. 9.

42. *Yildirim*, section 67.

43. Open Net Initiative 2013.

44. Council of Europe 2010, 17–18, part 72.

45. Rundle and Birding 2008, 73.

46. Macdonald 2013a, 5.2.8.
47. ECHR Neij and Sunde Kolmisoppi, p. 9.
48. Ibid.; ECHR Concurring Opinion of Judge Pinto De Albuquerque, Case of Ahmet Yildirim v. Turkey (Application no. 3111/10), Strasbourg, December 18, 2012, final March 18, 2013.
49. *Yildirim*, section 56.
50. *Yildirim*, p. 28; see also UN: United Nations 2011b of the Special Rapporteur on the Promotion and Protection of the Right to Freedom of Opinion and Expression, para. 60, Human Rights Council, Seventeenth Session, A/HRC/17/27, May 16, 2011.
51. *Yildirim*, p. 29.
52. ECJ case number C-70/10 in the European Court of Justice, Scarlet Extended v. Societe Belge des auteurs, compositeur, et editeurs (SABAM), section 52.
53. EDPS 2014.
54. *Scarlet Extended*, section 55.
55. Angelopoulos 2014, 4–5. It's also interesting to read the *Cartier International* judgment, starting at S.158 (Principles to be applied).
56. ECHR Neij and Sunde Kolmisoppi.
57. House of Lords, House of Commons 2010, S.1.37.
58. Rundle and Birding 2008.
59. *Scarlet Extended*, section 53.
60. Directive 2009/140/EC, article 1.3a. See Horten 2012.
61. See Giblin 2014.
62. Loi no. 2009-669 du 12 juin 2009 favorisant la diffusion et la protection de la Création sur Internet (Creation and Internet Law) (2009).
63. Bridy 2013, 31–33.
64. Horten 2013, chaps. 9–14.
65. House of Lords, House of Commons 2010, S.1.36. The committee was considering the Technical Measures in the Digital Economy Act, S.10, that include slowing down the broadband access service with intention to prevent the user from being able to use specific services, as well as disconnection from the network itself.
66. Barron 2010, 338.
67. ECHR, article 6.2.
68. Directive 2009/140/EC, article 1.3a.
69. See Horten (2012), chapter 12, for a full account of the Internet Freedom provision and its genesis in the European Parliament.
70. European Commission 2011c, p. 19, S3.5.3.
71. Matthews 2008, 30.
72. "Every natural or legal person is entitled to the peaceful enjoyment of his possessions. No one shall be deprived of his possessions except in the public interest and subject to the conditions provided for by law and by the general principles of international law. The preceding provisions shall not, however, in any way impair the right of a State to enforce such laws as it deems necessary to control the use of property in accordance with the general interest or to secure the payment of taxes or other contributions or penalties" (ECHR protocol 1, article 1).
73. Charter of Fundamental Rights of the European Union (2000/C 364/01), article 17:

1. Everyone has the right to own, use, dispose of and bequeath his or her lawfully acquired possessions. No one may be deprived of his or her possessions, except in the public interest and in the cases and under the conditions provided for by law, subject to fair compensation being paid in good time for their loss. The use of property may be regulated by law in so far as is necessary for the general interest.
2. Intellectual property shall be protected.

74. House of Lords, House of Commons 2010, S.1.33.
75. ECJ case of Promusicae v. Telefonica in the European Court of Justice (2008), case C-275/06. Referring court: Juzgado de lo Mercantil No. 5 de Madrid. Applicant: Productores de

Musical de España (Promusicae). Defendant: Telefónica de España. ECJ ruling of January 29, 2008.

76. *Scarlet Extended*, section 55.

77. Directive 2001/29/EC on Copyright in the Information Society.

78. Directive 2004/48/ec; Directive 2000/31/EC; Copyright, Designs and Patents Act 1988.

79. Anti-Counterfeiting Trade Agreement (ACTA), December 2010 version, article 12; Stop Online Piracy Act (SOPA), 12th congress, 1st session, HR 3261, A Bill to Promote Prosperity, Creativity, Entrepreneurship, and Innovation by Combating the Theft of U.S. Property, and for Other Purposes.

80. GoldenEye International Ltd v. Telefonica, no. A3/2012/1477, Court of Appeal, S.117; Twentieth Century Fox v. BT, no. HC10C04385, High Court of Justice, S.119.

81. Twentieth Century Fox v. Newzbin, no. H C08C03346, judgment of Kitchin J, March 29, 2010, S.135.

82. United Nations 2011a, I.A.1–2.

83. Directive 2000/31/EC of the European Parliament and of the Council of June 8, 2000, on Certain Legal Aspects of Information Society Services, in Particular Electronic Commerce, in the Internal Market (Directive on electronic commerce, OJ L 178, 17.7.2000), articles 12–15.

84. Ibid., article 15.

85. See European Parliament, Del Castillo report, March 26, 2014, amendment 241.

86. European Union 2001, article 16. This analysis draws on Angelopoulos 2014, 814.

87. Angelopoulos 2014, 814.

88. House of Lords, House of Commons 2010, S.1.19, S.1.33, S.1.36–1.37.

89. United Nations 2011a, II.A.11.

90. Macdonald (2013a, S3.9) and Macdonald (2013b, 2) provide an interesting insight into the issue of private actors being asked to act as censors.

91. United Nations 2011a, I.B.3, B.5.

92. Rundle and Birding 2008, 85.

93. UN: United Nations 2011b, S.69; Kuczerawy 2015, 55.

94. United Nations 2011a, I.B.3.

95. Rundle and Birding 2008, 85.

96. United Nations 2011a, I.A.1–2.

97. Macdonald 2013a, S.5.3.3.

98. The law is known as Ley Sinde, or Sinde's law. Its official title is Ley 2/2011, de 4 de Marzo de Economia Sostenible, Annex 43. It was appended to the Law on the Sustainable Economy, which was a much larger piece of legislation addressing the economy as a whole. Ley Sinde was derived from the name of the (then) culture minister, Angelez Gonzalez-Sinde. See Horten 2013, chap. 8.

99. Peguera 2010, 164, S.90.

100. Ibid., 163–64.

101. Consejo Fiscal 2010, 18, 25.

102. Kaminsky 2011, 21.

103. Research carried out by the author indicates that discussions were ongoing in Britain from 2007 to 2008 and in Spain from 2007 to 2009.

104. European Commission 2011a.

105. European Commission 2011b; and the author's personal conversations with participants.

106. United Nations 2011a, I.B.5.

107. Bridy 2011, 577.

108. United Nations 2011a, II.B.21.

Chapter Six

(Global) Internet Governance and Its Discontents

M. I. Franklin

Deliberations on the day-to-day running of the Internet that once took place in venues far removed from the public eye, presided over by technical and legal experts, now make the headline news around the world.[1] The amount of media attention currently being given to decisions about the Internet's design, access, and use is at a level unforeseen by those individuals and groups working to make what used to be referred to as *global media* policy agendas and that now go under the name of *Internet governance* more socioculturally inclusive and politically accountable. But it is only since 2013 when Edward Snowden, former contractor with the U.S. National Security Agency (NSA), leaked evidence of unlawful forms of mass online surveillance at the behest of the U.S., UK, and other governments that policy making at the nexus of human rights and the Internet have taken center stage.[2] These revelations and their political fallout around the world have provided an important impetus to efforts, from civil society as well as some intergovernmental organizations (IGOs), to see Internet policy making more consciously framed within international human rights law and norms.[3]

What this shift from behind the scenes to front of house means is that socioculturally inflected priorities for Internet policy making are now part of the agendas that have been largely framed by the technical and economic priorities of computer engineers and Internet businesses. Nongovernmental organizations (NGOs), grassroots groups, and other sorts of civil society organizations (CSOs), or hybrid advocacy networks, have also been making their voices heard in settings dominated by a constellation of intergovernmental and quasi-nongovernmental bodies primarily concerned with the *technical* or *legal* dimensions of the Internet as an *economic* undertaking. This shift to more diverse participation and topics on the agenda has been taking place over the last decade in particular. Nonetheless the view that decisions about the Internet's design, access, and use are primarily technical questions, and thereby socially and politically neutral, remains strong amongst those communities of engineers and computer programmers who have been at the forefront of the Internet's development.[4] Once a narrow term for these informal networks of experts and technical decision making based predominately in the United States, the term *Internet governance* now covers the full spectrum of activities pertaining to how the Internet works; at the level of national legislatures, there are UN agencies such as the International Telecommunication Union (ITU) and UNESCO, and other sorts of standards-making bodies such as the Internet Engineering Task Force (IETF).[5] An added factor in this diversifying landscape of Internet-governance processes, and actors looking to steer these outcomes, is the incumbent power of corporations that own and control the lion's share of the Internet's current configuration of "Web 2.0" generation of *social media* products and services.[6]

The increasingly proactive role of governments and UN agencies in promoting Internet governance as an international, and thereby geopolitical, undertaking collides in many respects with this way of doing business, based on the assumption that the Internet owes its existence to neoliberal, free market economics premised on minimal state intervention. Whilst others argue the converse, that the Internet owes its existence to government, research, and military funding, the arrival of civil society activists across the spectrum of Internet-governance venues underscores how these once expert-led and relatively inaccessible arenas for laypersons are now populated by technically and politically savvy participants looking to influence the terms of reference for a range of agendas. Civil society organizations and affiliated networks have become more organized, apparently better funded, and more visible in these intergovernmental and business-led settings.[7] The role and historical influence of civil society as a stakeholder of circumstance, as arbiter or co-accomplice in current and future decision-making, is a source of tension within these networks, fueling in turn scholarly debates about the past, present, and future of Internet governance as an implicitly *inclusive* and *participatory* rather than a predominately intergovernmental process.[8]

Meanwhile the historical heartlands of the Internet—as an idea, way of life, and business—the United States first and foremost but also western Europe, face stiff competition from other contenders in setting the intergovernmental, that is, global, agenda for the future of the Internet's design, access, and use. Whilst these UN member states variously stake their claims on the agenda as primarily a matter of national sovereignty, day-to-day decisions about the regulation of online content for commercial services such as Facebook or Twitter pay less heed to national boundaries. In addition, the incumbent powers in setting the agenda based in the United States, UK, and western Europe are facing increasing competition from major economies based in the Global South, such as Brazil, Russia, India, China, and South Africa (the so-called BRICS countries). These shifts were already in place before the events of 2013, the aforementioned "Snowden revelations" of mass surveillance online, saw human rights considerations come to the fore and so emerge as a "wild card into the mix" of Internet-governance geopolitics according to some observers.[9]

In short, Internet governance is being increasingly regarded as an international human rights affair.[10] How—and when—this shift took place is beyond the means of this chapter.[11] Suffice it to say that debates over the human rights implications for Internet design, access, and use now encapsulate Internet governance and its discontents at this historical juncture. This shift in the form and substance of policy agendas, for human rights and other issues around cyberveillance,[12] has also accentuated a number of ongoing and emergent issues about the constitution of Internet governance in terms of main actors and processes: for example, who rings any changes in how the Internet is run through, say, decisions made at ICANN meetings around the world on Internet domain names and addresses,[13] or standards-making organizations such as the International Telecommunications Union (ITU) as their work straddles transnational and national jurisdictions at cross-sector and cross-border events that are variously open to "stakeholders."[14] This means that Internet governance, as it is currently construed and practiced as both process and outcome, challenges technocentric, state-centric, and business-centric models for running the Internet simultaneously.[15] In this respect the involvement of civil society organizations has raised its own set of questions about accountability as these nonstate actors challenge, or affirm, ongoing "public-private partnerships" between government and business to roll out Internet access on a global level or provide content and other online services.[16]

CHAPTER RATIONALE

By now it should be apparent that the term *Internet governance* is the object of some debate as well as a set of hotly contested processes between diverse interests that both compete and cooperate with one another. This also means that like the history of the Internet itself, that of Internet governance is still being written. This chapter aims to pinpoint some of the most pressing issues that preoccupy the multisited (i.e., online and/or offline) cross-sector spaces in which agendas are set and decisions taken. It is a discussion that comes from a particular point of view, namely that of longstanding participant-observation research into the Internet-politics-society nexus and, more recently, direct involvement in human rights advocacy in some of these venues and processes from an engaged critical scholarly and lay perspective.[17]

First I provide some historical and definitional orientation points, in order to help the reader navigate the dizzying array of possible topics that jostle for attention in any discussion of Internet policy making. After a brief look at two milestones in the establishment of Internet governance as a global undertaking, we move to the participatory and conceptual issues that constitute different visions of Internet governance and the dynamics of agenda setting that fall under this rubric. For heuristic purposes, I will discuss these meta-level concerns in light of debates around *where* Internet governance takes place—or is seen to be taking place—*how* it is organized (as a conscious strategy, by convention, or in response to mobilization), and *who* gets to take part. This approach may seem counterintuitive in that identifying key issues usually starts with articulating these in substantive terms. But as Internet governance as a term takes leave of its once-narrow, engineering, and problem-solving definition and as its closed-shop, technophile, and expert-led venues go global, this undertaking becomes in itself an issue of some magnitude.[18]

Decisions, and intense debates about who gets to call the shots that have been taking place behind the scenes, at the "back end" of the Internet's daily operations,[19] have direct and indirect consequences for how individuals and communities are able to access and use the Internet of the day. As the human rights–Internet nexus shows, claims that Internet governance is primarily a technical problem-solving exercise, disconnected from the immediate or wider socioeconomic or political context in which said problem arises, no longer holds sway. For example, changes in the "privacy settings" of major service providers such as Facebook and Google in recent years have highlighted that the repercussions for how millions of people socialize, maintain family relationships, or get their work done go far beyond the technical parameters of software "upgrades."[20]

NAVIGATING DEFINITIONAL, AND INSTITUTIONAL TERRAINS

This chapter started with problematizing rather than defining Internet governance. However, a working definition does exist, a much-cited albeit circular articulation of this process. Established during the UN-brokered World Summit on the Information Society, or WSIS (2003–2005), that ushered in Internet policy making as an intergovernmental undertaking, the Working Group on Internet Governance set up as part of these meetings concluded that the term denoted the development and application by Governments, the private sector and civil society, in their respective roles, of shared principles, norms, rules, decision-making procedures, and programmes that shape the evolution and use of the Internet. . . . This working definition reinforces the concept of inclusiveness of Governments, the private sector and civil society in the mechanisms of Internet governance. [21]

It would not be exaggerating to note that a decade on, nearly every term in this working definition continues to be hotly contested; also debated is the extent of these "respective roles" in legal and technical terms, technological and commercial changes to the Internet since this working group's deliberations, which principles or norms are shared and by whom and in a so-called post-Snowden context, and who is responsible for restoring "trust" in this very model of governance.

To grasp the intensity of these ensuing debates, we need to move past this rather functionalist definition however. For the purposes of this discussion, let me offer an additional conceptualization. Internet governance can be taken as a rubric for a set of techno-economically and socioculturally constituted *political* processes that concern ownership and control of a planetary constellation of information and communication technologies (the Internet in short) and corollary service provisions that have transformed regulatory and conceptual conventions that separate pre-Internet media and telecommunications from computer-mediated ones. The way people, states, and businesses use the Internet in turn is in the process of transforming conventional understandings of national jurisdiction and sovereignty and with that the constitution of multilateral institutions such as the UN as ipso facto intergovernmental organizations. [22]

Getting to grips with struggles over the form and substance of *global* Internet governance at this historical juncture also means tackling those around the impact of Internet-dependent media and communications on "traditional" broadcasting and print media on the one hand and, on the other, telecommunications. In this respect the Internet, broadly defined, emerges in the scholarly and policy literature in various ways, for example, construed as "new media." [23] In practical terms, the converging of traditional media sectors with computing and Internet communications has had major repercussions for longstanding administrative and disciplinary separations between media policy and law on the one hand and, on the other, Internet policy and law. [24] Moreover, the Internet, and struggles over how it has been governed, alongside shifts in debates about how it should be governed, concerns a particular historical conjuncture of predominately computer-dependent modes of communication, knowledge exchange, human association, and sociopolitical organization that are now being put in place by design as much as they are unintended consequences. [25]

The terms of access and use and then the content that is produced online and then circulated as not only substantive material (words, images, and sounds) but also statistics of use, known as *metadata management* (the storage and use of digital information about where and how people, users, access the Internet as they produce both traffic and content), are important distinctions under the common use of the term *the Internet*. This has become a catchall term for what are planetary computerized communications with quite local, personalized characteristics that indicate who and what individual users are doing whilst they are online, and how and when they are online. All these data accrue through the ability of software applications to track, store, and process these burgeoning databases of our "digital imagination,"[26] without which the Internet as a globally distributed "thinking machine"[27] and imaginary would not be thinkable. From the World Wide Web applications that arguably turned the Internet from a computer geek tool to a mass medium and to the Google (search engine and allied services such as YouTube) dominance of how people surf/search the web and the social-networking tools such as Facebook (and allied mobile services such as WhatsApp), there is an intimate albeit noncontingent interrelationship between its physical and digital design and ways the people use its products and services. The shift in terminology from "the Internet" to "the World Wide Web" and to "social media" belies the fact that today's Internet still runs on early generations of software codes, computer communications protocols, and the physical (cable and satellite) networks that link computers with each other across a room, a floor, and now around the world. Whether or not it is written with a capital *I* or not, the Internet is much more than the sum of its parts, made up of software and hardware combinations that straddle the microscopic and the planetary. However defined, the Internet has well and truly left the ivory towers of its early years and has become the "mass media" of the early twenty-first century.[28]

As to where formalized processes of Internet-governance decisions take place when not occurring within national borders and legal jurisdictions, there are a number of organizations and corollary venues engaged. Some are part of emerging "multistakeholder" institutions, such as the Internet Governance Forum, whilst other venues are based at older UN agencies in the process of reinventing themselves as custodians of the Internet as a global or public good to varying degrees, such as UNESCO. Intergovernmental bodies such as the International Telecommunications Union (ITU), UNESCO, and the UN Conference on Trade and Development (UNCTAD), or the newest UN venue, the Internet Governance Forum (IGF), have divided their "roles and responsibilities" along the aforementioned divide between the technical, sociocultural, and legal dimensions to agenda setting for the Internet at the international level. For instance, ITU works with treaty-making powers; UNESCO has been charged with a caretaker role of education, development, and freedom of expression; and IGF is premised on being the UN host for consultations that aim to "build global consensus"[29] around the panoply of issues laid out in the Declarations of Principles and Action Plans of preceding UN initiatives.[30]

As more explicitly sociocultural agendas for running the Internet gather momentum, those focusing on human rights–based frameworks in particular, we can see how Internet governance has become a term and a locus for a range of competing visions for the future design, access, and use of the Internet for different interests. This pits supporters of pre-Internet notions of national sovereignty and corollary legal jurisdictions against the real-time power of corporate service providers and their copyright powers.

RECENT MILESTONES AT THE INTERNATIONAL LEVEL

To recall, public awareness and rise in the political and economic stakes of questions around who does, or should, run the Internet took off in 2013 and in the wake of the Internet's role in social unrest and political mobilization in recent years. These major events have unfurled alongside successive waves of furore over commercial service providers' overreaches (e.g., by tracking and archiving of metadata through implicit rather than fully informed consent). Given the impetus provided by the Snowden revelations, it may seem surprising to hear that human rights for the Internet continue to be a contested priority for Internet-governance consultations within technical communities as well as governmental sectors. In the case of rights-based policy agendas for the online environment, how to implement human rights norms, in the relative absence of case law to draw from,[31] and the centrifugal forces of national jurisdiction that pull away from fully fledged global governance institutions are debates that take place in a number of competing venues. These forces are evident within longstanding Internet-governance (IG) organizations such as ICANN, as opponents of national, government-led processes vie with UN agencies for precedence in setting both the agenda and the terms of reference at any given moment. Within this intense reshuffle of intergovernmental and international advocacy priorities and intensifying scholarly debates are those engaged in a range of human rights mobilization for agenda setting around Internet design, access, and use. Here the last few years have seen some substantial progress in the form of official, that is, intergovernmental, recognition that international human rights law and norms and Internet-governance agendas are mutually dependent.

Two events at the international level stand out in this regard. Their historical legacy is at time of writing still moot, but the intention of both initiatives provide two signposts for the future of Internet-governance institutions. First, as noted above, is high-level, intergovernmental recognition of human rights as a foundational, not just an add-on, element to how the Internet should be governed, Second is the official, that is, ostensible, recognition from major intergovernmental bodies such as ITU or UNESCO that Internet governance is also an inherently *multistakeholder* enterprise (more on this term below). The first milestone in this regard is the UN Human Rights Council Resolution of 2012.[32] Entitled "The Promotion, Protection and Enjoyment of Human Rights on the Internet," this resolution encapsulates efforts that both preceded and benefitted from the Snowden revelations of mass online surveillance in 2013 on behalf of putting human rights frameworks for the Internet on the agenda at the highest echelons of UN Human Rights agencies. Resolution A/HRC/RES/20/8

1. *Affirms* that the same rights that people have offline must also be protected online, in particular freedom of expression, which is applicable regardless of frontiers and through any media of one's choice, in accordance with articles 19 of the Universal Declaration of Human Rights and the International Covenant on Civil and Political Rights;
2. *Recognizes* the global and open nature of the Internet as a driving force in accelerating progress towards development in its various forms;
3. *Calls upon* all States to promote and facilitate access to the Internet and international cooperation aimed at the development of media and information and communications facilities in all countries.[33]

This resolution seals the commitment, in principle at least and in the most general of language, of those signatories to the premise that the online environment also falls under the international human rights law and norms. The ethical and legal issue that arises, however, is that these same states as custodians and generators of human rights under the UN system are also perpetrators of human rights abuses, again online and on the ground.[34] This conflict of interests affects moves by government agencies to prioritize state actors in the Internet-governance domain given their "roles and responsibilities" in enforcing human rights off line and ipso facto online according to international law.

A second milestone of another sort was the inaugural NETmundial, co-hosted by the Brazilian government and ICANN in April 2014, in São Paulo, Brazil. The outcome of this meeting was the finalization of the "NETmundial Multistakeholder Outcome Document."[35] Whilst some of the wording in the final text remains contested amongst civil society participants active in these negotiations,[36] two substantive aspects bear mentioning in terms of what they suggest about how prominent actors engaged in molding the "global Internet-governance" agenda see the future. Cohosts of this meeting, Brazil and ICANN, count as key actors in this regard. First, in stronger terms than the

UN 2012 Resolution discussed above, this Outcome Document underscores the formative, not simply corollary, role that international human rights law and norms have in this statement's articulation of a "set of common principles and important values" that "should underpin Internet governance principles."[37] The second aspect is the prominent place given to nonstate actors as playing a potentially *equal* role in decision making on Internet design, access, and use. A third point of note is the claim in the statement preamble that this meeting was "a bottom-up, open, and participatory process involving thousands of people from governments, private sector, civil society, technical community, and academia from around the world . . . the first of its kind."[38]

The provenance, organization, and eventual outcome of this meeting, one that took place outside the auspices of the UN's Internet Governance Forum and other UN agencies looking to set the agenda (UNESCO and ITU being two cases in point), deserves its own treatment.[39] Moreover fuller research into the power dynamics that became evident in the decisions taken in preparing for this event, and those emerging since participants at the conference agreed to this version as a "nonbinding" undertaking,[40] has yet to emerge. The point I want to make on going to press is that the future of the 2014 NETmundial participatory model as a serious contender to the one pioneered at the UN Internet Governance Forum is a moot point.[41] That said, so is the future of the IGF itself as its continued existence is up for renewal at the UN WSIS+10 meeting in New York, in December 2015.

It bears repeating that the first of these milestones was passed before the Snowden revelations in 2013 of governmental surveillance deep within the Internet's operational infrastructure without the knowledge let alone full consent of ordinary Internet users, albeit with the legal compliance of Internet companies. Critics note that high-level resolutions such as these, for all their symbolic power, only scratch the surface. They are far removed from the techno-legal and political practicalities of bringing human rights law and norms to bear on the complex, dense policy domain that encompasses both formal and informal decision making about how the Internet is run, or should be run, on the one hand and, on the other, on how people interact, present themselves, and produce content in public and private "cyberspaces."[42] These issues around implementation (how exactly) and the lack of feasible or affordable legal remedies remain unaddressed. However this first UN acknowledgment that human rights apply to the online environment is now public record, even if its substantive contribution to the implementation of human rights frameworks across the spectrum of Internet-governance agendas is unclear.[43] It thereby takes its place as part of the long trail of discourses and undertakings that the UN system as a whole and its respective agencies develop as they "frame the world,"[44] in this case in response to "increasing public concern at the national and international levels about the protection and enjoyment of human rights online as well as offline."[45]

For this reason, understanding how key issues divide and unite actors engaging across the spectrum of Internet governance as an emergent set of institutions can be divided into two streams: (1) those who take these processes to be a particular sort of inclusive process that sets out to achieve so-called concrete outcomes, and (2) those who focus on steering the discursive, policy-framing, and agenda-setting dimensions to these gatherings. Whether an IT engineer or IT lawyer, politician or career diplomat, or hactivist/activist or Internet policy director of an international NGO or think tank, both dimensions are increasingly important to balance; it is essential to engage in decisions that generate outcomes—policy and official undertakings—whether or not these are legally binding, and intervene in the narrative, larger and specific to any given issue area (e.g., net neutrality, cyberveillance).

RECURRING CONCEPTUAL AND
PARTICIPATORY CONUNDRUMS

There is a paradox at the heart of the term *Internet governance* in that it implies the Internet needs governing at all, that is, formal forms of political oversight that go beyond the informal, expert-run networks responsible for upgrading and maintaining the software codes on the one hand and, on the other, the physical, computer-mediated communications networks comprising successive generations of the Internet's design, access, and use. The aforementioned official definition of Internet governance states, despite evidence to the contrary, that there is a "common understanding of the Internet," whilst "there is not yet a shared view of Internet governance."[46] The latter differences mark out significant differentials in political and legal power over how decisions are taken, who takes those decisions, and on whose behalf.[47]

For instance, when it comes to participation in agenda setting, if not decision making, the remit of the Internet Governance Forum, called into being at the 2005 Tunis Summit of the World Summit on the Information Society, explicitly notes that this is to be a "forum for multistakeholder policy dialogue, that is, *multilateral, multistakeholder*, democratic *and* transparent."[48] The term "multistakeholder" has become increasingly politicized in Internet-governance deliberations and agenda setting for the future. For some, this term denotes an emergent form of global democracy whereby governments can be called to account for policy decisions that impact how the Internet works or is used. For others the same term is a euphemism for legitimating corporate ownership and control of Internet-dependent public services.[49] On this point government representatives differ as well, for such differences of policy and working principles are also differences in political ideology and worldview.

The other term—*multilateralism*—which once designated intergovernmental initiatives, or undertakings dependent upon governments' role in lawmaking (such as human rights), has become positioned as the polar opposite of multistakeholderism, for better or for worse and, again, depending on the point of view. However, as the Tunis agenda cited above shows, the historical record confirms that both terms have their place in these "founding documents" of the UN's establishment of the Internet Governance Forum as a place where member states are one rather than the only constituency. Scholars and activists will continue to wrangle over these two terms for some time to come because, when it comes to human rights, as a legal obligation of UN member states to protect citizens under international law, and businesses to respect these laws when providing goods and services, the tripartite issues of accountability, access to legal remedy (promised but yet to be delivered in web-saturated settings), and enforcement remain under-elucidated areas for consideration and action.

Whilst conceptualizing the "Internet" and its governance according to these contested criteria of participation and decision-making responsibilities continues to be grist to the mill for debates, those for whom these struggles are taking place point to the next issue around participation, the one-third of the world's population who are not yet online and who are positioned as either an inferior state of nonconnectivity or aspiring to go online. "Connecting the next billion"[50] is a catchphrase based in the very last of the UN Millennium Development Goals (MDGs) in which the UN undertakes in "cooperation with the private sector, [to] make available benefits of new technologies, especially information and communications" to the Global South.[51]

This project to connect the whole world has been reiterated in the last decade of Internet-governance events at the international level, the NETmundial included.[52] But as critics—including from the Global South—note, this emphasis on information and communication technologies (ICT), viz. *the Internet*, as a hi-tech solution for endemic socioeconomic equalities within the Global South as well as between Internet-"rich" and Internet-"poor" parts of the Global North, begs the question of the troubled historical legacy of international development programs that lean heavily on technological solutions.[53] In a year in which the UN Millennium Development Goals are being reviewed fifteen years later, the 1995 UN Beijing Conference on the Status of Women is twenty years on, and the World Summit on the Information Society undergoes its ten-year review, and with the future of the Internet Governance Forum itself up for renewal, a range of issues queue up to be taken into consideration, for example, around sustainable development, gender rights, access for persons with disability and young people, and increasingly the environmental costs of the electricity-dependent Internet servers and use of nonrenewable resources in the construction of computers and other hardware components. At the heart of these debates, about the viability of multilateral versus multistakeholder models for Internet-governance decision-making processes on the one hand and, on the other, the efficacy of Western, hi-tech modernization imperatives that position the Internet as the answer to global poverty, gender inequalities, and all other social injustices, is the role of governments—or to put it another way, the role of the private sector in providing essential goods and services, of which Internet access is now considered primary.

In the meantime, Internet-dependent societies have become mobilized by the human rights implications of both government-sponsored and commercially facilitated forms of mass surveillance and data mining. Internet for Development priorities, referred to as ICT for Development (ICT4D), and its environmental costs, still have some way to go. As such, these issues within or distinct from human rights frameworks for the Internet[54] call upon, indeed require, by international law the active rather than the passive role of governments in setting the rules, enforcing them, and being accountable. They also imply the cooperation of the same governments at the highest level about the key terms of reference of human rights and the Internet in practical terms, on content regulation and terms of use, for instance. And here, as is the case within civil society, intense disagreement is the rule. Moreover, there are powerful lobbies—involving those involved in the earlier prototypes of Internet technologies and the online communities that emerged in the Internet's earliest iterations as part of the U.S. West Coast IT-enthusiast countercultures in the 1980s—that would disagree with any need for regulation apart from technical maintenance. When the adjective "global" is included in the mix, particularly in the context of UN-hosted consultations, this paradox becomes a geopolitical bone of contention, not just a technical problem to solve.

This brings us to how participation is linked to location, for the term "global Internet governance" posits a process, a venue, and a constituency that operates in ways that are neither reducible nor confined to national institutions, jurisdictions, or citizenries.[55] Whilst national media and policy-making models continue to operate within pre-Internet-age imaginaries, as nation-based media discourses and electoral priorities, when it comes to Internet governance state actors do not dominate. How the Internet is run has meant a shift in venue, register, and forms of attendance. And these shifts affect how any given Internet-governance issue is understood, conveyed, and contested.

WHAT COUNTS AS A KEY ISSUE IS POLITICAL

Before concluding let me link the above conundrums to the equally vexed question of what counts as a key issue and who decides when it comes to setting these agendas, for example, (1) how decisions that appear to be purely technical, standard-setting face arguments that they have a role to play in the skewed geographies of Internet access and use; (2) when public services are pitted against for-profit business priorities in decisions where copyright law is involved; or (3) the ongoing standoff between advocates of open-source software and the proprietary software licenses of major corporate players such as Microsoft or Apple. All of these areas have implications for how people access the Internet and use the web as they produce, find, and then share content online.

Contentions about which issues are paramount and who decides on past, present, and future decisions about the Internet's design, access, and use have played a constitutive rather than a mimetic role in the history of Internet governance as a relatively new institutional process and, with that, an object of scholarly analysis. Right from the outset, if we were to date the origins of intergovernmental initiatives to institutionalize Internet governance in the ITU-hosted WSIS in 2003–2005,[56] we have seen in the official record debates taking place behind the scenes about the terms and participatory parameters of agenda setting.[57] In current Internet governance speak, the conventional term for these different positions is "stakeholders," according to three broad categories: public (governmental), private (business), and civil society (i.e., nongovernmental organizations).

As noted above, the term that encapsulates the notion of Internet governance as an inclusive process of consultation if not decision making, rather than one reserved for governmental representatives alone, is "multistakeholder participation,"[58] *multistakeholderism* for short. The way in which the latter term has been positioned at the opposite end of the spectrum to multilateralism is arguably one of the most contentious issues of Internet governance today—not just who *can* participate but also who gets to decide at the end of the day who *does* take part and consequently who can be called to account and by what means. With human rights now a clear fixture on the agenda, the "roles and responsibilities" of UN member states under international law to uphold and protect human rights as these arise online confront the de facto rule of private Internet service providers on the one hand and, on the other, claims by civil society organizations to be given more than a token role in these proceedings.

These debates, echoing precursor initiatives to forge an international consensus on "global media policy," highlight the different political stakes, techno-economic resources, and worldviews of protagonists.[59] Recall, there are those who regard the Internet and its governance as primarily a techno-economic concern and confront those who privilege the sociocultural—human—dimensions to decisions about the design, access, and use of Internet media and communications. These positions of relative influence (not the same as relative visibility) highlight the extent to which dominant actors work to shape the agenda with or without reference to a growing list of concerns that are anchored in the later treaties and covenants of international human rights law.[60] Containing the Internet-governance agenda within a strictly technical understanding is one way to keep out nontechnical concerns that are nonetheless affected by the way people use the Internet and the way power holders in turn deploy these technologies for various ends against citizens (including residents at home and citizens abroad), in the name of national security or public order, for instance. But these "power holders" who are referred to in these official statements are no longer nation-states, both in working practice and by volition. This means that a disconnect has opened between wider publics, usually addressed as national citizenries or local communities, and those agencies charged with Internet law and policy who are not, by law, directly answerable to these publics. So here we see how differing conceptualizations and models of democracy, or indeed any other political system, are becoming articulated as intrinsically Internet-governance issues. Incumbent UN powerbrokers (e.g., the United States and other permanent members of the Security Council) and voices from the Global South, those states that have a vote in the UN but relatively little say on setting the techno-economic agenda of current consultations, are particularly alert to this nexus.[61] A second point to note is that any decisions about an issue, once identified as significant and then put on the agenda, have repercussions for de jure (existing national and international legal mechanisms), and de facto decision making about the Internet's design, access, or use that also implicate online content production. Stronger still, active parties and analysts, like authors in this volume, have to take into account the recent sea change in popular imaginaries about the uncomfortable interconnection between how ordinary people use the Internet in everyday life and the pressing legal and ethical implications of how states and corporations have been deploying the Internet in turn.[62] Public attention being paid to human rights online in recent years belies, however, awareness by successive U.S. administrations of the Internet's economic implications and with that its political and military dimensions.[63]

This brings me to the third contentious issue: continuity and change in technical and legal terms, in other words, how to distinguish between existing and emerging—new—areas for consideration given the relatively short institutional history of "global Internet governance" consultations at the UN level within longstanding institutions, and the legacy of precursor initiatives to establish global agendas. This legacy is a contentious, indeed cantankerous, one that reaches back into the 1970s.[64] For one thing, the terms of reference have changed enormously, from "global media debates" to UN Summits on the "Information Society," and to "Internet Governance."[65] As the historical narrative around the origins of the Internet remains open to interpretation and contestation, so does that emerging around how the Internet has been, will be, and indeed should be governed, if at all. There are two dimensions to these debates and how they are articulated as agendas and outcomes. The first continues to concern process and participation. The second concerns substantive issues and outcomes in highly specialized areas that exercise participants in different degrees and in different locations, for instance, those advocating for the internationalization of ICANN.[66] Another example pivots on the technical specifications of national legislation on mandatory filtering of online content, seen as censorship for some, protection of minors for others.[67] In the wake of the Snowden revelations, media coverage of these measures pales in comparison though to those laws being put into place, in the United States and the UK, for instance, that grant law enforcement agencies increasing powers to track and collect users' personal data online in the name of national cybersecurity.[68]

Fourth, there are those issues that explicitly link techno-legal, regulatory, and sociocultural agendas under one rubric. Human rights frameworks that can be applied at all points of the Internet's governance are a principal approach in this respect, the gaps between this broad and comprehensive set of aspirations and their implementation in everyday decisions about running the Internet notwithstanding.[69] Whichever narrative holds sway within a respective moment, meeting, or outcome relating to Internet governance as a transborder undertaking, the thing to note is that whether they are couched in engineering, legal, or political terms, these narratives evoke competing visions of Internet futures. Those pivoting on an Internet premised on the historical conventions of national sovereignty—territorially bordered citizenries of "netizens"—have to deal with online and off-line spaces that are indelibly marked by substantial commercial ownership of the transborder, computer-mediated encounters, and transactions that characterize an Internet-dependent world.

IN CONCLUSION

> At least some procedural progress has been made. . . . New ways of participatory political action have been promoted: . . . a multistakeholder approach through the inclusion of all stakeholders, the private sector as well as civil society is being implemented. This is no small step. . . . Obviously we are still at the beginning of a very long process . . ., that is, in the very early stages of a possible transformation of the UN decision-making procedure, of the possible development of a new model of global governance which could have repercussions on national politics.[70]

The above observation is from the foreword to a set of critical essays by civil society participants on the first year of the World Summit on the Information Society. Twelve years on it is still pertinent. This chapter has discussed key issues for Internet governance, as a contested notion, within this wider historical context and in the wake of the 2014 NETmundial Outcome Document in which participating governments and other signatories agreed to a "nonbinding" undertaking to promote a model of Internet governance that "*should* promote sustainable and inclusive development and for the promotion of human rights" and do so in ways that ensure "the full involvement of all stakeholders in their respective roles and responsibilities."[71] Whilst the circular reasoning remains the same, there has been a subtle but concerted shift in language and emphasis from those of a decade earlier during the WSIS meetings. Statements that explicitly refer to both "multistakeholder" *and* "multilateral" participatory models have made way for those that omit the latter term altogether.[72]

The first point to make by way of a conclusion is to note that Internet governance, in form and substance, is political. By this I mean to say that how the Internet is run, by and for whom, and in which venue according to which rules of engagement has become an explicitly contested process that is subject to competing attempts to institutionalize, and thereby legitimate, the way respective interests wish to ensure "business as usual." How to reconcile this push-and-pull between innovative models (of which the IGF is a primary if much criticized example at the UN, and the recent NETmundial, a prototype that has yet to weather its first year) and established ways of doing things (e.g., at ITU or ICANN meetings) is what lies ahead for the architects of Internet policy making as a particular sort of model for computer-mediated global governance.

The second point is that many of the major political and sociocultural issues arising for the future of Internet policy making, as outlined here, are not new, even if their techno-legal implications may be. They articulate longstanding bones of contention that are now rendered for the digital, Internet-dependent Zeitgeist. The power ratio between states and markets (or government regulation versus market-based principles of self-regulation), private versus public ownership and control of critical resources such as the Internet's domain name system, or public service provisions of access and content in light of corporate power to dominate global market share, from Microsoft in the 1990s to Google this century are cases in point. For the Internet, however defined, is the object of political and economically motivated struggles for control of not only its design, access, and use quite literally but also the narrative. Internet governance is as much a battle of words as it is a technological or business decision.[73] As an object of analysis and advocacy, in practical and political terms the Internet is also both the means and the medium for how governance consultations take place, agendas can be influenced, and in turn where outcomes are archived and then accessed for future analysis.

This is not to suggest that terms of reference and these larger narratives are simply semantics. The Internet, as a communicative culture combined with the paraphernalia of physical cables, gadgets, and communities, is as material a structure as it is one based on "virtual" relationships. Substantive legal and technical decisions where experts command our attention make a difference to how people live their lives, polities maintain peace and order (as they see it), and businesses make money. Hence, the term "the Internet" and its "governance" are more than descriptive, unproblematic categories. They have come to encapsulate a cluster of political, economic, and sociocultural transformations that characterize our times. They are terms deployed by major players in the Internet-governance domain, such as ICANN, to conjure up the inevitable march of progress, for example, a future societal vision of the Internet as a transformative "tool" to engineer a particular world order. This epochal role is quite a large burden for an invention that first connected computers to one another so that computing experts could "talk" to each other via their consoles, and do so across physical space and different time zones. It is even quite a lot to carry for its next iteration, as a set of technologies that enabled ordinary people, nonexperts, to connect with one another, find information, and get other things done in relatively easy-to-use ways. Whatever the future may hold, the Internet's current iteration facilitates an ever-greater array of computer-dependent tools and applications that now "infuse our lives. Our homes, our jobs, our social networks—the fundamental pillars of our existence—now demand immediate access to these technologies."[74]

Finally, whilst states are charged with making and enforcing human rights law, and companies can call upon their proprietary rights as laid down by intellectual-property guarantees such as copyright, civil society representatives premise their claims on appeals to these laws and norms from a moral and ethical standpoint. This is to my mind the biggest issue for Internet governance from an international, or to put in the IG speak of the day, "global consensus building" perspective. From the point of view of how ordinary people, communities, and polities may use Internet-dependent goods and services, in order to survive if not prosper, the ways in which both states and businesses are seen (not) to carry out their respective responsibilities as "power holders" in their respective "roles and responsibilities to uphold, protect and respect human rights norms"[75] will preoccupy those working in and researching this domain for some time to come.

NOTES

1. This chapter is dedicated to the memory of Heike Jensen, critical Internet scholar and civil society activist at World Summit on the Information Society (WSIS) and Internet Governance Forum (IGF) events, who passed away in 2014. Heike championed both a social constructivist approach to Internet-governance research and work to have women's human rights be an integral element in all facets of the Internet's design, access, and use (Jensen 2005, 2006).

2. At the global level, these events encompass Wikileaks (2010), the Arab Spring (2010–2011), the Occupy Movement and related actions (2012 and ongoing), and the public furore at news in 2013 that a U.S.-led alliance of Western governments has been engaging in mass online surveillance at the global level; these are the most prominent cases in point at time of writing. In terms of where Internet-governance institutions have been evolving, one of these actors, the Internet Society (2014), has been developing an overview of these various agencies, now accepted as a reasonable representation of the main actors charged with, or assuming the leadership in key decisions about, the running of the Internet; see Franklin (2013, 226–27n3) and Kaspar, Brown, and Varon (2013). For historical accounts, and reflections on UN-hosted international consultations around global media/Internet policy agendas, see Frau-Meigs et al. (2012), Gerbner, Mowlana, and Nordenstreng (1993), Hamelink (1998), and MacBride (1980).

3. By this I am referring to the intersection between international human rights law and norms and how the Internet is designed, accessed, and used on the one hand and, on the other, to where international human rights advocacy communities and Internet policy makers converge.

4. See, for example, Cerf (2012).

5. See Council of Europe (2012, 2014a); Jørgensen (2013); Franklin (2013); and UN Frank La Rue Report of the Special Rapporteur on the Promotion and Protection of the Right to Freedom of Opinion and Expression, para. 60, Human Rights Council, Seventeenth Session, A/HRC/17/27, May 16, 2011. Standards-setting and treaty-making bodies such as the Internet Engineering Task Force (IETF) or the International Telecommunications Union (ITU) represent two distinct sorts of decision-making bodies in this regard. The Internet Governance Forum (IGF), the United Nations Educational, Scientific and Cultural Organization (UNESCO), and the Council of Europe are in turn another genus of intergovernmental venues, whilst the nongovernmental, private status of the Internet Corporation of Assigned Names and Numbers (ICANN) and its pivotal role in how the Internet works or the lobbying and research of Internet Society (ISoc) is another category again. See note 2 above.

6. Whilst not all elements in the Internet's history can be claimed as a U.S. invention—the World Wide Web protocols emerged from state-funded research in Europe, for instance, as did a precursor of the web: Minitel (a French initiative)—today's dominant tools and applications (said "social media") based on the "Web 2.0" design principles and business model (Mandiberg 2012) are predominately United States owned, by private corporations. And to date the main axis of the Internet's physical infrastructure and with that the bulk of its packet-switching traffic still run through the United States itself, passing under U.S. law. The literature on the skewed physical geography of the Internet and how this has impinged on how it has been managed to date is diverse. For celebratory accounts of the shift from the World Wide Web generation of goods and services to the "Web 2.0" social media that dominate today, see Mandiberg (2012); for an analysis of the history and policy implications of U.S. ownership of the domain name system, see Mueller (2002). For a range of views on the role of the state in running the Internet, see Eriksson and Giacomello (2009) as a response to Goldsmith and Wu (2006). And for two largely pessimistic views of the Internet's democratic potential given the U.S. technical and market dominance, see Morozov (2011) and Vaidyanathan (2012). And to get an immediate sense of how the Internet is a physical "network of networks" that spans some of the globe more than others, see the range of up-to-date and historical maps at https://www.telegeography.com/.

7. Evidence that the increase in civil society—and this includes academic—attendees at major events on the Internet-governance (IG) calendar is the result of increased funding can be gleaned from the rise in civil society attendance at conferences such as those provided by the Internet Governance Forum, or the European Dialogue on Internet Governance websites. An-

other indicator is the increase in professional campaigns for ostensibly civil society agendas, for example, the 2012 Internet Freedom campaign run by Access Now!, or the Necessary and Proportionate (2013) campaign on Internet privacy by an alliance of U.S.- and UK-based NGOs such as the Electronic Frontier Foundation Privacy International, and Article 19. Another indicator in recent years is the formal arrival of large human rights NGOs such as Amnesty International and Human Rights Watch at the 2014 IGF meeting in Istanbul. Debates as to the role of not only private sector but also governmental (e.g., the U.S. State Department) funding of civil society projects, that is, who funds whom and the ensuing agendas that are inferred from these relationships, are an ongoing source of concern within civil society/academic networks active in the IG domain. Journalists and other critics have also been following this "funding trail." The financial clout of companies such as Google (a proactive and prominent funder of research institutes, projects, and events with an Internet-governance theme), the Disney Corporation (a major funder of the 2015 UNESCO Internet Study Conference), and ICANN (co-organizer and major funder of the 2014 NETmundial Meeting in Brazil) as they become more active in supporting major international meetings such as these continues to exercise scholars and participants. See, for example, Guilhot (2005), Lipschutz (2005), and Becker and Niggemeier (2012).

8. More on the privileging of the role of governments vis-à-vis that of the private sector or civil society representation in agenda setting as well as decision making will follow. Suffice it to say that the research literature is characterized by a wide range of perspectives on just this point: see, for example, Jørgensen (2006, 2013), Franklin (2010, 2013), Mueller (2010), Dany (2012), Deibert (2000), Flyverbom (2011), and Singh (2012).

9. Deibert 2015, 15.

10. See Jørgensen (2013) and Council of Europe (2014b).

11. See chapter 3, by Roy Balleste, in this volume.

12. These issues are discussed in Balleste's chapter 3 and other chapters in this volume.

13. ICANN stands for the Internet Corporation for Assigned Names and Numbers, a U.S. nonprofit set up in the late 1990s to oversee the process of assigning Internet addresses and managing requests and revenues from their corresponding "domain names" (e.g., ".com" or ".NZ"). The *domain name system* is what makes the Internet as we know it and with that the way people navigate the web. See Mueller (2002) and Komaitis (2010) for two authoritative studies of this organization and its influence.

14. The IGF, for instance, is open to all-comers in that attendance is based on submitting a form based on self-identified affiliation rather than the need for full accreditation, as is the case with ITU or UN General Assembly events. That said, ensuring that meetings are considered suitably representative of all sectors also involves participation by invitation and funding support (see note 7 above); the 2014 NETmundial Meeting and 2015 UNESCO conference are two cases in point. See note 40 below.

15. I discuss the limitations of state-centric, techno-centric, and media-centric analytical models more fully in Franklin (2013, 13 passim). For a discussion of how the way a policy is "framed" plays a formative role in the outcomes of IG decision making and agenda setting, see Jørgensen (2013). See also the rationale behind the Charter of Human Rights and Principles of the Internet (IRP Coalition [2011] 2015) and Zalnieriute and Schneider (2014), examples of two responses to narrowly conceived understandings of Internet-governance priorities developed from within IGF and ICANN constituencies.

16. UN 2000; ITU/WSIS 2005; Jakubowicz 2009; Healy 2012.

17. Franklin 2004, 2005, 2007, 2013.

18. Global Partners 2013; Mueller 2010; Eriksson and Giacomello 2009.

19. Stalder 2012.

20. An example is the case of how to implement the right to privacy online in technical and legal terms, that is, encryption software that allows, by default and by law, for an Internet user to be anonymous when online. The legal and commercial issues that arise for implementing online anonymity as an operational principle of Internet access and web use (ironically for a communications system based on open, end-to-end computer communications across a network as it spans the globe) mean that right, principle, and legal guarantees do not necessarily work hand in hand. At the operational and international legal level, anonymity being deployed to

enable people to exercise their right to privacy online in an absolute sense is technically impossible on the one hand. On the other hand, it is legally and politically complex when applied across legal jurisdiction for those countries where anonymity is unconstitutional, as is the case in Brazil.

21. WGIG 2005, 4.

22. Elsewhere I explore how the term *Internet governmentality*, taking a cue from Michel Foucault and others, better encapsulates what is at stake (Franklin 2010, 2013; Lipschutz 2005).

23. Jakubowicz 2009; Mandiberg 2012.

24. Benedek and Kettemann 2014; Council of Europe (2014b); MacKinnon et al. 2014.

25. Mansell and Silverstone 1996.

26. Latour 2007; see also Lessig, 2006, and his arguments about how "code is law."

27. Quintas 1996.

28. Debates about capitalization of the term, aside from different grammatical conventions in different languages or English dialects (e.g., U.S. versus British English spelling), are beyond this chapter. Suffice it to say that they do relate to different conceptualizations of the object of analysis, as a singular or compound noun. For the record, I no longer use capitals (Franklin 2013) where publishing house styles permit.

29. This is in IGF's own words but also refers to the WSIS Tunis Agenda (IGF 2008, 2011; ITU/WSIS 2005).

30. For instance, from the ITU hosting of the WSIS process in the first decade of this century to the establishment in 2005 of the UN-based Internet Governance Forum (ITU/WSIS 2005) and its regional spin-off meetings such as the European Dialogue on Internet Governance (EuroDIG) and the Arab or Latin American Internet Governance Forum meetings, and to the changing role and ambitions of ICANN as co-instigator of the 2014 NETmundial Meeting in Brazil (NETmundial 2014) and its mooted successor, the NETmundial Initiative (NMI), to be based at the World Economic Forum in Davos, Switzerland. See ITU/WSIS (2003a, b, 2005), Gerbner, Mowlana, and Nordenstreng (1993), and Frau-Meigs et al. (2012) for more examples and case studies. For a careful reconstruction of the contentious developments around the outlook for the form and substance of the 2014 Brazilian NETmundial Meeting as it purportedly morphs into a World Economic Forum–sponsored project, see Corwin (2014).

31. This point is referred to in studies such as Benedek and Kettemann (2014) and the Council of Europe (2014b).

32. UN Human Rights Council (2012), A/HRC/RES/20/8.

33. Ibid., 2.

34. See Vincent (2010, 196) and Clapham (2007, 18–19) on this paradox.

35. NETmundial 2014.

36. The first is mention of future discussions on "the meaning and application of equal footing" between governments primarily and other protagonists, the private sector, in particular (NETmundial 2014, 11). The other sticking point, for governmental representatives, is mention of "mass and arbitrary surveillance" (ibid.) rather than simply "surveillance." The third contentious point pertains to the insertion of the term "creators" on the same footing as "authors," under the rubric of human rights, by including both the "rights of authors *and creators* as established in law" (ibid., 4) with respect to freedom of/access to information. Critics and observers were quick to note the legal and political problems arising from couching copyright (viz. "intellectual property rights") in the same breath as human rights and fundamental freedoms under international human rights law. Other key points, included as future agenda points or pending developments, were on how this meeting related to the future of the UN-hosted Internet Governance Forum and on changes in the ownership and governance structure of ICANN, the so-called IANA transition (ibid., 10).

37. NETmundial 2014, 4.

38. Ibid., 2.

39. The document is divided in two parts: "Internet Governance Principles" and "Roadmap for the Future Evolution of the Internet Governance" (NETmundial 2014, 4, 8). Human rights are framed as underpinning "Internet governance principles" (ibid., 4) in general, albeit fading from the explicit text as the document addresses "Internet governance *process* principles"

(ibid., 6, emphasis added). It is in the latter section and part 2 of the document that we see the term "multistakeholder" (discussed in the following sections) take over—four times in this one page. In total this term appears sixteen times in this twelve-page document, in virtually every major section, including the title. As for "human rights," this term appears nine times. As key word "visibility" is a key indicator of success in outcomes that are archived and accessed via the web's search engines, and "frequency" becomes a marker of failure or success (see Franklin 2007).

40. NETmundial 2014, 2.

41. Participation in the NETmundial was based on submitting an "expression of interest" in attending the meeting, from which "invitations" were issued and financial support was offered (ICANN being a key source of funding and supplier of organizational logistics such as travel bookings). Observers in the lead-up to the actual meeting noted that it took some time for governments to indicate their intention to participate. According to the NETmundial website, "1,480 stakeholders with active voices (including remote participation), from a diversity of 97 nations" took part (NETmundial 2015). Major powers such as the United States, the UK, and EU leader such as Germany, along with India and China, attended, which indicates a degree of success. For without governmental support the meeting would have not had the same traction in terms of its own claims to represent something new. On that point, it bears noting that participation at IGF meetings has always been open, based on submitting an application form (personal information such as passport number, nationality, and contact details). Once approved an interested party can attend. In short, NETmundial is not the first of its kind in terms of open-access attendance criteria for nongovernmental participants.

42. The term "cyberspace" evokes the phenomenological, experiential dimensions to what people do and where people go when "online"; see Franklin (2013, 53–55) for a fuller discussion.

43. In other words, a UN resolution is in itself only a start and for some human rights specialists a far cry from concrete moves to address pressing points of human rights law as they apply or not to the online environment, let alone Internet-governance processes. The ongoing lack of legal remedies that are affordable and accessible for ordinary Internet users who wish to seek redress from Internet giants such as Google or Facebook, or their own governments, continues to haunt critical commentaries on the burgeoning number of documents about Internet-governance "principles" (Jørgensen 2013, 61–62, 220 passim; IRP Coalition [2011] 2015). Court rulings pertaining to human rights online are also emerging as important nodes of debates amongst policy makers and legal experts (Council of Europe 2014b); my thanks to Joanna Kulesza for pressing me on this point.

44. Bøås and McNeill 2004.

45. IRP Coalition [2011] 2015, 1.

46. WGIG 2005, 4.

47. The Internet Society (ISoc), for instance, has shifted its stance of late, saying there is effectively "one single Internet" to promoting the term "the Internet ecosystem." As for definitions, as ISoc also admits "defining the Internet *isn't* easy" (Internet Society 2015, original emphasis). Hence the WGIG's optimism in 2005 that defining the Internet is not an issue continues to be problematic today. Moreover, definitions in this respect have geopolitical loadings within the UN. Whilst dominant countries such as the United States, the UK, and western European states tend to echo the sentiments above, other influential UN member states, China as a prime example but also Brazil and India, maintain that there is a distinction between a U.S.-centric "global" Internet, nation-based infrastructures with respective terms of access and use, and content regulation. Since the Snowden revelations, dominant EU states such as Germany have also shifted their view that a U.S.-centric infrastructure is appropriate given the jurisdictional power that accrues to the United States by having most of the world's Internet traffic pass over U.S. territory. In short, definitions as well as operations are now increasingly politicized even if they have always been political (Mansell and Silverstone 2006; Franklin 2013). If, as one of the core definitions of the Internet maintains, the term "Internet" refers to a "network of networks," then the notion of the Internet in the singular flies in the face of its multiplex historical and techno-economic trajectory to date.

48. ITU/WSIS 2005, para. 72 and 73, emphasis added.

49. The NETmundial Outcome Document (2014) discussed above is one. See Bellamy and McChesney (2011), Mueller (2010), and Singh (2012) for different views on this matter.

50. IGF 2008.

51. UN General Assembly 2000, target 8f.

52. NETmundial 2014, 4, 7.

53. Gurumurthy and Singh 2012; Jørgensen 2006; Jensen 2006.

54. For example, IRP Coalition [2011] 2015; Necessary and Proportionate 2013; and Council of Europe 2014a, 2014b.

55. Franklin 2013, 190 passim.

56. See Franklin (2013, 138–39). As to the origins and locus of Internet governance that predates UN involvement in this domain, these decisions date from the emergence of the Internet itself strictly speaking, that is, interoperable computer networks require agreements, and those agreements translate into code, Internet protocols being the basic building block to the Internet's supporting architecture (Mueller 2002). Internet-governance scholars and respective stakeholder interests in the IG domain disagree as to whether this early, narrow understanding of Internet governance should serve as the model for global undertakings that would put governments on a par with the "technical community," Internet businesses, and perhaps civil society representatives.

57. See Franklin (2005, 2007), WSIS Civil Society Caucus (2003, 2005), and Gurumurthy and Singh (2012).

58. IGF 2008, 2011; ITU/WSIS 2005; NETmundial 2014.

59. MacBride 1980; Frau-Meigs et al. 2012; Gerbner, Mowlana, and Nordenstreng 1993.

60. Vincent 2010; Clapham 2007; Jørgensen 2006, 2013; Benedek and Kettemann (2014).

61. Zalnieriute and Schneider 2014; Council of Europe 2014b; Gurumurthy and Singh 2012; Singh 2012; Goldsmith and Wu 2006.

62. The term "popular imaginary" refers to how these issues are conveyed in the mainstream media, in varying measures around the world, as online and traditional print and broadcasting outlets. An "imaginary" is qualitatively distinct from a political ideology in that an imaginary is embedded in layers of meaning making about how the world does, or should, work so it is susceptible to shaping and, as Edward Herman and Noam Chomsky argue, to the "manufacture" of consent (1988). This places language as the fulcrum of how ideas, and with that institutions, "frame" the terms of debate and thereby the world. As social and political theorists note, an imaginary (social, popular, and so on) constitutes "the creative and symbolic dimension of the social world, the dimension through which human beings create their ways of living together and their ways of representing their collective life . . . that can sustain or be asymmetrical to the organization of power" (Thompson 1984, 6). And if an imaginary encompasses the interplay between what people (say they) think about an issue and how an issue is framed and disseminated through the media, for instance, then human rights law and norms can be apprehended as changing imaginaries as well as institutions. For, as Andrew Vincent notes, rights have come to be as much about "the linguistic, grammatical, and logical usage of concepts and clarifying meanings" (2010, 19) as they are about "substantive content . . . as legal, moral, and political rights" (23). In this case of how human rights have been framed alongside, or for, Internet governance (Jørgensen 2013), a long-lamented "disconnect" between advocacy at Internet and media-governance consultations, at the UN level in particular (Franklin 2005), and how these admittedly arcane issues were not covered by major media players (e.g., the *Guardian* newspaper or the BBC in the UK, and the *New York Times* or the *Huffington Post* in the United States), has been assuaged by global coverage and campaigns about key rights issues and the online environment. This is the Snowden effect in other words.

63. See Gore (1994), Clinton (2010), and Obama/the White House (2015).

64. See Gerbner, Mowlana, and Nordenstreng (1993), MacBride (1980), and more recently, Frau-Meigs et al. (2012).

65. Gerbner, Mowlana, and Nordenstreng 1993; ITU/WSIS 2003a, 2003b, 2005; WGIG 2005.

66. Mueller 2002, 2010.

67. Civil liberty debates around successive attempts by the UK Conservative government to require filters on Internet content by law, as opposed to parents applying these tools, in order to

prevent children accessing unwanted content, is a case in point. See Paton-Williams (2013) for an overview in the UK context, and the Council of Europe for an international comparison (2014b, 12–14, 24 passim, 66 passim).

68. This topic is exercising legal professionals, human rights advocates, and scholars in particular. In the UK context, a number of bills have been proposed, or passed into law, that continue to stir ongoing controversy for civil liberty organizations. The 2013 Draft Communications Data Bill, the so-called Snoopers' Charter, and the 2014 Data Retention and Investigatory Powers (DRIP) Bill have been the main focus for ongoing public campaigns against this legislation. Liberty, a prominent civil liberties organization in the UK, has started to group all such bills looking to increase governmental powers to "snoop" on people's lives online under the "Snoopers' Charter" rubric (Liberty 2014).

69. IRP Coalition 2011; Jørgensen 2006, 2013; Council of Europe 2014b.

70. Fücks and Drossou 2005, 6.

71. NETmundial 2014, 8, emphasis added.

72. In the NETmundial Outcome Document, multilateral does not appear at all. Neither does it in another more recent statement from a UN-hosted IG event: the 2015 UNESCO Internet Study Conference. "Multistakeholder" does appear in this outcome document, twice (UNESCO 2015).

73. Jensen 2005.

74. Deibert 2015, 9.

75. IRP Coalition 2011, 2015, article 20, 26. See also the Universal Declaration of Human Rights (UN 1948, article 30).

Chapter Seven

Walled Gardens or a Global Network?

Tensions, (De-) centralizations, and Pluralities of the Internet Model

Francesca Musiani

IN THE BEGINNING

The principle of decentralization has been one of the cornerstones of the Internet's genesis: the primary objective of the "network of networks" was indeed to enable communication between heterogeneous and remote machines, without mandatory transit points.[1] Today, concentration models dominate, around a handful of macro-actors—*giants* equipped with extensive server farms—managing most of the Internet traffic. However, the original principle has not been entirely abandoned, and in all areas of application, developers explore decentralized alternatives, relying on cooperation between users (and their computers). These *dwarfs* of the network can form the basis of search engines, social networks, and storage platforms that—contrary to the services proposed by the main digital actors of today, such as Google and Facebook—allocate resources and tasks equally among participants in the network.

This chapter draws upon some of the results of a six-year-long (and ongoing) investigation of alternative, decentralized, and peer-to-peer approaches to Internet services, and of the social and organizational forms they propose.[2] It discusses the extent to which the Internet, as we know it today, is shaped by an ongoing tension between "walled gardens" on one hand—the giants of information and networking platforms, a quasi-monopolistic tendency subtending their business model—and a global network on the other hand, one that draws inspiration from the symmetrical, transparent Internet of

129

the pioneers. Looking back to some elements of the history of the "network of networks," as well as some of the tensions that permeate its present and are likely to shape its close future, this chapter shows how the Internet's technical shaping is less based on the domination of a single organizing principle than one might think—and more so on the coexistence of (and tension between) a plurality of levels of centralization, hierarchy, and cooperation of resources, power, and users.

PEOPLE AND PLATFORMS: WHEN THE INTERNET
BECAME PUBLIC

In the mid-1990s, the commercial explosion of the Internet entailed some radical changes to its model and structure, turning a tranquil utopia of passionate scientists into an agitated and powerful mass medium.[3] Millions of new users make their first appearance on the Net, many of them sporting a new kind of profile: that of the "ordinary people" interested in the ease with which one can get in touch, visit information pages, and make online purchases, rather than in the details subtending the structure and functioning of a complex network of networks. Thus, the procedures of adoption and appropriation of the network by the users (and of users by the network) evolve profoundly. On one hand, since 1994, the general public begins to join en masse the clusters of computers that constitute the Internet, posing problems for the sustainability of the most basic of resources—bandwidth. On the other hand, the growing confidence that users bestow upon the Internet for a number of uses and applications, both fundamental and critical, leads to new security requirements, leading to the establishment of firewalls that strongly divide the Internet into self-sufficient, self-feeding regions.

In several respects, the transformation of the Internet into a mass culture phenomenon occurs through radical changes to the network architecture, entailing a double phenomenon: the growing asymmetry of traffic flows and the erection of barriers to free movement of content and data. This change leads to a reconfiguration of what we have called the "principle of cooperation" of the Internet: the processes through which, in the early Internet, priority was assigned primarily to issues of efficiency and technical optimization of the system.[4] While the original purpose of the "collective intelligence" of man and machine that built the Internet can fairly easily be identified in the construction of a reliable, efficient, and powerful network, the entrance of the Internet in its commercial phase modifies balances, benefits, and structures; it causes many points of stress and weakness.

This reconfiguration of the network multiplies the organizational arrangements of the Internet, while at the same time calling into question its very model.[5] While the quasi-monopolies of the Googles and Facebooks of today arguably set the scene of the digital economy, and make it harder, because of network and "snowballing" effects, for new actors to rise to prominence, the Internet's technical shaping is still not based on the domination of a single organizing principle. It was not the case originally, with a model that is assumed to have been completely decentralized, and it is not the case today, with a supposedly pervasive hierarchical model. In contrast, the Internet model is based on the coexistence of (and tension between) different levels of centralization, hierarchy, and cooperation of resources, power, and users, revealing an ongoing dialectic between the "walled gardens" and a global, open network.

COOPERATION: THE CORE OF THE EARLY INTERNET MODEL

Since the development of ARPANET in the late 1960s, the network of networks has challenged the sustainability of the technical and economic models underpinning data-flow management, and in turn its status as a "collective good."[6] The Internet was originally built on the principle of decentralized circulation of transmission and communication. Its main users, researchers, designed extremely pragmatic and at times somewhat precarious data-sharing and charging modes: spreading news from site to site through flooding,[7] complex routing tables, and constantly evolving and approximate charging of usage, relying on the goodwill of the pioneer centers and of a community of interest. In the 1980s, the "Internet model" had an open, distributed architecture that readily embraced *best effort*[8] and the loss or redundancy of data packets, preferring the principle of *running code*[9] to protocols founded on technical ecumenism and robustness developed within traditional standardization agencies.

Thus, populated by a highly homogeneous group of users—homogeneous in both profiles and objectives—the initial model of the Internet was based on a primarily decentralized and symmetrical organization, not only in terms of bandwidth, but also in terms of connection, relationship, and communication between machines.[10] The purpose of the original ARPANET was to share computing resources within the territory of the United States. The main challenge this effort has faced has been the integration of different types of existing networks, as well as the projection of possible future technologies, into a common network, allowing each host to be an equal participant in the game. At this stage, protocols and systems were sufficiently obscure—and required technical skills sufficiently specialized—to make security breaches rare and, for the most part, negligible. While the first mainstream Internet applications, FTP and Telnet, were programmed according to a client/server model, usage patterns as a whole were symmetrical: each host on the Internet could connect to another host, and in the early days of personal computers and mainframes, servers often behaved as clients. The Usenet system, which made its first appearance in 1979, eventually influenced some of the most successful examples of decentralized control structures on the Net.[11] The first visions of the web, since 1990, drew a portrait of a great "equalizer of communications"—a system that allowed any user to make his or her views public, instead of acting merely as a consumer of media.[12]

The TCP/IP protocols (Transmission Control Protocol/Internet Protocol) illustrate this cooperative model, with its fundamental principle of Internet design, the abovementioned *best effort* of packet delivery. The higher-level protocols of the Open Systems Interconnection (OSI) model, such as TCP, create reliable connections by detecting when a packet is lost and tries to send it again. The collective behavior of many individual TCP connections, which slow down independently, causes a decrease in the saturation at the level of Internet routers; thus, the algorithm subtending TCP is, in fact, a way for different peers to manage a shared resource, without a central coordinator .

The efficiency of TCP across the entire Internet required and still requires, fundamentally, cooperation. Each network user was asked to play by the same rules, yet this was feasible since anyone working on the Internet shared the same motivation: to maximize efficiency and optimize the device technologically to build a reliable, efficient, and powerful network.[13] But it would be quite possible to "develop other protocols that do not follow this equation, and that will imposingly try to consume more bandwidth than they should. These protocols can wreak havoc on the Net," says a developer.[14]

The growing concern that hostile protocols may begin to interfere with the Internet's core functioning is well illustrated by the controversy that took shape in 1996 around the functionality added by Netscape to its pioneer browser, which provided the ability to upload multiple files simultaneously.[15] Netscape engineers discovered that if you downloaded images integrated in a page in parallel, rather than one at a time, the entire page loaded faster, a feature that users obviously appreciated. But a question arose: was this pattern of bandwidth use fair? Not only was the server forced to send multiple images simultaneously, but also the TCP channels multiplied, and the download bypassed the TCP algorithms aimed at preventing saturation. The controversy eventually subsided once Netscape made the specifications of its browser public, and it was found, in practice, that the strategy of parallel downloads did not unduly prejudice the Internet. However, the controversy reveals, once again, the centrality of the cooperation model and its vulnerability to technical evolutions, as well as the massification of uses.

The organizational model based on cooperation was also questioned by user practices and their business models, as it encompassed a shift to a model where data download became more important (if only in terms of data flows circulating on the network) than the publication or upload of information.

This reflected the uses and practices that would eventually become dominant, especially (but not exclusively) with the exchange of cultural content beyond the frame of copyright.[16] The commercial "explosion" of the Internet would rapidly redirect the vast majority of traffic toward a downstream paradigm, typical of television and traditional media; however, the creation of ad hoc content, related to the specificity of each query and contribution initiated by users, remained an evolution of the Internet model—an evolution that would be here to stay.

SLOW EROSION

From the 1990s, the Internet's principles were gradually eroded as it moved toward tools that afforded greater data-flow management and security. Numerous analogies, especially spatial, have been used to describe the evolution of the Internet in the nineties: the shift from a horizontal model to a vertical model, from a *bazar* model to a *cathedral* model,[17] the "*minitelization*" or "broadcastization" of the Internet,[18] the fast track to a "civilized Internet," balkanization, and the transformation of *Netville* into conglomerations of sanitized suburbs. All these images suggest that the Internet, the interconnection of over forty thousand different networks, is under considerable pressure from the growing desire to manage and control its data flows—and from the reconfigurations of its model brought on by its own success.

The initial model of cooperation became challenged by its own founding principle: indeed, it required proactive behavior from users—*all* users. If in the first cooperative model, each host assumed responsibility for its connections and exchanges, this model soon revealed its limitations in terms of the functioning of the network and its usability for a large number of users. The Internet started to become populated by choke points, especially Internet service providers (ISPs), and became subject to a much stricter regulation, particularly in terms of constraints imposed on data transfers—which grew, in turn, into a breaching of the symmetry of flows. Starting from the mid-1990s, the principle that if a host could access the network, everyone on the network could reach this host, became increasingly eroded.

The most flagrant case study that can illustrate this trend is the web browser. Like many other applications that arose in the early stages of commercialization of the Internet, the browser is based on a simple client/server protocol: the client initiates a connection to a known server, downloads data, and disconnects. This model is simpler, although often less transparent, and it works without the user having to get involved in the setup process. This model is a straightforward way to implement many applications that involve a service to the user, from web browsing to the streaming of videos, quickly accompanied by shopping carts, transactions of stocks, interactive games, and many other "goods." Machines hosting a web client do not require a stable or permanent address. They do not need a permanent connection to the Internet, or to manage the needs of many users. They just have to "know how to ask the good question, and how to listen and understand the answer."[19]

To maximize the effectiveness of the available Internet "plumbing," providers of broadband chose, meanwhile, to use asymmetric bandwidth. The typical residential installation of an ADSL line or a cable modem was designed to provide three to eight times more bandwidth for downloads of data from the Internet than for sending the data to the network, thus promoting client-based uses rather than server-based ones. The reason for this imbalance between downloads and uploads, widely accepted by the public, was linked to the supremacy of the World Wide Web among Internet applications; most web users very rarely have the need for their machines to be more than clients. Even users who published their own web pages usually did so not directly from their home broadband connection but from dedicated servers owned by third parties, including GeoCities or Exodus. If in the early days of the web the situation was less clear—the possibility that many users would equip themselves with a personal web server was not rejected out of hand—it soon became clear that the commercial web had, in itself, elements of asymmetry (many clients for few servers) and that most users were, in this context, well served by asymmetric bandwidth. But the beginnings of peer-to-peer (P2P) applications for file sharing, exploding with Napster in 1999,[20] which we will come back to, would radically challenge anew the approach according to which end users conduct almost exclusively operations involving downloads, not uploads.

The fight against spammers, flamers, and the newborn "vandals" of the network of networks also showed the rise of this trend.[21] During the precommercial phase of the network, unsolicited advertising was generally received with surprise and indignation. This era ended on April 12, 1994, when lawyers Laurence Canter and Martha Siegel individually posted an advertisement across all Usenet newsgroups—thereby initiating events that became the first spam operation. Electronic mail and Usenet counted on the active cooperation of individuals, and their individual and collective will, to avoid flooding valuable and common resources with undesirable advertising mail: it is this principle of cooperation, human and technical at the same time, that failed with this unwanted and pervasive post and raised new questions about the lack of attribution of responsibility within the architecture of the Internet. Since any host could connect to any other host, and the connections were almost anonymous, users could insert spam into the network at any time. Thus began a sort of "arms race" to try to increase users' perception of their responsibility vis-à-vis the broader network, or to enforce it outright: the closure of open relays for sending messages, the monitoring of spam sources on Usenet, and the retaliation against spammers.[22]

The spread of spam and the operation of the TCP algorithm shared a common feature: they demonstrated the fragility of the sustainable functioning of the Internet and the need for cooperation that it implied. But they differed on another account: in the case of TCP, the system resisted, and the network was preserved. In the case of spam, however, the noncooperative behavior persisted—and persists to this day, partially due to the very "cooperative" features of the network that made it possible in the first place.

POWERFUL AND CONTROVERSIAL "FENCES"

While the cooperative nature of the Internet was put into question, various fences and barriers came into place: a rise in the number of dynamic IP addresses, an increasingly frequent deployment of firewalls, and the popularity of Network Address Translation (NAT).[23] The development of these new methods and procedures was surrounded by controversy—which did not prevent them from evolving and spreading.

As average users could not independently manage threats against the security of their machines, managers turned to various network management measures, which affected in particular the openness and the symmetry of the network, yet it appeared to require a structurally more mature Internet, hosting increasingly varied practices. Firewalls found themselves at the point of contact between each network (private, internal, etc.) and the outside Internet. They filtered packets and chose what traffic should pass and what should be denied access. A host protected in this way would not easily function as a server: it could only be a client.

Preventing a host from being a server, and allowing it to be just a client, became a transversal theme to many changes in the Internet after its commercial explosion. With the increasing number of users equipped with a connection to the Internet via modem, the practice of giving each host a fixed IP address became impractical, as the number of IP addresses was no longer sufficient.[24] The IP address assignment in a dynamic manner took hold, until it became the norm for many hosts on the Internet, where the address of a particular computer was now able to change even once a day. Bandwidth providers, on their part, found dynamic IP addresses useful for the deployment of services that could be constantly available. The end result is that many hosts on the Internet, constantly moving, were not easily accessible, affecting again the principle of cooperation. In particular, this was a problem for peer-to-peer applications destined to purposes such as instant messaging and file sharing, which, in order to work around this problem, were since then constrained to build dynamic host directories.

This trend increased even more in subsequent phases, when NAT started to be used—the process by which addresses were hidden behind a firewall instead of attributing a public, valid Internet address to its host. As mentioned, a router utilization of NAT methodology allows it to match internal, often not routable, and nonunique IP addresses of an intranet to a range of unique and routable external addresses. This mechanism, notably, permits to have one visible external public address on the Internet correspond to a set of addresses of a private network. From the perspective of direct communication between clients, such as in peer-to-peer traffic, NAT combines the problems of firewall and those of dynamic IP addresses: the real address of the host is not only unstable but also no longer accessible. All communications must speak a relatively simple language that the NAT router will be able to understand, causing a great loss of flexibility in communications between applications.

When firewalls, dynamic IP addresses, and NAT technology were each tested with its specific characteristics, the original core model of the Internet showed that some regions of the network could no longer communicate with complete freedom with other regions or components. Security tools and methods, very useful in other respects, posed many serious obstacles to direct, symmetrical, peer-to-peer communication models—models that, nonetheless, "kept trying," as the remainder of this chapter will show.

PRESENT AND POSSIBLE FUTURE(S) OF INTERNET ARCHITECTURES

The current innovation trajectories of the network of networks are said to make it increasingly clear that its evolutions and (in-volutions) will probably depend, both in the medium and long term, on the topology and organizational and technical models of Internet-based applications, and on its underlying infrastructure.[25] Indeed, the current organizational and economic models adopted by the most widespread Internet services of today—and of the structure of the network allowing them to function, with its obligatory points of passage, its more or less constrained crossroads, and its "toll roads"—raise many questions about the optimal use of storage resources and about the fluidity, speed, and efficiency of electronic exchanges, as well as the security of exchanges and the network's stability.

These questions largely influence the balance of power among network developers, users, and operators, and ultimately connect to issues related to the neutrality of the Internet. This is the case, for example, of operators "clamping" certain specific uses, or of the optimization of the network for certain types of traffic or protocols at the expense of others.[26] As Barbara van Schewick emphasizes, by influencing users' appropriations of Internet—creating more or less openness, exchange, and sharing—changes in the architecture of the network of networks influence its "social value":

> But the social value of architectures . . . goes beyond that. The Internet has the potential to enhance individual freedom, provide a platform for better democratic participation, foster a more critical and self-reflective culture, and potentially improve human development everywhere. The Internet's ability to realize this potential, however, is tightly linked to features—user choice, non-discrimination, non-optimization.[27]

These characteristics can be studied from various angles, depending on how the underlying technical architecture is understood.[28] Different types of architecture and other forms of organization of the network therefore offer an alternative way of addressing some critical issues surrounding the network's management, with a focus on efficiency, security, "sustainable digital development" through enhanced resource management, and the maximization of Internet's value for society.

The first part of this chapter consisted of a brief recollection of some salient episodes in the Internet's history, which hopefully has shown that the technical architecture underpinning the current Internet—that of the global Internet and of the networks, systems, and services populating it—is neither static nor intrinsically technically superior. As we have seen, the history of the "network of networks" is one of constant evolution based on de facto normalization. It is linked to changes in uses—particularly their massification—and to a number of technical as well as economic, political, and social changes. Just as the architecture of the Internet and its services sparked controversies in the past, so too there is tension surrounding its future. Now that its status as a political regulation mechanism has been acknowledged, its full importance as a lever for development and economic constraints is also starting to be recognized,[29] along with its aptitude "by design" to be changed and modified.[30]

DISTRIBUTION AS "ALTERNATIVE"?

For years now the development of services based on—at least partially—decentralized network architectures or P2P has been recognized as a lingering "alternative" for modes of communication and digital content management on the Internet. These architectures advocate placing responsibility for exchanges and communication at the margins or periphery of the system, and not having all of the system's resources in the same physical location but rather distributed across several machines.

While there is no standard definition of these architectures, some common elements underlying the various terms can be identified, such as the multiple units comprising the network, often called nodes, which each have a local memory, and the completion of the application's objectives through the sharing of resources—which can be of several types—to serve a *common goal*, such as the resolution of a large-scale computational problem, or *individual needs* through the *coordination* of shared resources. There is also the tolerance for faults in the individual nodes and the subsequent lack of a single point of failure, flexible scaling, and the constant change in the system's structure—the network's topology and latency, the number of computers connected—and the attribution of an incomplete or limited vision of the system to each node.

As previously discussed, the concept of distribution and decentralization was in a sense embedded in the early days of the Internet, particularly in the organization and circulation of data flows. The integration of this structuring principle into its current topology is however—as argued by several experts—limited.[31] The limits of the current Internet model, which has been central since the start of its commercial phase and its adoption by the public, are regularly highlighted by specialists, particularly in view of the spectacular success of certain services such as social media. Indeed, as every Internet user is now at least potentially not only a consumer but also a distributor and a producer of digital content, this organization of the network has led to the centralization of the masses of data in certain regions of the Internet, even though they are almost immediately redistributed to multiple places in today's global network.[32] The Internet services that gained a foothold in the early to mid-2000s, such as social networks, messaging tools, and digital content storage applications, were based on technical and economic models in which users requested information, data, and services from powerful "farms" of servers storing information and managing the network's traffic.[33] Issues of resource allocation, fluidity, and efficiency have been compounded by concerns regarding the security of exchanges and the network's stability. A series of dysfunctions (e.g., doubts about Twitter's sustainability raised by its repeated blackouts) and breakdowns with global consequences (e.g., early 2008, the global paralysis of YouTube and Pakistani networks following the routing of Border Gateway Protocol requests,[34] to limit the sharing of certain content in that country) have drawn attention to issues of data security and protection, inherent to the current structure of the Internet.

Even if the global circulation of Internet traffic still follows the principle of generalized distribution, it nevertheless coexists with an organization of services concentrated around servers or data centers providing access to content. The significant increase of spam, along with the growing presence of bandwidth-intensive protocols jeopardizing the smooth running of the Internet as a "common resource,"[35] are calling into question the network's cooperative nature.[36] At the same time, the management measures eroding its symmetry keep on developing. At the points of interface between internal networks and the external Internet, network managers are deploying increasingly strict firewalls. The increase in dynamic IP addresses, useful to bandwidth providers for the permanent deployment of Internet services, is forcing decentralized applications to build dynamic directories of the hosts to which to connect. Finally, the popularity of Network Address Translation is leading to a situation where hosts' real addresses are no longer just unstable but also inaccessible.

With the great enclosure movement constantly raising content protection levels, private regulations are replacing intellectual property rights management by public authorities through the enactment of laws.[37] Meanwhile, "best effort" is making way to the prioritization, both "conditional" and "active," of traffic by network operators.[38] While there has been little reaction to the former—ad hoc network optimization based on requirements at a given moment—having resolved congestion issues, the latter has received more criticism: by deliberately prioritizing certain packets or, on the contrary, by discriminating against others and slowing them down, Internet access providers have called into question the neutrality of the "network of networks." This is currently a subject of intense controversy.[39] Sustainability challenges are being created by the high demands on servers providing access to services and content, by the growing number of bandwidth-intensive applications, and by users' growing trust in the "network of networks" for applications. These applications and its uses require new security criteria, resulting in firewalls that divide the Internet into self-sustaining and self-sufficient networks or regions, or yet create further changes of scale for the Internet.

For all these reasons, many actors in the IT sector are reflecting on the organization of services and the network's structure, and are identifying specific issues challenging the Internet's architecture in its current "concentration" scenario. Many projects, companies, and services are therefore considering resorting to decentralized network architectures and to distributed forms of organization for Internet services, as a possible way to remedy certain network management difficulties, from a local to a global scale. Their aim is to achieve differently efficiency, security, and sustainable digital development. The search for alternatives to the dominant organization of services and structure of the network—seeking efficiency and sustainability—is ongoing,[40] and to find better solutions, some are turning back to the Internet of fifteen or twenty years ago, that is, to the lasting qualities of an old technology. They are thus reembracing the precommercial topology of the Internet and turning to good account the "margins" of the network, via peer-to-peer technologies.

THE MARGINS OF THE NETWORK AND THE INTERNET'S "CLOUDY" FUTURE

Peer-to-peer (P2P) architecture refers to a network model designed to facilitate communications or exchanges between nodes that control the same task within the system. The dichotomy between servers providing resources and clients requesting them, characteristic of the *client-server* model, is replaced by a situation where all peers have the resource and all peers request it.[41] P2P architecture embraces the principle of decentralization, using the network differently from client-server applications. In this architecture, users request services from servers with a limited capacity, and as a result, added clients can slow down the transfer of data for all users.

In P2P architecture users not only use resources to access content (bandwidth, storage space, and computing capacity) but also provide them: if the demand to be met by the system increases, the system's total capacity also increases. Furthermore, P2P systems may offer greater stability and endurance, including in cases of failure of one of the nodes, because their distributed nature improves their strength, while preventing their total invalidation. P2P's efficiency as a distribution model is strictly linked to the sharing of computing capacity and bandwidth between all of the system's components. This changes the distribution structure and cost allocation by increasing bandwidth use at the network level rather than the server level. Moreover, P2P systems' potential vulnerabilities mostly lie with nonsecure code, likely to authorize remote access to the computers that form the network, and even to compromise it. Consequently, security and file verification mechanisms (such as the hash function,[42] the verification of the fragments that will recompose a file, and various encryption methods) are the domains in which P2P-based applications are currently evolving the most. Over the course of their still relatively brief "public" history, P2P networks have been considered almost exclusively as a threat to the digital content industry. With the public mainly using these networks for the unauthorized sharing of music or video files, the issue of intellectual property rights, particularly copyright, has been the predominant media and political framing of P2P networks and their uses.[43] This reputation has especially developed with the rise, at the turn of the twenty-first century, of content-exchange practices on a global scale, involving millions of users. The most emblematic case was the extraordinarily fast growth of the service Napster: with sixty million "sharers," this service allowed files to be stored and distributed among several nodes. But the presence of a central server to facilitate the identification of content, being an obligatory point of passage for each exchange of information, became an easy target for "eligible parties," ultimately causing its downfall. The second generation of P2P file-sharing systems, used for example by Gnutella, overcame the need for a central server and demonstrated the advantages and robustness of a decentralized system. There were also third-generation systems that, being hybrid, combined the former two, noted by their extensive use by KaZaA and other file-sharing applications.[44]

The importance of the debate surrounding copyright violations, which facilitated these exchanges, motivated the media and public opinion, propelling research priorities for technical projects, economics, and social sciences research. Yet alone this cannot sum up the philosophy of P2P systems. Authors such as jurist Niva Elkin-Koren or computer scientist and sociologist David Hales have adopted an original approach to highlight that these systems' political and technical significance lies elsewhere, particularly in a set of "virtues,"[45] reflected by their efficiency, stability, and endurance, which are at once technical, social, financial, and legal.

The direct transmission of data between computers in a decentralized network, oftentimes coupled with the file-fragmentation principle, gives way to new definitions of "sharing"—ones that do not only involve content but also extend to computing capacity and infrastructure—and, potentially, to the emergence of new organizational, social, and legal principles. Beyond these benefits, of importance in the sharing economy, it has also been stressed that peer-to-peer systems can provide specific solutions for the protection of personal freedoms,[46] or for the emergence of alternative decision-making processes and of participatory environments[47] afforded by the direct exchange of content between the different nodes of the network.[48] This has multiple implications, not only in terms of technical performance, but also in redefining concepts such as security and privacy, and reconfiguring the location of data and exchanges, the boundaries between users and network, and available tools. In short, P2P can have an impact on the attribution, recognition, and modification of rights between the users of services and service providers.

While P2P models offer new pathways to explore and maintain the equilibria of the Internet ecology, the current major actors in the IT market have set their own conditions. Would a "P2P turn" still be possible at a time when cloud computing seems to be taking over, thereby reinforcing an economic and technical model in which final users rely on powerful server centers that store information and manage traffic on the network?

Although there are currently intense controversies surrounding the very definition of the cloud (a specialized journal, in 2008, listed over twenty different definitions of the concept[49]), it is a shared starting point where, within this model, the supplier generally offers the physical infrastructure and the software product, thus hosting both applications and data in a remote location (the so-called cloud), while interacting with the latter through a client interface. This leads toward a model of removal of information toward processing servers traditionally located on the user's computer, and of growing distance between the performance of the operations needed for the service to run and the personal/local equipment of clients of that service.

However, the decentralized cloud is equally conceivable and would be designed to distribute the cloud's computing power and resources across all users'/contributors' terminals. This was the intention of Eben Moglen, the inspirer of the decentralized social network project Diaspora*. The researcher and activist noted that, as it stands, the cloud has benefited only the major players: "*Cloud* means servers have gained freedom, freedom to move, freedom to dance, freedom to combine and separate and re-aggregate and do all kinds of tricks. Servers have gained freedom. Clients have gained nothing."[50] This is a very strong assertion and perhaps an oversimplification, for the cloud's model, even without envisaging a decentralized version, does provide final clients/users with something: permanent access to the service in mobile situations.[51] However, it is still worth noting that decentralization stands in parallel and in dialogue with the Internet's "cloudy" future, rather than in opposition to it—and may therefore be likely to reconnect the major unknowns of this model—particularly those who are responsible for data processing and flows, and the how—to users' machines.

CONCLUSIONS

Security measures such as firewalls, dynamic IP addresses, and Network Address Translation were born out of a need to secure Internet architecture and allow for the evolution of the instruments preserving the very principle of cooperation, while at the same time the network evolved and was populated by an increasing number of users. The implementation of these "barriers and walls" of the Internet has doubtlessly contributed in a significant way to bringing millions of "client" computers onto the network of networks, in a rapid and flexible manner. However, these same technologies have also profoundly reconfigured the balance of Internet infrastructure as a whole, "relegating" the majority of personal computers and devices to client-only status and perhaps reducing the inherently global reach of the network of networks.

If asymmetric connections and a strong imbalance between uploads and downloads have been widely tolerated by the public, the reason lies in the role of "killer application" that the web has held during all these years vis-à-vis the rest of the Internet ecosystem: most web users (and their equipment) do not, in the overwhelming majority of cases, need to be more than a client. Self-publishing practices certainly became more popular with the advent of the commercial Internet, but users spend essentially, in any case, most of their online time reading (and downloading) information and less on publishing. Service providers and access providers now build their services, from both a technical and an economic point of view, based on this very asymmetry.

However , P2P applications have again been put to the test[52]—and by a radical approach—shown today, for example, by two of the most popular P2P applications: the Tor network and the electronic currency system Bitcoin. Within those, the architectural choices and political choices mingle and overlap. P2P applications that enjoy considerable success since the early 2000s are bearers of an "intermediate" reality between the supposedly ideal case of the origins, "everybody publishes," and the apparent reality of the commercial Internet, "everybody consumes." P2P applications make it easy for users to publish data they have not created or authored and, at the same time, for users' machines to be leveraged as points of relay for retransmission of the data they receive. This development puts back in discussion the design of a commercial network based on the existence of a limited number of data "originators" or sources and asymmetric bandwidth as an optimization principle. A significant portion of networks becomes overloaded; the "arms race" dynamism is reproduced; and in practice, the "pure" or integral P2P—one that uses a completely decentralized network structure—is almost never used, for the benefit of hybrid solutions or trade-offs between centralized and decentralized components. The coexistence of different levels of centralization, hierarchy, and cooperation—in a "ballet between programmers, software and users"—is once again demonstrated.[53] The overall trend, exemplified by the giant-controlled "clouds," with a tendency toward concentration, centralization, and the predominance of data and processes, has increasingly removed itself from the edge or the margins of the network and cannot be doubted today.[54] It is remarkable, however, that despite the rise of anti cooperative models, the ability of the Internet (or Internets, as the plural may now seem necessary) to serve as a fertile ground for the production of alternative models remains strong. The current architecture of the network of networks, although fraught with asymmetries and fences, can still be put to the service of projects that seek to circumvent these barriers—in order to propose alternatives to today's predominant centralized infrastructures.[55] It is perhaps through these projects that openness and plurality of choice may be preserved for the information and communication networks of tomorrow—and thus, allow for technical solidarity[56] and technical democracy[57] to keep thriving there.

NOTES

1. This chapter owes greatly to joint work with Cécile Méadel (F. Musiani and C. Méadel, "Asymétrisation et barrières: évolutions d'architecture et reconfigurations de la « coopération » dans l'internet des origines," paper prepared for the annual symposium of the Société Française des Sciences de l'Information et de la Communication [SFSIC], Toulon, France, June 4–6, 2014), Valérie Schafer (F. Musiani and V. Schafer, "Le modèle Internet en question [années 1970–2010]," *Flux* 85–86, nos. 3–4 [2011]: 62–71), and Laura DeNardis (DeNardis and Musiani 2014). Previous versions of it were presented at the Fifth Tensions of Europe conference

(Paris, December 2013) and in my book *Nains sans géants. Architecture décentralisée et services internet* (Paris: Presses des Mines, 2013).

2. Musiani, *Nains sans géants.*

3. Janet Abbate, *Inventing the Internet* (Cambridge, MA: MIT Press, 1999).

4. Musiani and Méadel, "Asymétrisation et barrières."

5. Musiani and Schafer, "Le modèle Internet."

6. P. Mounier, *Les maîtres du réseau. Les enjeux politiques d'Internet* (Paris: La Découverte, 2002).

7. Information-diffusion protocol was used both to send content and for distributed or parallel computing, where each node sends the information to all its neighbors in a single time step.

8. *Best effort* is a network routing model designed to ensure that each element playing a role in the routing does its utmost, "everything it can," to take these data from the source to the destination. It offers no guarantee as to the quality of the routing, nor even of its success.

9. *"We believe in rough consensus and running code,"* a part of the famous sentence by David Clark, pioneer of Internet and of the Internet Engineering Task Force (IETF), indicates that the IETF is particularly interested in setting up flexible systems that can rapidly be implemented and changed.

10. N. Minar and M. Hedlund, "A Network of Peers: Peer-to-Peer Models through the History of the Internet," in *Peer-to-Peer: Harnessing the Power of Disruptive Technologies*, ed. A. Oram, 9–20 (Sebastopol, CA: O'Reilly, 2001).

11. B. Pfaffenberger, "If I Want It, It's OK: Usenet and the (Outer) Limits of Free Speech," *Information Society* 4, no. 12 (1996): 365–73. http://pfaff.sts.virginia.edu/.

12. P. Flichy, *L'imaginaire d'internet* (Paris: La Découverte, 2001).

13. A. Oram, "From P2P to Web Services: Addressing and Coordination," O'Reilly XML.com, April 7, 2004, http://www.xml.com/; A. Oram, ed., *Peer-to-Peer: Harnessing the Power of Disruptive Technologies* (Sebastopol, CA: O'Reilly, 2001); I. Taylor and A. Harrison, *From P2P to Web Services and Grids: Evolving Distributed Communities*, 2nd exp. ed. (London: Springer-Verlag, 2009).

14. Interview by author, October 2, 2009.

15. Minar and Hedlund, "A Network of Peers."

16. F. Dauphin and E. Dagiral, "P2P: From File Sharing to Meta-information Pooling?" *Communications and Strategies* 59, no. 3 (2005): 35–51.

17. E. Raymond, *The Cathedral and the Bazaar: Musings on Linux and Open Source by an Accidental Revolutionary* (Sebastopol, CA: O'Reilly, 1997).

18. V. Schafer and B. G. Thierry, *Le Minitel. L'enfance numérique de la France* (Paris: Nuvis, 2012).

19. P2P developer, interview with author, March 19, 2009.

20. J. Farchy, *Internet et le droit d'auteur: la culture Napster* (Paris: CNRS Editions 2003).

21. F. Brunton, *Spam: A Shadow History of the Internet* (Cambridge, MA: MIT Press 2013).

22. R. Everett-Church, "The Spam That Started It All," *Wired*, April 1999, http://www.wired.com/.

23. Network Address Translation is a procedure aimed at modifying network address information in packet headers, while transiting across a device that routes Internet traffic, for the purpose of remapping one IP address space into another. See "Network Address Translation," *Wikipedia*, last updated September 5, 2015, http://en.wikipedia.org/.

24. L. DeNardis, *Protocol Politics: The Globalization of Internet Governance* (Cambridge, MA: MIT Press, 2009).

25. P. Aigrain, "Another Narrative: Addressing Research Challenges and Other Open Issues," presentation at the PARADISO Conference, Brussels, September 7–9, 2011.

26. V. Schafer, H. Le Crosnier, and F. Musiani, *La neutralité de l'Internet, un enjeu de communication* (Paris: CNRS Editions/Les Essentiels d'Hermès, 2011), 66–68.

27. B. van Schewick, *Internet Architecture and Innovation* (Cambridge, MA: MIT Press 2010), 387.

28. E. Moglen, "Freedom in the Cloud: Software Freedom, Privacy, and Security for Web 2.0 and Cloud Computing," ISOC Meeting, New York, February 5, 2010, Software Freedom Law Center, https://www.softwarefreedom.org/.

29. Van Schewick, *Internet Architecture.*

30. S. Braman, "Designing for Instability: Internet Architecture and Constant Change," presentation at the Media in Transition 7 (MiT7): Unstable Platforms; The Promise and Peril of Transition conference, Cambridge, MA, May 13–15, 2011.

31. Minar and Hedlund, "A Network of Peers"; T. Berners-Lee, "Long Live the Web: A Call for Continued Open Standards and Neutrality," *Scientific American*, December 2010, http://www.scientificamerican.com/.

32. Moglen, "Freedom in the Cloud."

33. Van Schewick, *Internet Architecture*, 70.

34. Border Gateway Protocol (BGP) is a standardized exterior gateway protocol designed to exchange routing and reachability information between autonomous systems on the Internet.

35. E. Ostrom, *Governing the Commons: The Evolution of Institutions for Collective Action* (Cambridge: Cambridge University Press, 1990).

36. M. Mueller, "Property and Commons in Internet Governance," in *Governance, Regulation and Powers on the Internet*, ed. E. Brousseau, M. Marzouki, and C. Méadel (Cambridge: Cambridge University Press, 2012).

37. J. Boyle, "The Second Enclosure Movement and the Construction of the Public Domain," *Law and Contemporary Problems* 33 (2003), http://www.law.duke.edu/.

38. N. Curien and W. Maxwell, *La neutralité d'Internet* (Paris: La Découverte, 2011), 43–44.

39. C. Marsden, *Net Neutrality: Towards a Co-Regulatory Solution* (New York: Bloomsbury Academic, 2010); Curien and Maxwell, *La neutralité d'Internet*; Schafer, Le Crosnier, and Musiani, *La neutralité de l'Internet.*

40. P. Aigrain, "Declouding Freedom: Reclaiming Servers, Services, and Data," 2020 FLOSS Roadmap (2010 version, 3rd ed.), accessed August 28, 2015, https://flossroadmap.co-ment.com/; Aigrain, "Another Narrative"; Moglen, "Freedom in the Cloud."

41. R. Schollmeier, "A Definition of Peer-to-Peer Networking for the Classification of Peer-to-Peer Architectures and Applications," *Proceedings of the First International Conference on Peer-to-Peer Computing*, Linköping, Sweden, August 27–29, 2001.

42. For a piece of data provided, the hash function computes a *fingerprint* used for the rapid though incomplete identification of the data from which it originated. In informatics, this function is used to speed up the identification of data; the time needed to compute the fingerprint of a piece of data is negligible compared to the computation of the initial piece of data.

43. N. Elkin-Koren, "Making Technology Visible: Liability of Internet Service Providers for Peer-to-Peer Traffic," *New York University Journal of Legislation and Public Policy* 9, no. 15 (2006): 15–76.

44. J.-S. Beuscart, "Les usagers de Napster, entre communauté et clientèle. Construction et régulation d'un collectif sociotechnique," *Sociologie du Travail* 44, no. 4 (2002): 461–80.

45. Elkin-Koren, "Making Technology Visible."

46. J. A. Wood, "The Darknet: A Digital Copyright Revolution," *Richmond Journal of Law and Technology* 16, no. 4 (2010), http://jolt.richmond.edu/.

47. N. Elkin-Koren and E. M. Salzberger, *Law, Economics and Cyberspace* (Cheltenham, UK: Edward Elgar, 2004).

48. D. Hales, "Emergent Group-Level Selection in a Peer-to-Peer Network," *Complexus* 3, nos. 1–3 (2006): 108–18.

49. "Twenty-One Experts Define Cloud Computing," *Cloud Computing Journal* (2008), accessed August 28, 2015, http://cloudcomputing.sys-con.com/.

50. Moglen, "Freedom in the Cloud."

51. M. Mowbray, "The Fog over the Grimpen Mire: Cloud Computing and the Law," *Scripted Journal of Law, Technology and Society* 6, no. 1 (2009): 132–46.

52. Musiani, *Nains sans géants.*

53. Abbate, *Inventing the Internet.*

54. Moglen, "Freedom in the Cloud."

55. T. M. Egyedi and D. C. Mehos, eds., *Inverse Infrastructures: Disrupting Networks from Below* (Cheltenham, UK: Edward Elgar, 2012).

56. N. Dodier, *Les Hommes et les Machines. La conscience collective dans les sociétés technicisées* (Paris: Métailié, 1995).

57. M. Callon, P. Lascoumes, and Y. Barthe, *Agir dans un monde incertain. Essai sur la démocratie technique* (Paris: Seuil, 2001). (English translation available as *Acting in an Uncertain World: An Essay on Technical Democracy* [Cambridge, MA: MIT Press, 2009]).

Chapter Eight

National Security and U.S. Constitutional Rights

The Road to Snowden

Richard B. Andres

In 2013, Edward Snowden released a trove of classified National Security Agency (NSA) documents describing ways the agency uses cyberspace to gather information.[1] The disclosures created a firestorm in the media and Congress, and raised questions about the constitutionality of the methods the U.S. government uses to gather information on its citizens and the wisdom of its methods of collecting intelligence on allied nations. Throughout the debate, human rights groups attacked the NSA's techniques mainly with regard to privacy, and the Obama administration defended the methods in terms of the number of terrorist operations foiled. While these are relevant arguments, they are only part of a larger picture.

This chapter examines the four-year legislative and diplomatic fight between cybersecurity and citizens' rights that preceded the Snowden leaks. It characterizes the battle as a classic contest between national security and civil and property rights. This struggle had two aspects. The first involved attempts to determine the magnitude of the foreign threat and decide what concessions would be necessary to protect the United States from attacks by foreign adversaries. The second had to do with choosing which groups voters would force to make these concessions. The chapter concludes that the militarization of cyberspace presented the United States with the choice of losing rights to the federal government or losing them to foreign attackers and that, faced with this dilemma, its institutions repeatedly failed to find a practicable solution.

The chapter is divided into four sections. The first places the current cyber debate in the context of the classical trade-off between national security and citizens' rights in U.S. history. The second describes attempts by U.S. policy makers to assess the magnitude of the cyberthreat and communicate their assessment to the American people. The third follows the series of failed attempts by Congress to pass legislation to mitigate the cyberthreat and diplomatic attempts by the administration to use diplomacy to force foreign opponents to halt attacks. The chapter concludes with a brief analysis of the implications of the government's legislative and diplomatic failure for national security and civil rights.

THE HISTORICAL TENSION BETWEEN U.S. NATIONAL SECURITY AND CIVIL RIGHTS

For the past two years, the United States has been embroiled in a debate over how much power U.S. intelligence and law enforcement agencies should have to monitor cyberspace. The controversy has proven particularly thorny because it has defied traditional left-right political framing, often placing both left and right on the same side of cyber-related issues. On the left side of the aisle, groups such as the ACLU have proposed that current cyber policy threatens citizens' constitutional right to privacy as described in the Fourth Amendment and elsewhere. On the right, groups have argued that current policy increases federal power over citizens in ways opposed to constitutional notions of limited government. Overall, in a country that forbids warrantless searches of known criminals, protects the rights of private citizens to bear arms, and declined to create a national identification card even in the aftermath of the 9/11 attacks, citizens on both the political left and right wonder how much power they should concede to the federal government to monitor their behavior in cyberspace.

The current debate is far from the first in U.S. history over the tension between national security and citizens' rights. For the past two centuries, U.S. voters have regularly been forced to make decisions of this type. At its base, the problem is that voters prefer not to concede rights to the government but understand that, if the government does not have enough power to protect them from foreign opponents, their overall loss of rights could be even greater.

National security debates are sometimes caricatured as fanciful or paranoid scenarios about war and invasion, but the reality is more nuanced. Although war is the most obvious type of national security threat, it is not the only one or even the main one. While wars are relatively rare events, military bargaining (deterrence and coercion) is constant. During the Cold War, for instance, American policy makers did not fear that the Soviet Union would invade the United States, but they did believe that American arms could help to deter the USSR from invading or using threats of violence against allies. This argument persuaded voters to sacrifice some rights to enhance U.S. military power. Citizens understood (with various levels of sophistication) that if the Soviet Union triumphed abroad, eventually their own security and rights would be placed at risk. In the current era, the United States helps to uphold a prosperous global system that is often at odds with Chinese, Russian, and Islamist views about what the world should look like. If the United States failed to push back against these alternative visions, they would inevitably begin to replace the current Western centric world order. Such changes would almost certainly impact U.S. citizens.

The tension between rights and security has played out in different ways at different points in American history as voters have determined which rights to surrender and which to maintain in the face of foreign threats. The main sacrifice Americans have agreed to make in the face of national security threats has involved surrendering property rights in the form of higher taxes and demands of eminent domain. However, during extreme circumstances, the country has gone further. In 1798, during the Quasi-War with France, for instance, Congress passed the Alien and Sedition Acts to limit free speech, and in 1917, during the First World War, it enacted the Espionage Act to prohibit speech undermining the war effort.

In debates that pit civil rights against national security, not everyone is forced to pay equally; part of the debate inevitably involves deciding which groups will pay the bulk of the costs for defending the country and which will ride free. During the First and Second World Wars, the country required a disproportionate sacrifice from its wealthy, raising the highest marginal tax rate from 15 to 77 percent during the First World War and to 94 percent during the Second (with President Franklin Delano Roosevelt pressing for a 100 percent rate on the highest earners). At various times in U.S. history, the government has appropriated or assumed some level of control of individual firms and entire industries in the name of national security. During World War II, U.S. voters interned citizens of Japanese ancestry. And although few Americans might view it as such, the greatest discriminatory appropriation of citizens' rights in American history probably involves military drafts in which voters required young men (and only young men) to surrender their liberty and often their lives for the good of the nation.

In regard to the actions described above, modern Americans are likely to see some historical decisions to infringe on citizens' rights as more justified than others. At the time these decisions were made, however, they all involved rancorous constitutional debates.

One dimension of debates over national security involves rational calculations about how to achieve the greatest gains in national security at the lowest cost to citizens' rights. Such decisions depended to a large extent on the character of military technology and techniques at the time the policy was enacted. For instance, when massive armies were the key to military power, during the Industrial Age, the United States chose to draft its citizens; but early in the Information Age, as skilled troops and superior technology came to play an increasingly important role in war, it transitioned to a much more expensive all-volunteer force that shifted the burden from young men to older tax payers of both sexes. Similarly, during the first half of the twentieth century, when propaganda was seen as a key to national power, the government sometimes censored mass media during crises; but as early as the beginning of the Cold War, when education and other factors increased citizens' confidence in each other's ability to deal with information, the country usually rejected government censorship. To a large extent, the current debate involving cyberspace is about how to achieve the greatest security against opponents using new militarized cyber technology at the lowest overall cost to citizens.

But beyond rational calculations, when new military technologies emerge, raw interest group politics also play an important role in determining which rights citizens forfeit and which groups forfeit them. The problem here is that national security generally involves a public goods problem. Since, as a general rule, no group can be excluded from the benefits of national security, each has an incentive to shift the burden of paying for it elsewhere. Thus, while part of the decision to surrender rights in the name of national security is based on rational strategy, another part is based on the push and pull of interest groups attempting to influence the argument in order to shift the burden onto other groups. This type of politics can lead to fierce struggles, and while it is comforting to believe that some groups are motivated by the good of the country as a whole, it is not always easy to find groups completely oblivious to their own interests either in or out of government.

Taken together, the above arguments suggest that in dealing with the tension between a new military technology and citizens' rights, the United States goes through three stages. The first involves attempts by the government to assess the magnitude of the threat and to communicate that information to voters. The second comprises determining the technical characteristics of the new technology and developing options for mitigating the threat. The third and most difficult requires making a decision about which groups within the United States will bear the cost of protecting the country as a whole. If the process works well, it finds a balance between protecting citizens from foreign adversaries and from loss of rights to their own government. If it works badly, it either leaves citizens exposed to attacks by foreign enemies or unnecessarily deprives them of their rights. Each of these three stages is explored below with regard to U.S. cybersecurity policy.

ASSESSING THE MAGNITUDE OF INVISIBLE CYBERTHREATS

Assessing the magnitude of national security threats is seldom easy. As late as December 6, 1941, U.S. factions in Congress argued that their opponents were exaggerating the threat from Nazi Germany and Imperial Japan, and scholars still debate how great of a threat the Soviet Union represented during the Cold War. Gauging the magnitude of cyberthreats is particularly difficult because virtually everything involved with both cyber offenses and defenses depends on stealth. Technically, attackers attempt to conceal their methods because targets that learn how they are being attacked are better at defending themselves. Defenders prefer not to reveal that they have been attacked to avoid cueing attackers that they have been discovered. Politically, attackers do not admit they are attacking, to avoid diplomatic, legal, or financial retaliation; defenders do not divulge that they have been attacked to avoid the political, legal, and financial liability associated with the appearance of incompetence. These dynamics apply equally to public and private actors. As a result, cyberthreats are generally invisible to the general public.

Democracies do not deal well with invisible threats. Democratically elected policy makers have trouble developing defenses and find it nearly impossible to allocate costs if they cannot inform the public about what they are doing or why they are doing it. The United States, in particular, has enormous technical assets in the public and private sector—from the world's best universities to Silicon Valley—but can only utilize them if it publicizes the problem that it wants them to solve. It also has the world's largest economy and one of the most patriotic populations but can only ask them to support defenses if it can persuade them the county needs to be defended.

As countries increasingly militarized cyberspace in the first two decades of the cyber age, the U.S. government played the cyber game quietly. By the end of the last decade, however, many of those involved in cyber policy began to believe that this method was failing. In 2009, at the urging of senior intelligence and military leaders, President Barack Obama addressed the nation in a speech warning of national security threats to the United States from adversaries using cyberspace.[2] While the speech discussed threats to critical infrastructure and intellectual property (IP), it did not go into technical details of foreign attacks or U.S. defenses. The clear intent behind the speech was to galvanize America to act in cyberspace while preserving the secrecy required to compete in this domain.

The precedent Obama set by openly discussing cyber conflict was followed by a series of current and former national security leaders. In 2010, former director of National Intelligence Admiral Mike McConnell revealed more about why Obama had gone public when he warned that the United States was losing a cyberwar. Still somewhat ambiguously, he noted that a cyberwar could have implications on par with a nuclear war.[3] Over the next few months, military and civilian government officials from both the Democratic and Republican parties offered similar warnings.

The specific threats government officials pointed to tended to fall into three categories. The first involved attacks on critical infrastructure. The danger, officials warned, was that the United States depended on the critical infrastructures that provided communications, finance, transportation, drinking water, and electricity for its survival. Of these, electricity was the most important; if it failed, all other critical infrastructures would stop working as well. Over the last two decades, all infrastructures have been connected to computer networks. If an opponent could hack into the computer, it could destroy the physical infrastructure. In a worst-case scenario, the loss of life resulting from such attacks would run into the tens of millions.[4]

In 2009, despite official warnings, private experts expressed doubt about the ability of malware to destroy physical infrastructure. However, one year after Obama's speech, a Belarussian computer security company discovered that military-grade malware designed to destroy centrifuges (Stuxnet) had infected an air-gapped Iranian computer network at its Natanz nuclear facility.[5] The centrifuges utilized the same SCADA (Supervisory Control and Data Acquisition) infrastructure as most electric grids, and the malware had spread and infected thousands of power utilities around the world. If malware could be designed to physically destroy air-gapped, ultrasecure, Iranian military hardware, it could be built to destroy standard unprotected power grids. Over the next two years, power companies increasingly scanned their systems for intrusion. Nearly two-thirds found malware on their systems designed for sabotage.[6]

Malware of the type discovered in U.S. critical infrastructure could potentially be used to attack the country in two ways. The first involves a massive coordinated attack akin to a nuclear strike. A successful attack of this nature could result in massive financial costs and loss of life. The second involves a modulated attack of the type Stuxnet executed against Iran's nuclear program. The idea here would be to create damaging effects beneath the threshold that would invite conventional or nuclear retaliation from the United States. Although either type of attack would be difficult to execute, this type of malware potentially presents state and nonstate adversaries with the ability to inexpensively project destructive power into the United States. Proposed defenses against this type of attack usually involved private U.S. companies paying a good deal of money to fight off attacks and allowing significant government regulation and intrusion into their systems.

The second type of threat the U.S. government warned of involved espionage. Throughout the early 2000s, Chinese and Russian cyber-spying activities had often been publicized in the news. Government officials and organizations successfully targeted included Barack Obama and John McCain during the 2008 presidential race,[7] the French prime minister's office, the office of German chancellor Angela Merkel, and most U.S. departments and agencies.[8] Not surprisingly, given that the United States also engages in espionage, U.S. officials seldom made much of this type of spying. What U.S. officials did begin to protest around 2010, however, involved foreign militaries engaged in corporate espionage against private U.S. citizens, IP-producing businesses, and news organizations.[9]

From the U.S. perspective, espionage against government organizations is an accepted part of international relations, but using state power to conduct corporate espionage is not. However, China and other nations do not make this distinction. In 2009, Obama warned of the threat of cyber espionage and placed global annual financial loss due to intellectual property theft at one trillion dollars; NSA director Keith Alexander placed annual U.S. losses at $338 billion.[10] Given that the United States mainly produces IP for international trade rather than physical goods, they warned that the massive loss of IP is a significant threat to its economy. It could be argued, for instance, that the $338 billion in annual losses Alexander describes equate to around half of all U.S. unemployment and virtually the entire economic slowdown after 2008.

Along with protests about economic espionage, the administration pointed to China's hacking of U.S. organizations to gather information to use against its own dissidents. These actions became public knowledge in 2010 when Google announced that the Chinese government hackers had gained access to the Gmail accounts of Chinese human rights activists.[11] The attack on a U.S. news media represented an attack on freedom of speech. The incident provoked a strong statement from the State Department, which China appears to have disregarded.[12]

Detecting and preventing attacks by foreign militaries on private U.S. citizens and firms would be difficult. If citizens could not protect themselves, the alternative involved the U.S. government monitoring private networks with whatever that might imply for loss of privacy.

The third threat described by government officials involved terrorism. The main threat described involved Al-Qaeda and similar groups using the Internet as virtual territory. In the wake of 9/11, U.S. military operations in Afghanistan and the threat of reprisal against governments that harbored terrorists deprived Al-Qaeda of physical geography. Subsequently, the organization moved its operations to cyberspace.[13] Within a few years of the Twin Towers attack, it would not be unreasonable to describe Al-Qaeda as mainly a cyber-based organization. More recently, ISIS/Daesh has taken this to a new level by using cyber recruiting to gain an army from around the globe large enough to hold physical territory in Iraq and Syria.

Al-Qaeda and similar groups used cyberspace in two main ways. First, these organizations began to reach out to potentially sympathetic population groups around the world using web pages, chat groups, online videos, and related means. The individuals and groups hosting this content were difficult to stop because most were only indirectly affiliated with the individual who performed violent acts, and all were located within the territory of sovereign nations. Beyond recruiting, terrorist groups coordinated their operations online. They sometimes did so overtly, but even when they did not send their plans digitally, they coordinated online to make members aware of whom to contact and how to obtain information.

Terrorists' use of the Internet represented a particularly thorny problem for the U.S. government. These groups were widely seen as impossible to deter through normal means. They were dispersed globally and camouflaged their online activities within the background noise of the billions of telephone, text, and e-mail messages that cross cyberspace daily. It would be impossible to locate or track their activities without affecting the privacy of other Internet users.

By the end of 2010, the administration had laid out its argument, and it was left to the American people to determine what they would make of it. But while government officials had offered warnings, they provided little concrete evidence, and citizens were left to form their own opinions about the magnitude of the threat. Cyber conflict remained essentially invisible. Americans could believe that their critical infrastructure was infested with malware, but the infrastructure continued to function. Americans could accept that Chinese soldiers were stealing hundreds of billions of dollars in IP each year, but the link with unemployment and lower wages was ephemeral. And while a quick search of Google could pull up terrorist recruiting videos of Americans being beheaded, proving that they themselves were threatened was another matter. Thus, government attempts to render cyberthreats visible to the general public were only partially successful at best.

THE FAILURE OF U.S. CYBER LEGISLATION AND DIPLOMACY: 2010 TO 2013

The United States has a good deal of experience balancing the trade-off between security and rights with regard to the traditional technologies of violence. From its inception, the United States regularly sacrificed military efficiency to civil rights; the Third Amendment of the U.S. Constitution deals with this type of problem when it forbids the military from quartering soldiers in private homes. When the U.S. military builds bases, executes military patrols, and engages in military operations, to the extent possible, it does so in spaces not owned by private citizens.

The fundamental constitutional dilemma associated with cyber conflict is that it occurs almost entirely within privately owned computers and networks.[14] There are no commons in cyberspace. If a foreign military or terrorist group used traditional means to attack the United States, it would be forced to traverse oceans, roads, or air space that is either an international common or publicly owned border. This type of geography can usually be patrolled by the military without violating citizens' property and privacy rights. However, when an opponent attacks the United States through cyberspace, the attack flows through privately owned cables and computers to privately owned cables and computers. There are virtually no spaces in U.S. cyberspace in which the military can operate without violating property and privacy rights.

Given the above problem of lack of commons, the United States has three options for defending against foreign attacks through cyberspace. It can pass legislation requiring the private persons that own and use computer networks to pay for the costs of stopping attacks passing through them with the cost counted in money or lost privacy. It can use diplomacy to attempt to compel foreign governments to halt attacks. Or it can do nothing. In the wake of Obama and other policy makers' warnings, each of these was tried.

The Legislative Option: Who Pays?

Before 2011, the question of allocating responsibility for defending cyberspace against foreign attacks seldom made headlines. After two years of warnings from national security officials, however, it entered the public sphere when a bipartisan group of thirty-seven Democrat and twenty-six Republican representatives and senators sponsored legislation labeled the Stop Online Piracy Act (SOPA) in the House, and Protect IP Act (PIPA) in the Senate.[15] The legislation aimed at preventing IP theft by forcing Internet service providers (ISP) and content providers to police content flowing through their networks. Its main targets were overseas torrent sites. Specifically, it required U.S. search engines, advertising networks, and other providers to withhold their services from pirate servers located in other countries.

It would be difficult to calculate how much IP theft the legislation might have prevented or how many jobs it might have saved if it had been implemented. The groups it aimed to protect mainly included entertainment IP producers. Given the size of the market for this type of IP, it is almost certain that tens of billions of dollars were at stake, but it is not clear that the legislation would have done much to alleviate the larger IP theft problem facing Silicon Valley and other technology IP producers. The solution the legislation offered to IP theft was to shift the cost of securing IP to U.S. ISPs and content providers by making them legally liable for illegal content crossing their systems. The legislation also forced consumers to give up privacy by requiring companies to monitor content going into private homes. Again, it is unclear precisely how much the legislation would have cost ISPs and content providers, but it would almost certainly have run into the billions and required significant changes in business models and Internet architecture. As might be expected, IP producers and business groups in general largely supported the legislation while ISPs, content providers, and privacy groups opposed it.[16]

In November 2011, the debate over SOPA and PIPA moved from lobbying to civil dissent. Content-providing companies labeled November 16, 2011, "American Censorship Day." More than six thousand websites joined the protest. Tumblr blocked all user-generated content to draw attention to the legislation. Google, Facebook, Twitter, Yahoo, and other groups ran full-page ads in the *New York Times*, the *Wall Street Journal*, the *Washington Post*, and the *Washington Times*. On January 18, 2012, *Wikipedia* along with dozens of prominent sites led an Internet blackout by shutting down for twenty-four hours. *Wikipedia*'s normal content was inaccessible; others posted protest messages on their home page. Participants included Google, Reddit, Craigslist, Wordpress, Imgur, Pinterest, Flickr, and Amazon. According to one count, more than seventy-five thousand websites temporarily went dark.[17] A Google online petition to Congress gained 4.5 million signatories. Four million people used *Wikipedia*'s blacked-out page to look up contact information for their local representatives. In some cases, physical demonstrations took place.[18] Bowing to pressure from business and privacy lobbies, Congress permanently tabled both bills on January 20. The government had asked ISPs and content providers to pay for defending Hollywood and to spy on their customers; the companies had used twenty-first-century protest technology to fight off the request.

About the time SOPA and PIPA protests reached their zenith, Congress introduced the Cyber Intelligence Sharing and Protection Act (CISPA) in the House. While SOPA had aimed mainly at protecting the entertainment industry against IP thieves, CISPA was more ambitious. It proposed to defend all U.S. IP and critical infrastructure against attacks emanating from China, Russia, Iran, and other nations.[19] The bill would do so by facilitating and incentivizing sharing of Internet data between the government and the private sectors.

CISPA directly focused on the types of threats Obama had warned of in his 2009 speech and administration officials had warned of since that time. It promised to significantly improve the government's ability to find and halt foreign actors attacking through cyberspace. Unlike SOPA/PIPA, CISPA placed the financial costs of implementing the security requirements on the U.S. government; corporations could choose to share information with the government but would not be liable for attacks crossing their networks. Like SOPA/PIPA, however, the legislation would have resulted in a significant loss of privacy for individual Internet users by freeing ISPs and content providers to share customers' data (including Internet search terms) with the government.[20]

Not surprisingly, CISPA was hugely popular with the business community, particularly the banks, energy utilities, defense corporations, and technology IP producers that were suffering the most grievous losses from foreign cyber attacks. The ISPs and content providers that had fought against SOPA/PIPA almost universally supported CISPA.[21] Also unsurprisingly, the legislation was opposed by privacy rights groups including the American Civil Liberties Union (ACLU), the Center for Democracy and Technology, the Electronic Frontier Foundation, and the Libertarian Party.[22] Siding with privacy groups, President Obama promised to veto the legislation, and the Senate leadership chose not to vote on it.[23] CISPA passed the House by a bipartisan vote of 248 to 168 in April 2012. It was later modified to reduce privacy concerns and passed again in February 2013 but was never voted on by the Senate. The bill would have solved part of the cybersecurity problem, but privacy advocates were unwilling to pay for greater security with less privacy.

At the same time CISPA was making its way through the House, the Senate began work on the Cybersecurity Act of 2012. The idea behind this legislation was to protect businesses from IP theft and critical infrastructure companies from attack by foreign governments and criminal networks. As Obama passionately explained in a *New York Times* op-ed, this bill was about national security.[24] Like SOPA/PIPA, the Cybersecurity Act of 2012 proposed that the cost of the added security should be footed by a small set of companies. This time the bill payers would be utility and finance companies and the bill would be paid in greater regulation and forced information sharing by business entities.

Faced with a potential loss of revenue, utility and finance companies brought their massive lobbying power to bear against the Cybersecurity Act of 2012. While they could not shut down the Internet as the content providers had done, they did have enormous influence on Capitol Hill. On the other side, the bill received support from tech companies and privacy groups. Eventually, in a misguided effort to placate utility companies, the bill's sponsors watered it down by making its requirements voluntary. As companies could already volunteer to share information about cyber attacks but generally refused to do so, the amendment made the bill almost entirely irrelevant, and most backers removed their support in disgust. In November 2012, the Senate bill was defeated by a vote of forty-one to fifty-seven.

As an alternative to the Cybersecurity Act of 2012, Senator John McCain introduced the SECURE IT Act in March 2012. This act had the same goals as the Cybersecurity Act of 2012 but, rather than increasing government regulation, attempted to remove legal barriers that prevented government and industry from sharing information. But while the legislation reduced the burden on businesses, its critics argued that it did so by giving the government more power to access and share private information. Groups with concerns over national security opposed the bill because it did not provide enough regulation of the businesses responsible for critical infrastructure, and privacy groups opposed it for the potential harm it would do to civil rights.[25]

Each of the bills described above proposed a novel solution to the problem of preventing foreign adversaries from using privately owned computer networks. Each ran afoul of a combination of companies unwilling to be the bill payer for U.S. national security and privacy advocates unconvinced that the cyberthreat warranted companies sharing information with the government. As 2012 drew to a close, it became clear that Congress would not be able to solve the problem.

Diplomacy: Deter China

As Congress worked to allocate liability for defending against foreign attacks, the administration contemplated diplomatic options to deter aggression. Perhaps because Chinese hacking was more aggressive and less stealthy than Russian attacks, almost all diplomacy related to cyberspace focused on China.

Visible evidence that the administration was willing to use coercive diplomacy first surfaced in 2010 when Google, after having its networks penetrated, discovered the attacks had been conducted by the Chinese government in an attempt to spy on human rights activists. Breaking precedent, Google alerted the U.S. government and agreed to work with it to stop further Chinese attacks.[26] Shortly thereafter, Secretary of State Hillary Clinton officially rebuked China and demanded that it halt its attacks. Clinton's demands were accompanied by neither threats nor promises, and China formally responded that it did not engage in cyber espionage and continued its attacks.[27]

For a number of reasons, compelling China to halt its attacks would be difficult. First, China's ruling party appeared to be convinced that its survival depended on maintaining robust economic growth and that economic growth depended on stealing U.S. IP. From their point of view, giving in to U.S. demands would risk internal political instability. Second, for a U.S. threat to have any chance of succeeding, it would have to be backed by a credible threat. For a threat to be believable, the United States would have to convince China that it was willing to go through with it. At the time, the United States was engaged in partisan political turmoil at home, two wars, and a deep and prolonged economic recession. Under these conditions, it was not plausible that the president would enter a trade war or cyber conflict with China. Bereft of more tangible options, Obama, via Clinton, responded to Chinese intransigence with a string of speeches in support of Internet freedom.[28]

Given this background, the problem involved the trade-off between democracy and cyber secrecy. To build up enough support from voters to be able to threaten China credibly, the administration would have to reveal specific evidence of the methods China was using to attack. The more specific the information it released, the more credible it would be to the American people, but the more damaging it would be to America's cyber defenses.

As it turned out, at least part of the decision about whether to talk about China's methods was taken out of the administration's hands. In August 2011, the computer security company McAfee released a report describing widespread state-sponsored espionage of U.S. companies.[29] In October, House Intelligence Committee chairman Mike Rogers (R-MI) publicly labeled China's IP theft program a "massive trade war" and called on political leaders to band together to confront China.[30] In October, the Office of the National Counterintelligence Executive revealed that China was "the world's most active and persistent perpetrators of economic espionage."[31] Industry lobbyists and Republican and Democratic policy makers began a drumbeat of calls for the administration to confront China and Russia.[32] In January 2012, a collection of America's most respected former government officials publicly labeled China's massive cyber theft campaign a national strategy and called on the United States to confront it.[33] In October, Secretary of Defense Leon Panetta announced that intruders had gained access to U.S. critical infrastructure and warned of a possible future cyber Pearl Harbor.[34]

By the end of 2012—almost a year after Congress had given up on any real hope of passing cybersecurity legislation—the public had begun to take note of the cyberthreat. The straw that finally broke the camel's back came in January 2013, when the *New York Times* announced that the People's Liberation Army (PLA) had executed a sustained attack on its systems for four months. The *New York Times* announced that after detecting hackers in its systems, it had hired the firm Mandiant to determine the hackers' identity. Mandiant found incontrovertible evidence that the hackers belonged to China's PLA.[35] Over the next few months, many other U.S. news organizations announced that the PLA was also hacking their computer networks, and a picture emerged of a massive Chinese military hacking campaign against America's media.[36]

Throughout the spring of 2013, an increasingly irate U.S. media worked to galvanize the American public against Chinese government hackers. While Wall Street had long been aware of the threat Chinese hackers represented to intellectual property rights, the angry news campaign showed Main Street the threat hackers represented to the Fourth Estate and, by extension, to their privacy and freedom of speech.[37] Particularly galling was that the PLA's hacks on the *New York Times* appeared to have been conducted to defend a particular corrupt Chinese government official.[38]

In February, soon after the *New York Times*' announcement, in a press conference, White House spokesman Jay Carney described the danger of cyber espionage against the U.S. economy and identified China as the primary culprit. Empowered by an energized media, the administration stated that it would raise its concerns "at the highest levels about cyber theft with senior Chinese officials, including in the military."[39] As public outrage increased, on March 11, in a speech, national security advisor Tom Donilon bluntly demanded that the Chinese government stop theft of data from American computer networks and agree to "acceptable norms of behavior in cyberspace."[40]

As the White House ramped up diplomatic pressure, Beijing appeared unmoved. In February, following Mandiant's description of attacks on the *New York Times*, the PLA removed its malware from the *Times'* computers. In May, however, Mandiant reported that China had resumed its spying operations.[41] In response to the report, the administration noted that naming and shaming was clearly not enough and that China would "have to be convinced there is a real cost to this kind of activity." The *Christian Science Monitor* described the mounting tension as cyber storm clouds and the U.S. public coming to a slow boil as it woke to the magnitude of China's theft.[42]

At the end of a tense spring, anger over China's hacking program appeared destined to culminate in a scheduled June 7–8 meeting between President Obama and China's newly appointed President Xi Jinping. In the lead-up to the meeting, U.S. senators pressured Obama to act and proposed a bill that would empower the president to impose heavy costs on China if it did not relent.[43] As the meeting approached, over the strong opposition of the Chinese, the United States insisted that the summit include cyber diplomacy and eventually that the summit focus primarily on U.S. complaints about Chinese military hacking. After heated diplomacy, China agreed that this meeting would be the first in a series of conferences aimed at settling the cyber dispute.[44]

By June 4, the agenda for the historic cyber summit was mainly set.[45] At the beginning of 2013, the prospects of deterring Chinese hacking had seemed as remote as the prospects of Congress passing meaningful cyber defense legislation. After a six-month-long drumbeat of protests against the PLA in the U.S. news media, however, it finally looked like diplomacy might work. If the public and Senate would stand behind the president, there was a very good chance that China would back down. Once the precedent was set with China, Russia would almost certainly feel pressure to reduce its attacks on U.S. private industry and media. None of this was to be.

On June 5, the *Guardian* published a story it claimed was based on a classified NSA document describing a program the NSA used to secretly collect data on millions of American citizens.[46] On June 6, the *Guardian* published a second story, this one describing an NSA program to gather information from Google, Facebook, Apple, and other Internet companies that allowed officials to access users' private search history, e-mails, files, and live chat.[47] On June 7, as the summit between Obama and Xi began, the

Guardian published a presidential directive for the military to draw up a list of foreign targets for cyber attacks.[48] On June 8, it published a description of an NSA program that detailed how the agency collected information on U.S. citizens and allies.[49] Over the next few days, the media revealed that the *Guardian* had received its information from a U.S. defense contractor named Edward Snowden who had secretly downloaded thousands of NSA documents onto a hard drive and subsequently fled to China.

Whatever the motives behind the timing of Snowden's actions, the leaks removed any hope that U.S. diplomacy could be used to reduce foreign hacking. Within hours of Snowden's leaks, both Congress and the public changed the focus of their anger from China to the administration. Deprived of its public backing, Obama made no meaningful demands of Xi at the June conference, nor did the high-level bilateral cyber talks envisioned in the run-up to the conference occur. The dispute was, for all practical purposes, tabled. Over the next year, Congress and the media indignantly focused their attention on the U.S. government and why an administration and content providers that had lobbied so hard for privacy had engaged in the types of activities that came to light in subsequent congressional testimony. In the ensuing turmoil, the spotlight was removed from China. For the foreseeable future, diplomacy would not be an option.

THE "DO NOTHING" OPTION

Sometimes a decision by the government to do nothing is the best option available; at other times it is not. While the U.S. decision to do nothing since 2009 has helped to safeguard U.S. citizens against losing rights to the U.S. government, it has required them to endure further loss of rights to foreign governments.

The first rights foreign attacks affect involve risks to liberty and life insofar as extortion represents threats to the first and attacks on critical infrastructure represent risks to the latter. During the four years of failed attempts at cyber legislation and diplomacy after 2010, America's cybersecurity situation worsened. In August 2012, as Congress argued over SOPA/PIPA and other legislation, organizations widely believed to be fronts for the Iranian military launched the largest Distributed Denial of Service (DDoS) attack in history against the U.S. banking system.[50] In December 2014, North Korea was so emboldened by U.S. docility that it attacked the Sony Corporations, destroyed its computers, blackmailed its staff with stolen records, and succeeded in extorting the U.S. movie industry into cancelling a motion picture.[51] Throughout this period, attacks on U.S. critical infrastructure increased in magnitude and sophistication. In congressional testimony in November 2014, director of the NSA Admiral Michael Rogers bluntly stated that he believed a cyber attack on the electric grid is inevitable.[52]

A second set of rights lost to foreign hackers involves freedom of the press and speech. After a brief pause in 2013, China recommenced its attacks on U.S. news agencies. While the U.S. government is prohibited from demanding that U.S. news organizations divulge their sources, today autocratic foreign governments hack U.S. media nearly at will creating a pall of fear over reporters and sources dealing with issues involving the hacking governments.

A third set of rights at stake involves property rights. Since 2010, U.S. industries have worried that new legislation would unfairly damage their companies. ISPs, content providers, utilities, and the finance industry have all worked to prevent Congress from unfairly saddling them with the bill for defending cyberspace. Even as Congress has agreed to their demands, however, China and Russia have ruthlessly plundered privately owned American IP. If the size of this theft is even close to what U.S. officials claim, it has cost hundreds of thousands of Americans their private property and millions of Americans their jobs.

Finally, cyber attacks have had a severe cost in lost privacy. While the U.S. data-collection methods described by the *Guardian* in 2013 raise constitutional questions about privacy, U.S. privacy concerns have not prevented Chinese and Russian hackers from downloading the personal information of tens of millions of U.S. citizens. Cases of foreign hackers seizing payroll, tax, and health-care databases have become so ubiquitous as to barely rate as news stories.[53] While it is difficult to grasp the scale of these programs, anecdotes come to light from time to time providing scattered glimpses. In 2014, for instance, a computer security researcher discovered that, of the top ten flashlight apps listed in the Android Apps Store, all ten were malware designed to steal users' personal information and send it to China, Russia, or India.[54] Keeping in mind that a massive number of apps must be released to place one in the top ten and hundreds of data intrusions often take place for every one that is detected, the magnitude of the violation of U.S. citizens' privacy by foreign government can only be described as breathtaking.

CONCLUSION: NATIONAL SECURITY OR CIVIL RIGHTS

For the past two years, the controversy over cybersecurity in Washington has centered around the Snowden leaks and their implications for U.S. privacy rights. The debate is one of the most important in civil rights history. From its inception, the United States has treated the right to privacy as akin to life, liberty, and speech. Beyond this, information is power. An information age country like the United States cannot increase its government's authority to gather information without changing the relationship between citizens and state. At the same time, however, America's foreign adversaries are currently depriving U.S. citizens of the same rights the country fears to give its own government.

This is not the first time in U.S. history the country has faced hard trade-offs between national security and citizens' rights. In the past, in the face of external threats, the United States has had to decide whether to confiscate private property, censor speech, draft young men, and imprison ethnic minorities. Sometimes it has chosen well, and sometimes it has not. What is different this time is that the threats posed by cyber technology are far more likely than previous threats to be invisible to the general public; and the solutions, to require the military and police to operate in spaces owned by private citizens. For the last half decade, these characteristics of the new technology have short-circuited the democratic process and resulted in extraordinarily poor foreign policy legislation and diplomacy.

While Snowden's leaks are viewed by the U.S. intelligence community as one of the greatest blows to U.S. national security in the nation's history, they did have the salutary effect of opening important constitutional issues to debate by the American people. But the leaks tell only half of the story. Snowden did not release documents describing ways Chinese and Russian cyber programs attack U.S. infrastructure, intellectual property, and citizens' privacy. National security creates hard trade-offs. Assessments of NSA programs are only meaningful if they can be conducted in light of the rights these programs help to preserve from attacks by foreign governments. This aspect of the debate is likely to remain lacking until China or Russia presents the West with Snowdens of their own.

NOTES

1. The views expressed in this chapter are those of the author and do not necessarily represent those of the U.S. Department of Defense or any federal entity.

2. Barack Obama, "Remarks by the President on Securing Our Nation's Cyber Infrastructure" (speech), White House East Room, May 29, 2009, http://www.whitehouse.gov/.

3. Mike McConnell, "Mike McConnell on How to Win the Cyber-War We're Losing," editorial, *Washington Post*, February 28, 2010, http://www.washingtonpost.com/.

4. While little is published describing the specific techniques or mechanisms a cyber attacker could use to cause this outcome, after studying this type of scenario, the U.S. Defense Science Board recommended that the United States prepare to use nuclear weapons against opponents using attacks of this type. Defense Science Board, "Task Force Report: Resilient Military Systems and the Advanced Cyber Threat," U.S. Department of Defense, January 2013.

5. For a detailed history, see Kim Zetter, *Countdown to Zero Day: Stuxnet and the Launch of the World's First Digital Weapon* (New York: Crown, 2014).

6. Stewart Abercrombie Baker, Natalia Filipiak, and Katrina Timlin, "In the Dark: Crucial Industries Confront Cyber Attacks," McAfee, 2011, http://www.mcafee.com/, 6.

7. "Highlights: Newsweek's Special Elections Project," *Newsweek*, November 4, 2008, http://www.newsweek.com/.

8. For a list of significant known cyber incidents, see Center for Strategic and International Studies, "Significant Cyber Incidents Since 2006," last updated August 7, 2014, http://csis.org/.

9. China, in particular, had been called out for hacking into U.S. companies to gain information on Chinese human rights activists with the goals of silencing them.

10. Estimates about U.S. financial losses are controversial and vary widely. See, for instance, Josh Rogin, "NSA Chief: Cybercrime Constitutes the 'Greatest Transfer of Wealth in History,'" *Foreign Policy*, July 9, 2012.

11. David Drummond, "A New Approach to China," Google: Official Blog, January 12, 2010, http://googleblog.blogspot.co.uk/.

12. Mark Landler, "Clinton Urges Global Response to Internet Attacks," *New York Times*, January 21, 2010, http://www.nytimes.com/.

13. Catherine A. Theohary and John Rollins, "Terrorist Use of the Internet: Information Operations in Cyberspace," Congressional Research Service, March 8, 2011, http://www.fas.org/.

14. Small parts of the Internet are owned by the U.S. military and government, but even these entities rely on privately owned networks for external communications.

15. The legislation reiterated much of the less well-known Combating Online Infringement and Counterfeits Act (COICA) legislation of 2010 that failed in the Senate.

16. For a list of groups supporting and opposing the legislation, see "List of Organizations with Official Stances on the SOPA and PIPA," *Wikipedia*, last updated May 9, 2015, http://en.wikipedia.org/.

17. Alan Fram, "SOPA and PIPA Bills: Online Companies Win Piracy Fight," *Huffington Post*, January 21, 2012, http://www.huffingtonpost.com/.

18. Jenna Wortham, "With Twitter, Blackouts and Demonstrations, Web Flexes Its Muscle," *New York Times*, January 18, 2012, http://www.nytimes.com/; Jennifer Martinez and Tony Romm, "SOPA Blackout Leads Co-sponsors to Defect," *Politico*, January 18, 2012, http://www.politico.com/.

19. Dave Smith, "CISPA 2013: Google, Apple Top Massive List of Supporters Favoring the Controversial Cybersecurity Bill," *International Business Times*, April 12, 2013, http://www.ibtimes.com/.

20. Dave Smith, "RIP CISPA: Senate Expected to Kill 2013 Cybersecurity Bill," *International Business Times*, April 26, 2013, http://www.ibtimes.com/.

21. Andrew Couts, "CISPA Supporters List: 800+ Companies That Could Help Uncle Sam Snag Your Data," *Digital Trends*, April 12, 2012, http://www.digitaltrends.com/; "Cyber-Security Bill Cispa Passes US House," *BBC News*, April 26, 2012, http://www.bbc.com/; Smith, "CISPA 2013." Supporters included the Business Software Alliance, the Internet Security Alliance, the National Cable and Telecommunications Association, the U.S. Chamber of Commerce, AT&T, IBM, Intel, Oracle Corporation, Symantec, Verizon, and Facebook. While Google, Yahoo, Apple, and Microsoft did not officially support the bill, TechNet, a trade group on which leading executives from all three companies serve, sent a letter of support.

22. *BBC News*, "Cyber-Security Bill."

23. Ibid.; Gerry Smith, "Senate Won't Vote on CISPA, Deals Blow to Controversial Cyber Bill," *Huffington Post*, April 25, 2013, http://www.huffingtonpost.com/.

24. Barack Obama, "Taking the Cyberattack Threat Seriously," *Wall Street Journal*, July 19, 2012, http://www.wsj.com/.

25. William Jackson, "McCain's Retooled Secure IT Act Still a Privacy Threat, Critics Say," *GCN*, July 2, 2012, http://gcn.com/.

26. Kim Zetter, "Google Asks NSA to Help Secure Its Network," *Wired*, February 4, 2010, http://www.wired.com/.

27. Tania Branigan, "China Responds to Google Hacking Claims," *Guardian*, January 14, 2010, http://www.theguardian.com/.

28. Hillary Clinton, "Secretary of State," Remarks on Internet Freedom from US Department of State, Washington, DC, January 21, 2010. See also Fergus Hason, "Internet Freedom: The Role of the U.S. State Department," 2012, accessed June 29, 2014, http://www.brookings.edu/.

29. Ellen Nakashima, "Report on 'Operation Shady RAT' Identifies Widespread Cyber-Spying," *Washington Post*, August 3, 2011.

30. Josh Smith, "Rogers: U.S. Must Confront 'Intolerable' Chinese Cyberespionage," *National Journal*, October 4, 2011, http://www.nationaljournal.com/.

31. Office of the National Counterintelligence Executive, "Foreign Spies Stealing US Economic Secrets in Cyberspace: Report to Congress on Foreign Economic Collection and Industrial Espionage, 2009–2011," National Counterintelligence and Security Center, October 2011, http://www.ncix.gov/. See also Patrick Smith, "Stealing America: China's Busy Cyber-Spies," *Fiscal Times*, November 7, 2011, http://www.thefiscaltimes.com/.

32. Ken Dilanian, "U.S. Lawmakers Demand Action over Alleged China Cyber Attacks," *Los Angeles Times*, October 4, 2011, http://articles.latimes.com/. See also Ken Dilanian, "Russian and China Accused of Cyber-Spying Campaign to Steal U.S. Secrets," *Los Angeles Times*, August 12, 2011, http://articles.latimes.com/.

33. Mike McConnell, Michael Chertoff, and William Lynn, "China's Cyber Thievery Is National Policy—And Must Be Challenged," *Wall Street Journal*, January 27, 2012, http://www.wsj.com/.

34. Leon E. Panetta, "Remarks by Secretary Panetta on Cybersecurity to the Business Executives for National Security, New York City" (speech), October 11, 2012, http://www.defense.gov/.

35. Nicole Perlroth, "Hackers in China Attacked the Times for Last 4 Months," *New York Times*, January 30, 2013, http://www.nytimes.com/; David E. Sanger, David Barboza, and Nicole Perlroth, "Chinese Army Unit Is Seen as Tied to Hacking against U.S.," *New York Times*, February 18, 2013, http://www.nytimes.com/; Mark Landler and David E. Sanger, "U.S. Demands China Block Cyberattacks and Agree to Rules," *New York Times*, March 11, 2013, http://www.nytimes.com/.

36. "New York Times, Wall Street Journal and Washington Post Hacked," *Guardian*, February 20, 2013, http://www.theguardian.com/.

37. In the United States, the press is sometimes referred to as the Fourth Estate. The idea behind this label is that the press is on par with official government institutions in terms of its importance to democracy.

38. Sebastian Anthony, "China Continues Cyberwar Campaign, Hacks the New York Times," ExtremeTech, January 31, 2013, http://www.extremetech.com/.

39. Ken Dilanian and Christi Parsons, "White House Adopts New Strategy to Safeguard Intellectual Property," *Los Angeles Times*, February 20, 2013, http://articles.latimes.com/.

40. Tom Donilon, "Remarks by Tom Donilon, National Security Advisor to the President: 'The United States and the Asia-Pacific in 2013'" (speech), White House, Office of the Press Secretary, March 11, 2013, http://www.whitehouse.gov/.

41. David E. Sanger and Nicole Perlroth, "Hackers from China Resume Attacks on U.S. Targets," *New York Times*, May 19, 2013, http://www.nytimes.com/.

42. Mark Clayton, "Obama Pressured to Confront China's Xi Jinping on Cyber Spying," *Christian Science Monitor*, June 7, 2013, http://www.csmonitor.com/.

43. Ibid.

44. David E. Sanger and Mark Landler, "U.S. and China Agree to Hold Regular Talks on Hacking," *New York Times*, June 1, 2013, http://www.nytimes.com/.

45. Aamer Madhani, "Cybersecurity Will Loom Large at Obama-Xi Summit," *USA Today*, June 5, 2013, http://www.usatoday.com/; Scott Wilson and William Wan, "Obama, Xi Summit Could Help Define U.S.-China Relationship for Years to Come," *Washington Post*, June 5, 2013.

46. Glenn Greenwald, "NSA Collecting Phone Records of Millions of Verizon Customers Daily," *Guardian*, June 5, 2013, http://www.theguardian.com/.

47. Glenn Greenwald and Ewen MacAskill, "NSA Prism Program Taps in to User Data of Apple, Google and Others," *Guardian*, June 7, 2013, http://www.theguardian.com/.

48. Glenn Greenwald and Ewen MacAskill, "Obama Orders US to Draw Up Overseas Target List for Cyber-Attacks," *Guardian*, June 7, 2013, http://www.theguardian.com/.

49. Glenn Greenwald and Ewen MacAskill, "Boundless Informant: The NSA's Secret Tool to Track Global Surveillance Data," *Guardian*, June 11, 2013, http://www.theguardian.com/.

50. Nicole Perlroth and Quentin Hardy, "Bank Hacking Was the Work of Iranians, Officials Say," *New York Times*, January 8, 2013, http://www.nytimes.com/.

51. Ellen Nakashima, "White House Says Sony Hack Is a Serious National Security Matter," *Washington Post*, December 18, 2014, http://www.washingtonpost.com/.

52. Siobhan Gorman, "NSA Director Warns of 'Dramatic' Cyberattack in Next Decade," *Wall Street Journal*, November 20, 2014, http://www.wsj.com/.

53. Michael A. Riley and Jordan Robertson, "Why Would Chinese Hackers Steal Millions of Medical Records?" BloombergBusiness, August 18, 2014, http://www.bloomberg.com/; Michael A. Riley and Jordan Robertson, "Chinese State-Sponsored Hackers Suspected in Anthem Attack," BloombergBusiness, February 5, 2015, http://www.bloomberg.com/.

54. SnoopWall, "Consumer Digital Privacy Protection Advisory: Top Mobile Flashlight Applications Spy on Users, Warn SnoopWall Cybersecurity Experts," October 2, 2014, http://www.snoopwall.com/; Tom Fox-Brewster, "Check the Permissions: Android Flashlight Apps Criticized over Privacy," *Guardian*, October 3, 2014; Robert McMillan, "The Hidden Privacy Threat of . . . Flashlight Apps?" *Wired*, October 21, 2014.

Chapter Nine

Attribution Policy in Cyberwar

Kalliopi Chainoglou

THE TWENTY-FIRST CENTURY BEGINS

During the first decade of the twenty-first century, the security landscape has changed irrevocably; traditional and nontraditional security challenges compel us to revisit many of the assumptions that have served as the foundations of the Westphalian international system. As sovereign states are more dependent on cyberspace, they are more vulnerable to cyber operations launched by an opponent operating asymmetrically through cyberspace. Computerized flight-control systems, power networks, Internet-enabled home-security systems are only a few of the possible targets of the hostile use of cyberspace; even so, cyber attacks can have disastrous results without incurring loss of lives or physical destruction. Cyberthreats expose national sovereignty to ever-changing challenges; constantly evolving and reformulating diminishing distance, and with unprecedented speed and scope, cyberthreats threaten traditional sovereign prerogatives of states.[1]

The existing international legal framework—including the UN Charter, the law of state responsibility, and the rules of international humanitarian law—was set up in view of preserving and reaffirming the tenets of national sovereignty. However, it has often been criticized with regard to the available options for states to address attacks or threats emanating from the cyber domain.[2] Many of the arguments stem from a persistent fear or concern that the UN Charter, the law of state responsibility, or the international humanitarian law lack clarity vis-à-vis the new forms of cybersecurity threats[3] and the cyber tactics employed.[4] Additionally, concerns are expressed that stretching the existing international legal framework to accommodate the various forms of threats and attacks from the cyber domain would simply end up compromising the "normative integrity of the existing system for limiting the use of force and . . . further militarize the cyber domain."[5]

Indeed, it has often been the case that states, policy makers, or scholars have advised that there is every need to adopt an international cyber treaty[6] or that the UN Charter is not flexible enough to be applied in this cyber context. On the other hand, it has also been argued that these ambiguities surrounding cyber attacks "simply reflect the challenges in applying the [UN] Charter framework that already exists in many contexts."[7] To date, the majority of the member states of the international community have affirmed the validity of the UN Charter in the cyber context,[8] while they have also stressed the need for international cooperative action against threats resulting from the malicious use of information and communication technologies (ICTs) to reduce risk and enhance (cyber) security.[9]

The aim of this chapter is to present a perspective as to how international law meets twenty-first-century expectations, taking into consideration scholarly comments and policy makers' concerns regarding cyber attacks. This chapter has two parts. The first section presents the cyber challenges posed to sovereignty and the technical and legal issues on state attribution. The second section explores the jus ad bellum perspective.

SOVEREIGNTY AND CYBERSECURITY, STATE ATTRIBUTION, AND STATE RESPONSIBILITY

The law of state responsibility concerns the internationally wrongful acts that have been committed by states when violating their international obligations vis-à-vis other states. State responsibility, a set of rules stemming from customary law, was codified in the International Law Commission's "Draft Articles on Responsibility of States for Internationally Wrongful Acts" in 2001.[10] More than a decade ago, when the 9/11 attacks were carried out against the United States, legal scholars were striving to ascertain whether the right of self-defense could be exercised against nonstate actors; along those lines, legal literature was exploring the attributability of the perpetrators' 9/11 attacks to the state of Afghanistan and scholars were in favor of "indirect responsibility." The normative impact of the 9/11 attacks on the law of state responsibility and the frequency of nonstate actors' conventional and nonconventional attacks in the international system have heralded a shift in international law toward a model of indirect state responsibility based on a state's failure to meet its international duties. On a similar note, during the past few years, the issue of attributability in the cyber context has attracted the interest of both legal scholars and policy makers. Although at the UN level it has been affirmed that states must meet their international obligations regarding internationally wrongful acts attributable to them even in the cybersecurity context,[11] difficulties arise with regard to the applicability of the state responsibility in the cyber domain.

Cyberspace is practically borderless and beyond the territorial sovereignty of states[12]—at least in terms of geographical delimitation of sovereign boundaries. The intricacies of applying state responsibility in the cyberspace context revolve around two pillars: sovereignty and the nature of cyberthreats.

Cyberspace is not essentially limited to the territorial or geographical aspects of sovereignty.[13] The physical dimension of cyber infrastructure (i.e., routers, servers, computers, and network/IP connections), which is essentially regulated by the legal framework of the state that is located therein, is intertwined with the virtual dimension of the cyber attacks (for example, the transboundary transfer of packets of data and the ideas or information that the data represent). President Obama has voiced his concerns over "how the Internet and cyber operates" and did not hesitate to describe the situation as "sort of the Wild West," where there are "weak States that can engage in these kinds of attacks, [and] non-State actors that can do enormous damage."[14] Although states may exercise sovereign control over infrastructure, people employed therein, or data (e.g., "Chinese firewall"), states do not necessarily have control over the actors (e.g., numerous hackers) or the content (e.g., terrorist rhetoric) disseminated over the Internet. The use of cyberspace changes itself; it becomes a theater of terror and propaganda for motivating recruits and providing them a form of "distance learning" in terrorist tradecraft, a call for jihadists and supporters around the world to take action themselves. The inability of states to exercise sovereign control over them renders cyber-jihadists stateless, if not unaccountable for these cyber operations.[15] The impact of the web on individual would-be jihadists and the accessibility of terror-related content encourage further radicalization and engagement in terrorist violent or nonviolent, cyber,[16] or conventional operations.[17] The challenges to sovereignty are perhaps best reflected in the recent plan of the leaders of the Islamic State of Iraq and Syria and Al-Qaeda to set up a digital, cyber, caliphate with appointed (but stateless), cyber jihadi leaders.[18] It is also within this context that an ongoing online conflict (initially with website defacements and Distributed Denial of Service [DDoS] attacks) between Islamist and pro-Western hactivists has been taking place within hours after the Charlie Hebdo attacks.[19]

The clandestine nature of cyber attacks and the evident difficulty in tracing the authors of such attacks appear to be the Gordian knot in international law, specifically the law of state responsibility and the law of use of force. Legal and technical issues of attribution are naturally interrelated to the ambiguities pertaining to cyber attacks and cyber infrastructure. For example, it is often difficult to determine the origin, identity, sponsorship, or motive behind the cyber attack.[20] Or the purpose, location, or activity related to cyber infrastructure can change with overwhelming ease,[21] making technical attribution difficult with cyber operations even when states are involved. However, it has to be emphasized that attribution of cyber attacks is central to the desired regulation and governance of cyberspace and mitigation of the occurrence of cyber attacks.[22]

Under article 2 of the International Law Commission (ILC) Articles, a state will have committed an internationally wrongful act when its conduct consists of an action or omission that is attributable to the state under international law and constitutes a breach of an international obligation (whether by treaty or customary law) of the state.[23] It should be noted that the act or omission must be in violation of international law; following the Kosovo Advisory Opinion interpretive line, if a particular act is not prohibited under international law, then it is possible that this act is not contrary to international law.[24] In cyberspace, an international wrongful act may consist of a violation of the UN Charter, for example, article 2 (4) on the threat or use of force, article 2 (7) on intervention in the domestic affairs of another state,[25] or violation of law of sea or of international humanitarian law, for example, attacks on civilians.[26] For the purposes of the law of state responsibility, attribution is independent of the legality of the conduct in question. For attribution to be effective, it needs to be established that there is an act (or an omission) of the state.[27]

Article 4 (1) of the ILC Articles provides that "the conduct of any state organ shall be considered an act of that State under international law, whether the organ exercises legislative, executive, judicial or any other functions, whatever position it holds in the organisations of the state, and whatever its character as an organ of the central Government or of a territorial unit of the State." Paragraph 2 of article 4 defines as an organ "any person or entity which has that status in accordance with the internal law of the state." This is a clear-cut case for state organs and state agencies, including the military, intelligence, or internal security that have established cyber departments or cyber units/centers; their conduct is attributable to the state by virtue of article 4 of ILC.[28] The conduct of individuals or legal persons that are not organs of a state in the sense of article 4 of ILC can still be attributable to the state if the individuals or legal persons were acting in that capacity in the particular cyber context (article 5 of ILC). In real-life terms, that would include national Computer Emergency Response Teams or contractors or personnel engaged with cyber units (not necessarily on a contractual or payroll basis) mandated to conduct cyber defense of governmental networks. It is mentioned in this context that article 5 could be applicable where persons or entities are in public-private partnership with the purpose of enhancing preparedness during a crisis situation or volunteers that serve in units that in wartime would be coordinated under a unified command.[29] Furthermore, ultra vires acts of state organs or entities empowered to exercise elements of the governmental authority, perhaps in the due course of covert cyber operations, will still be attributable to the state (article 7 of ILC).

Attribution of cyber attacks can be fraught with challenges as to the identification of the original or multiple sources. A state may incur responsibility for the conduct of both de jure and de facto organs. In the latter case, the nexus between the state and the de facto organ must be compelling for attribution to suffice; as the court has stated, it has to be proved that the de facto organ has acted in "complete dependence" on the state.[30] Article 8 of the ILC Articles provides that "the conduct of a person or group of persons shall be considered an act of a State under international law if the person or group of persons is in fact acting on the instructions of, or under the direction or control of that state in carrying out the conduct." Article 8 of ILC would be applicable in cases where private actors are contracted by the state to launch cyber operations or even in cases where private actors are called upon to conduct cyber attacks against other states; it is within this context that numerous people have been "recruited" to join a cyber jihad against the United States and other Western countries in the past few years. However, this may differ from a situation where cyber volunteers acting in the name of patriotism merely conduct cyber operations under their own initiative and without any control or direction by the state. The most recent example would have to be when Ukrainian cyber volunteers were reported to have blocked bank accounts that financed the conflict in Eastern Ukraine.[31] The commentary to the ILC Articles clarifies that evidence must support that the state was involved with the private actor's action in question and that essentially the state "has directed or controlled the specific operation and the conduct complained of was an integral part of that operation."[32] The ICJ has similarly pointed out in the *Nicaragua* case that the state must have had effective control of activities in the course of which the international obligations were violated.[33] The principle of "effective control" was reaffirmed in the Armed Activities case where the court examined whether the conduct of the perpetrators was carried out "on the instructions of, or under the direction or control of" the state.[34] Later on in the Genocide case, the ICJ stated that it had to be shown that "effective control was exercised or that the state's instruction were given, in respect of each operation in which the alleged violations occurred, not generally in respect of the overall actions taken by the persons or groups of persons having committed the violations."[35] Even though the insistence of the court on "effective control" has clashed in the past with the divergent standpoint of the International Criminal Tribunal for the former Yugoslavia (ICTY) in the *Prosecutor v. Tadic* case, where the principle of "overall control" was proclaimed,[36] the International Court of Justice (ICJ) has taken a firm stance in the Genocide case.[37] In the court's words, "Persons, groups of persons or entities may, for purposes of international responsibility, be equated with State organs even if that status does not follow from internal law, provided that in fact the persons, groups or entities act in 'complete dependence' on the State, of which they are ultimately merely the instrument."[38] Even though the *Tallinn Manual* does not shed any further light on the issue, there is some support in favor of applying "different attribution criteria to different situations."[39] Perhaps this is a legal void that should be filled in by the International Law Commission or an international treaty in the near future.

A state may be held responsible for wrongful acts perpetrated by nonstate actors, which the state subsequently approves or endorses, even tacitly. In the Tehran Hostages case, the ICJ held that while Iran was not responsible for the acts of individuals, and therefore not for the takeover of the U.S. embassy in Tehran, subsequent encouraging statements in the face of the incidents, including hostage taking by students, created liability on the part of the state.[40] The general rule arising out of this case is in line with article 11 of the ILC Articles, which reads: "Conduct which is not attributable to a State under the preceding Articles shall nevertheless be considered an act of that State under international law if and to the extent that the State acknowledges and adopts the conduct in question as its own." In the cyber context, where a state has expressed its support to cyber operations and where a state could have been considered capable of putting a stop to the situation and instead chooses to endorse it, then what is originally deemed to be a nongovernmental act becomes a governmental act.[41]

As opposed to conventional terrorist attacks, for example, by an extremist jihadist group that could be averted or at least traced back to the perpetrator through intelligence, cyber attacks cannot always be traced back to their source. The collection of evidence on such complex and sensitive security matters can often be staled. The ICJ has affirmed this problem in the *Nicaragua* case where it admitted that "the problem is not . . . the legal process of imputing the act to a particular State . . . but the prior process of tracing material proof of the identity of the perpetrator."[42] In the case of a cyber attack, the lack of or the existence of patchy intelligence and evidence—for example, due to a multiple front (spoofing) or traveling through many different jurisdictions—may render it impossible to identify the physical operator of the cyber attack and his or her affiliation to other state or nonstate entities. Furthermore, missing or disrupted data commands could render the claim for state sponsorship or state control unsuccessful.[43] For this reason, attribution claims should be substantiated by the victim state with any clear and unequivocal evidence (following the principle of "actori incumbit onus probandi") in the form of official statements, witnesses (if available), and experts' and technical evidence, which would attest to the perpetrators of the cyber attacks.

Imputing cyber attacks to a particular state may be time consuming vis-à-vis (the attributability of) other conventional threats to which states have traditionally been subjected. For cyber attacks, the origins of which are either well covered through "spoofing" or anonymized through "Tor,"[44] it may be difficult to physically obtain both intelligence and evidence as to the authors of the attacks and their connections to other state or nonstate entities. Moreover, a certain degree of transnational cooperation will be expected—especially if the attack has seen the light of the day through spoofing. Unfortunately, there are still geographical regions of this world that have not prioritized cybersecurity or may not have addressed the possible legal lacunae that exist with regard to the criminalization of certain cyber activities. Furthermore, if cyber attacks have taken place in parallel with a conventional terrorist attack, it is likely that intelligence services would seem to prioritize on tracing the perpetrators of the conventional attacks rather than the perpetrators of cyber attacks. Michael Schmitt correctly points out that in such cases "publically disclosing whether, and how, a target State knows the source of a malicious operation may reveal that State's cyber capabilities, [and] its response to a cyber attack may appear to be either an unlawful first-strike or precipitous response."[45] A recent example would have to be the jihadist cyber attacks taking place within hours after the Charlie Hebdo attacks in January 2015. Furthermore, legal and political hurdles or interstate intelligence communications mishaps may impede or delay the process of collecting evidence.

If the cyber attack is indeed unattributable to a state, the question remains as to the identity of the attacker, both the physical operator and the coordinator of this attack. Is it a nonstate actor? What are the possible connections to the state(s) in which this nonstate actor operates, that is, if the cyber operations are routed through another state other than the one that cyber infrastructure is located? Is there still a window of attributability for the cyber attack in question? These issues need to be addressed as states cannot respond to a cyber attack with countermeasures without establishing state responsibility for the cyber attack.[46] Under article 2 of ILC, a state will have committed an internationally wrongful act even when its conduct consists of an omission that is attributable to the state under international law and constitutes a breach of an international obligation (whether by treaty or customary international law) of the state.[47] In the Corfu Channel case, the court held that every state is under an obligation "not to allow knowingly its territory to be used for acts contrary to the rights of other states."[48] It was in this case that the court found that Albania should have known of the existence of mines in the Albanian territorial waters and should have warned third states with regard to the imminent danger in its territorial waters; it is this duty of the state "not to tolerate the preparation in its territory of actions which are directed against a foreign government or which might endanger the latter's security" that will raise the responsibility of the state for the international wrongful act of omission.[49] In the case of the 9/11 attacks, even if the terrorist acts could not be attributable to the state of Afghanistan, the state still incurred liability for violating its international obligation as established by the General Assembly Declaration on Principles of International Law concerning Friendly Relations and Cooperation among States and reaffirmed in resolution 1373 (2001).[50] A state may incur primarily responsibility because of a breach of an international obligation, despite this obligation arising out of the situation created by a nonattributable act.[51] The toleration by a state of such activities or the state's failure to prevent attacks directed against another country is unlawful;[52] the obligation to prevent such activities from occurring is one of conduct, that is, a matter of exercising due diligence, and not of result.[53] This is in line with the finding in the S.S. *Lotus* case where it was held that "a state is bound to use due diligence to prevent the commission within its dominions of criminal acts against another nation or its people."[54] Thus, a state may be responsible for failing to prevent a nonstate group from using its territory as a base for attacks against another state.[55] This is in line with one of the five principles for cyber peace enunciated by the International Telecommunications Union secretary-general, namely, that "every country will commit itself not to harbour terrorists/criminals in its own territories."[56] Equally, if a state fails to fulfill one of its duties, in particular the duty to prevent nonstate actors from conducting cyber attacks against another state, there will be responsibility under international law.[57] The duty to prevent cyber attacks ranges from restricting access to Internet without prejudice to constitutional or human rights law,[58] prohibiting the use of its cyber infrastructure for attacks against other states,[59] passing criminal legislation, conducting criminal investigation, and prosecuting to preventing cyber attacks emanating from the territory of the state itself. However, it seems almost impossible to extend the duty of a state to prevent cyber attacks to the prohibition of passage of data (part of the cyber attack) via the routers located in the territory of the transit state.[60] Rule 8 of the *Tallinn Manual* is correct in stating that "the fact that a cyber operation has been routed via the cyber infrastructure located in a State is not sufficient evidence for attributing the operation to that State"; however, I am of the view that the commentary on rule 8 is exaggerating in suggesting that "the State of transit will bear responsibility for failing to take reasonable measures to prevent the transit."[61] Unless an international convention regulates these aspects of data transit or sets up the minimum standards for cybersecurity vis-à-vis data traffic and the governance of states' informational space, it would be wise to refrain from interpretive statements that could create further discomfort with the applicability of the law of state responsibility in this context.[62]

JUS AD BELLUM

The prohibition of the use of force stands as one of the most significant and challenging cultural and political achievements of the twentieth century. The threat or use of interstate force is prohibited under both article 2 (4) of the UN Charter and customary international law. The task of maintaining international peace and security is within the realm of the Security Council under article 24 of the UN Charter. Under article 39, the Security Council is "to determine the existence of any threat to the peace, breach of the peace or act of aggression" and can make recommendations or adopt measures under articles 41 and 42. The very fact that article 39 gives the Security Council the power to determine but does not necessitate it to act (i.e., to determine the means and the extent of measures aimed to eliminate the threat) has prompted states in the past to take law in their own hands when facing a grave threat, to arrogate to themselves the right to use force to maintain and restore international peace and security occasionally by interpreting unilaterally the Security Council resolutions as authorizing the use of military force. In any case, the broad powers of the Security Council guarantee that the latter can act and determine as threats to peace even novel threats, including hostile cyber operations.

The cardinal question in jus ad bellum traditionally addresses whether the use of force in question reaches the threshold of an armed attack. This part discusses whether cyber attacks can fit within the paradigm of the UN Charter's provisions as there is a certain reluctance to categorize cyber attacks as armed attacks under article 51 or as threats to international peace and security that would even necessitate a Security Council authorization for military intervention under article 42.[63]

Armed Attack

Pending the Security Council action, a state may exercise the right of individual or collective self-defense under article 51 of the UN Charter—a right that is also well founded in customary law and is subject to the criteria of imminence, proportionality, and necessity as promulgated in the *Caroline* case.[64] Not any threat or use of force, which is a violation of article 2 (4), will justify the exercise of self-defense under article 51 unless it amounts to an "armed attack."[65] As Derek Bowett has observed, "There is no necessary correlation between aggression and self-defence, so that the one concept is not always the counterpart to the other."[66] Indeed, aggression is a wider concept than an armed attack,[67] and aggression per se would have to amount to an armed attack for the right of self-defense to be exercised. If "aggression" and "use of force" were found to coincide with an armed attack, they would serve as a precondition for the exercise of self-defense, and the concept of the "armed attack" would include other prohibited uses of force, which are beyond its scope.[68]

The international community accepts that the concept of armed attack must be of "sufficient gravity" in view of its scale and effects, possibly involving loss of life or significant destruction of property.[69] The ICJ jurisprudence suggests that the term "armed attack" be construed to mean an attack of a significant scale across international borders.[70] In *Nicaragua*, the court held that states do not have a right to exercise the right of individual or collective self-defense against acts that do not amount to an "armed attack."[71] This was upheld in the *Oil Platforms* case where the court also stated that for a state to attack another state it has to show that there was an armed attack for which the other state holds the responsibility. In *Nicaragua*, the ICJ considered that only uses of force of particular scale and effects will qualify as armed attacks: "It will be necessary to distinguish the most grave forms of the use of force [those amounting to an armed attack] from other less grave forms."[72]

Although the ICJ did not provide a complete list of what may constitute an armed attack, it found that mere frontier incidents would not amount to armed attacks; the ICJ noted that "the prohibition of armed attacks may apply to the sending by a State of armed bands to the territory of another state, if such an operation, because of its *scale* and *effects*, would have classified as an armed attack rather than as a mere frontier incident had it been carried out by regular armed forces."[73] However, the court has also noted that even the "mining of a single military vessel" may be sufficient to activate the inherent right of self-defense.[74] In 2007, the Institut de Droit International proclaimed that "an armed attack triggering the right of self-defence must be of a certain degree of gravity. Acts involving the use of force of lesser intensity may give rise to countermeasures in conformity with international law."[75] Cyber attacks that cause human or property destruction of sufficient gravity may be equated to an armed attack for the purposes of article 51 and activate the individual or collective right of self-defense.[76] What remains unsettled though is whether hostile cyber attacks that do not result in material damage but rather have a disruptive effect on economy or debilitating impact on essential state functions could cross the threshold of an armed attack.[77] Although there is a growing number of scholars and states that are in favor of expanding the concept of an armed attack, the majority of the states and international jurisprudence do not concur to this opinion.[78] A simple example would have to be the 2010 Stuxnet incident: even though it has been found by some to amount to an armed attack, the victim state, Iran, desisted from reaching such conclusions and reportedly used cyber counteroffensive moves against U.S. targets.[79]

Progressively legal scholars and the ICJ have come to accept that the inherent right to self-defense is not limited to a single, direct "armed attack" but also applies to a series of acts—below the threshold of an armed attack—culminating in a single armed attack.[80] This approach may be challenging in the cyber context. It gives rise to a number of questions that will need to be assessed on a case-by-case basis: How can the alleged victim state know if a second cyber attack or a second kinetic attack will follow the first cyber attack? What should the frequency of the cyber operations be before they are aggregated (to constitute a single armed attack)? Finally, international experts correctly observe a "determinative factor is whether the same originator (or originators acting in concert) has carried out smaller scale incidents that are related and that taken together have the requisite scale. If there is convincing evidence that this is the case, . . . there are grounds for treating the incidents as a composite armed attack."[81]

However, if the use of force in questions falls below the "armed attack" threshold, then the state may still bring the matter to the attention of the Security Council or act against the perpetrator state by employing countermeasures.[82] Should the matter fall within the jurisdiction of an international judicial body, the state could also bring action against the perpetrator state (in this scenario, it would be ideal if a new cyber treaty established such a court).

Finally, it should be kept in mind that the essence of the UN Charter, the mechanisms established under it, and even the language of article 51 indicate that states should (ideally) always opt for collective security action and that the collective security mechanism should assume its role at the earliest possible opportunity. This entails that states acting in self-defense will have to report to the Security Council any measures taken, including cyber measures. Article 51 provides that the state will exercise the right of self-defense until the Security Council takes action.

Anticipatory Self-Defense

Throughout the literature there is some support that the right of self-defense does not arise except in the case where an armed attack has occurred. In particular, in 1963 Ian Brownlie noted that "the view that Article 51 does not permit anticipatory action is correct and . . . arguments to the contrary are either unconvincing or based on inconclusive pieces of evidence."[83] Accordingly, article 51 is envisaged to limit self-defensive action to those situations where the victim state is subject to a large-scale use of force, such as the ones that were experienced in 1945, that is, an invasion or a bombardment. In such cases, when the potential victim state would understand that an invasion was planned and was underway, it was expected that the first thing the victim state would do would be to inform the Security Council.[84] The ICJ has also taken a narrow approach regarding the right of self-defense.

A narrow interpretation of article 51 has never gained much support in state practice or in literature.[85] Instead, state practice and a number of the academics accord a more lax interpretation of the right of self-defense. Following the 9/11 attacks and the U.S. military operation in Afghanistan, legal literature has explored other legal bases for the use of force stemming from nonconventional sources, that is, terrorist groups like Al-Qaeda. Indeed, a number of scholars have examined the legality of uses of force in anticipatory or even preemptive self-defense.[86]

To provide some flexibility to article 51 in the light of the contemporary threats, the UN High-Level Panel and the secretary-general have identified the right of anticipatory self-defense as part of the right of self-defense; this could mean that the strict approach to the right of self-defense has seriously started losing support.[87] According to the High-Level Panel Report, "A threatened state" can "take military action as long as the threatened attack is imminent, no other means would deflect it and the action is proportionate."[88] According to the secretary-general's report, "Imminent threats are fully covered by Article 51, which safeguards the inherent right of sovereign States to defend themselves against armed attack. Lawyers have long recognised that this covers an imminent attack as well as one that has already happened."[89]

Indeed, in a more lenient interpretation of articles 2 (4) and 51, the latter permits the right of anticipatory self-defense (but not preemptive or preventive self-defense[90]) because article 51 confirms the natural-law right of each state to defend itself against an existing attack or an imminent threat of attack. The right of anticipatory self-defense expands the meaning and content of the response to an "armed attack." An armed attack can be impending and unavoidable even if it is not materialized and accomplished. In this sense the attack is pictured as a multistep process on a time line from peacetime to conflict. So anticipatory self-defense is concerned with the temporal aspect of the threat; it must be tightly connected in time and space with the awaited use of force.[91] A typical exercise of the right of anticipatory self-defense was the 1967 Six-Day War.

In a post-9/11 world, the dividing line drawn by the jurisprudence of the ICJ between armed attacks and "less grave forms" on the use of force may not be reasonable anymore.[92] From a security and strategy angle, there is every need to allow for a natural evolution of the right of self-defense. Using as a platform the fact that customary international law develops to respond and to adjust to challenging circumstances, it can safely be argued that the concept of armed attack includes the concept of "imminent threat." Furthermore, the target of armed attack is not anymore only the political independence of the sovereign state or a strict conceptualization of the territorial integrity. The legal construct of self-defense now entails an enlarged "self" and a projected reach upon which the sovereign state seeks to protect itself and that corresponds to the challenges that the sovereign state faces in an international system with nonstate actors and statist proxies engaged in cyberwarfare.[93]

The *Tallinn Manual* raises the issue of the applicability of anticipatory self-defense within the cyberwarfare context.[94] According to the *Tallinn Manual*, in the scenario that a state has information of an imminent cyber attack against its critical infrastructure, it would be justified in using force in anticipatory self-defense should no other means be adequate to eliminate the imminent attack. Even though anticipatory self-defense has received support in state practice and *opinio juris*, it is highly unlikely that the international community would approve or condone the use of force against a cyber attack in the absence of (1) a previous conventional attack and (2) clear and un-equivocal evidence of the imminence and scale and effects of such an at-tack.[95] Even if the state claimed that the necessity of anticipatory self-de-fense was indisputable and that the forcible measures taken were proportion-ate, state practice so far has indicated that states that have been subjected to cyber attacks, that is, the United States, China, and Russia, have refrained from claims to use force in such context.

Self-Defense against Nonstate Actors

Prior to the 9/11 attacks, legal scholars were reluctant to accept that the right to self-defense applied to attacks that did not originate from a state;[96] the UN Charter lacked any reference to nonstate actors. The ICJ has also maintained a strict view of article 51 and has accordingly pronounced that self-defense is available only against an armed attack by one state against another state,[97] adding that when an attack is carried from within the territory of the victim state, article 51 is not applicable.[98] However, the customary law of self-defense going back to the *Caroline* case has long established that the authors of armed attacks can be nonstate actors too. Furthermore, state practice and *opinio juris* has now well accepted that armed attacks can be carried out by nonstate actors[99] and has placed terrorist groups and nonstate actors in the jus ad bellum realm.[100] In 2001, both Security Council resolutions 1368 and 1373 recognized Al-Qaeda, a nonstate group with quasi-state functions and an advanced organization, as author of the 9/11 attacks and affirmed the inherent right of self-defense. Should a cyber attack perpetrated by a nonstate actor cross the threshold of an armed attack, the inherent right of self-defense should be applicable even against a nonstate actor.[101] If the armed attack cannot be attributed to a state from where it emanates, the potential of the nonstate actor must not be dismissed. If the state is unable to prevent or terminate the attack or if the state is unaware of the cyber terrorist action, then the act cannot be attributed to the state. To infer the opposite would place a heavy precedent on the rules on attribution, if not challenge the normative settings of the right of self-defense. Hence, it would serve best to acknowledge the right of self-defense against a nonstate actor in the event of a cyber armed attack on the condition that the requirements of necessity, proportionality, and imminence are met.[102]

CONCLUSION

Admittedly, the unique and unprecedented features, actors, and means of cyberspace expose national sovereigns to new challenges. It has already been pointed out that "no explicit state practice has crystallised concerning the exercise of the right of self-defence against cyber armed attacks"; even more, various scholarly comments have been presented in this chapter as to the scope and content of the rules on state responsibility and self-defense.[103] Not all of the issues that have been brought up in this chapter are susceptible to clear legal answers derived from existing precedents; however, it transpires that attribution is central to the legal framework on the use of force as it is formed by the UN Charter and the customary international law framework. Till the dust settles, states and international organizations would have to make case-by-case assessments of the occurring hostile, maybe noninjurious or destructive, cyber operations. Yet, it is reassuring that there is an ongoing dynamic and insightful dialogue between the academic world and policy makers that will contribute to the clarification of the applicability of the existing rules on state attribution and self-defense *de lege lata* or *de lege ferenda* in the cyber attacks' context.

NOTES

1. Peter Margulies, "Sovereignty and Cyber Attacks: Technology's Challenge to the Law of State Responsibility," *Melbourne Journal of International Law* 14, no. 2 (2013): 496–519.

2. Matthew J. Sklerov, "Solving the Dilemma of State Responses to Cyberattacks: A Justification for the Use of Active Defenses against States Who Neglect Their Duty to Prevent," *Military Law Review* 202 (2009): 1–85.

3. Michael Gervais, "Cyber Attacks and the Laws of War," *Emory International Law Review* 26 (2012): 825–90; Heather Harrison Dinniss, *Cyber Warfare and the Laws of War* (New York: Cambridge University Press, 2012); Michael N. Schmitt, "Cyber Operations and the *Jus in Bello*: Key Issues," *Israel Yearbook on Human Rights* 41 (2011): 113–35; Scott J. Shackelford and Richard B. Andres, "State Responsibility for Cyber Attacks: Competing Standards for a Growing Problem," *Georgetown Journal of International Law* 42, no. 4 (2011): 971–1016; Scott J. Shackelford, "From Nuclear War to Net War: Analogizing Cyber Attacks in International Law," *Berkeley Journal of International Law* 27, no. 1 (2009): 192–251; Michael J. Glennon, "The Road Ahead: Gaps, Drips, and Cyber-Conflict," *Israel Yearbook on Human Rights* 43 (2013): 1–22; Joanna Kulesza, "State Responsibility for Cyber Attacks on International Peace and Security," *Polish Yearbook of International Law* 29 (2009): 139–52; Marco Roscini, "World Wider Warfare: Jus Ad Bellum and the Use of Cyber Force," *Max Planck Yearbook of United Nations Law* 14 (2010): 85–130; Williams C. Banks, "The Role of Counterterrorism Law in Shaping Ad Bellum Norms for Cyber Warfare," *Israel Yearbook on Human Rights* 43 (2013): 45–80; Jenny Döge, "Cyber Warfare: Challenges for the Applicability of the Traditional Laws of War Regime," *Archiv des Volkerrechts* 48, no. 4 (2010): 486–501; Robin Geiss, "Cyber Warfare and Non-international Armed Conflicts," *Israel Year-*

book on *Human Rights* 43 (2013): 141–58; Herbert S. Lin, "Offensive Cyber Operations and the Use of Force," *Journal of National Security Law and Policy* 4 (2010): 63–86.

4. For example, ISIS sympathizers or ISIS cyber jihadis have been organizing "hashtag campaigns" to raise the online profile websites as opposed to older tactics such as bombarding Twitter and Facebook with automated messages or disrupting/defacing websites. See Jamie Bartlett, "Why Terrorists and Far-Right Extremists Will Be Early Adopters," *Telegraph*, November 4, 2014, http://www.telegraph.co.uk/; Jamie Bartlett, "The March of the Armchair Jihadis," *Financial Times*, January 13, 2015, http://www.ft.com/.

5. Mary Ellen O'Connell, "Cyber Security without Cyber War," *Journal of Conflict and Security Law* 17, no. 2 (2012): 190–91, 199.

6. Stephen Moore, "Cyber Attacks and the Beginnings of an International Cyber Treaty," *North Carolina Journal of International Law and Commercial Regulation* 39, no. 1 (2014): 228–29; Heather Harrison Dinniss, *Cyber Warfare and the Laws of War* (New York: Cambridge University Press, 2012), 38.

7. UN Doc A/66/152, July 15, 2001, 18.

8. UN Doc A/68/98, July 24, 2013, 8.

9. UN Doc A/68/98, July 24, 2013, 2, 6–7.

10. UN International Law Commission, Report of the International Law Commission, Draft Articles of State Responsibility, UN GAOR, 53rd Sess Supp. No. 10, UN Doc. A/56/10 (2001), http://www.un.org/law/ilc/ (hereafter ILC Articles). See James Crawford, *State Responsibility: The General Part* (Cambridge: Cambridge University Press, 2013). Despite the Draft Articles reflecting the customary rules, states have not expressed their support for the convening of a diplomatic conference of plenipotentiaries to adopt a convention on the responsibility of states for internationally wrongful acts. See Laurence T. Pacht, "The Case for a Convention on State Responsibility," *Nordic Journal of International Law* 83, no. 4 (2014): 439–75.

11. UN Doc A/68/98, July 24, 2013, 8; Margulies, "Sovereignty," 505.

12. David Midson, "Geography, Territory and Sovereignty in Cyber Warfare," in *New Technologies and the Law of Armed Conflict*, ed. Hitoshi Nasu and Robert McLaughlin, 75–94 (The Hague, Netherlands: TMC ASSER, 2014), 75, 76.

13. On the subject, see for Wolff Heintschel von Heinegg, "Legal Implications of Territorial Sovereignty in Cyberspace," in *2012 4th International Conference on Cyber Conflict*, ed. Christian Czosseck, Rain Ottis, and Katharina Ziolkowski (Tallinn, Estonia: NATO CCD COE Publications, 2012), https://ccdcoe.org/, 11–12; Yoram Dinstein, "Sovereignty, the Security Council and the Use of Force," in *Redefining Sovereignty: The Use of Force after Cold War*, ed. Michael Bothe (Ardsley, NY: Transnational, 2005), 111.

14. Barack Obama, "Remarks by the President in Year-End Conference," December 19, 2014, http://www.whitehouse.gov/.

15. On the power of social media and attracting potential followers and "lone wolves" to commit individual acts of jihad, see Gabriel Weimann, "Lone Wolves in Cyberspace," *Journal of Terrorism Research* 3, no. 2 (2012), http://ojs.st-andrews.ac.uk/.

16. See, for example, Bartlett, "March of the Armchair Jihadis," commenting on the changing nature of militants and the many uses of cyberspace today: "Like everyone else, the militants have moved online. You no longer need to fly halfway across the world to join your chosen extremist cause. You do not even need to leave the house. You can join the jihadis from behind your screen, contributing to the effort with freelance propaganda or cyber attacks. [On January 13, 2015,] someone, somewhere, did just that, hacking into the U.S. Central Command Twitter and YouTube accounts, posting propaganda for Islamic State of Iraq and the Levant (Isis), and replacing the logo with an image of an Islamist fighter."

17. Jerome Bjelopera, "American Jihadist Terrorism: Combatting a Complex Threat," in *The Changing Nature of War*, ed. Kristen E. Boon, Aziz Huq, and Douglas C. Lovelace (Oxford: Oxford University Press, 2012), 112 et seq.

18. Pierluigi Paganini, "ISIS Is Ramping Up Efforts to Mount a Massive Cyber Attack," *Security Affairs* (blog), September 14, 2014, http://securityaffairs.co/.

19. In the immediate aftermath of the Charlie Hebdo attacks, an active cyber group, known as "AnonGhost" started defacing French websites. The anonymous group launched a cyber counterterrorist operation as part of its efforts to protect freedom of speech, named "OpCharlie-

Hebdo," but in the meantime other pro-Islamic and religious-motivated hactivist groups have joined forces with AnonGhost. See Lorenzo Franceschi-Bicchierai, "Islamist Hackers Deface French Sites in Response to 'Operation Charlie Hebdo,'" Mashable, January 13, 2015, http://mashable.com/. See also Harriet Line, "Charlie Hebdo Attack: Anonymous Claims First Victory in 'War' on Jihadi Websites," *Telegraph*, January 14, 2015, http://www.telegraph.co.uk/.

20. Such a case has been the cyber attack "Flame," which was believed to have been launched in 2010 but was only revealed in 2012. See Dave Lee, "Flame: Massive Cyber-Attack Discovered," *BBC News*, May 28, 2012, http://www.bbc.com/.

21. Midson, "Geography, Territory," 77–78.

22. Scott J. Shackleford, "State Responsibility for Cyber Attacks: Competing Standards for a Growing Problem," in *Conference on Cyber Conflict Proceedings 2010*, ed. Christian Czosseck and Karlin Podins, 197–208 (Tallinn, Estonia: CCD COE Publications, 2010), https://ccdcoe.org/.

23. The present analysis makes reference to the *Tallinn Manual on the International Law Applicable to Cyberwarfare* (ed. Michael Schmitt [Cambridge: Cambridge University Press, 2013]) prepared by an international group of experts and published by the NATO Cooperative Cyber Defence Centre of Excellence (NATO CCD COE), based in Tallinn, Estonia. Even though the document is nonbinding, it is this author's view that it represents an academic effort to analyze whether the existing law applies to cyber issues at all and, if so, how. The *Tallinn Manual* is available at https://ccdcoe.org/.

24. See ICJ Accordance with International Law of the Unilateral Declaration of Independence in Respect of Kosovo (Request for Advisory Opinion), July 22, 2010, General List No. 141, para. 56: "It is entirely possible for a particular act . . . not to be in violation of international law without necessarily constituting the exercise of a right conferred by it."

25. ICJ Case on Military and Paramilitary Activities in and against Nicaragua (Nicaragua v. US), jurisdiction, judgment, November 26, 1984, ICJ Reports (1984), para. 205: "The principle [of nonintervention] forbids all States or groups of States to intervene directly or indirectly in the internal or external affairs of other States." See also UN Declaration on Principles of International Law concerning Friendly Relations and Cooperation among States in Accordance with the Charter of the United Nations, GA Res 2625, December 17, 1970.

26. It should be noted that this is a nonexhaustive list of what may amount to an international wrongful act. On cyberwarfare and humanitarian law, see Kalliopi Chainoglou, "An Assessment of Cyberwarfare Issues in Light of International Humanitarian Law," in *The Liberal Way of War: Legal Perspectives*, ed. Robert P. Barnidge Jr. (Farnham, UK: Ashgate, 2013), 189.

27. See UN Materials on the Responsibility of States for International Wrongful Acts, UN Legislative Series (New York: UN, 2012), ST/LEG/SER B/25, pp. 27–28, paras. 3–5, http://legal.un.org/.

28. See Schmitt, *Tallinn Manual*, rule 6, para. 6.

29. Marco Roscini, *Cyber Operations and the Use of Force in International Law* (Oxford: Oxford University Press, 2014), 35–36. He mentions therein the Cyber Unit of the Estonian Defence League (http://www.kaitseliit.ee/en/cyber-unit). Furthermore, the *Tallinn Manual*, rule 6, para. 8, cites as examples "a private corporation that has been granted the authority by the government to conduct offensive computer network operations against another State, as well as a private entity empowered to engage in cyber intelligence gathering."

30. See *Nicaragua*, paras. 110, 193; ICJ Application of the Convention on the Prevention and Punishment of the Crime of Genocide (Bosnia and Herzegovina v. Serbia and Montenegro), merits, judgment, February 26, 2007, ICJ Reports (2007) (hereafter Genocide), paras. 392–93.

31. See "Ukrainian Volunteers Join Cyberspace War in Bid to Stop Insurgency Funding," *Ukraine Today*, November 20, 2014, http://uatoday.tv/. The head of Ukraine's security service, Valentyn Nalyvaichenko, denied any control exercised from Ukrainian authorities but still praised the impromptu actions of the cyber volunteers: "People are writing, sending very important information under various names and nicknames. For those groups of young people that help us in blocking the bank accounts of the separatists, we are truly thankful!" See also Schmitt, *Tallinn Manual*, rule 6, para. 11.

32. UN Doc A/56/10, 2001, chap. 4, commentary to article 8 (3). See also Michael Schmitt, "'Below the Threshold' Cyber Operations: The Countermeasures Response Option and International Law," *Virginia Journal of International Law* 54, no. 3 (2014): 711 et seq.

33. *Nicaragua*, para. 115.

34. ICJ Armed Activities on the Territory of the Congo (DRV v. Uganda), judgment, December 19, 2005, ICJ Reports (2005) (hereafter Armed Activities), 226.

35. Genocide, para. 400. See commentary on article 8 of the ILC Articles, 45, 104–5.

36. ICTY, Prosecutor v. Tadic, IT-94-1-A, Appeals Chamber judgment, July 15, 1999, para. 131: "A state wields overall control over the group, not only by equipping and financing the group, but also by coordinating or helping in the general planning of its military activity."

37. The overall control "stretches too far, almost to a breaking point, the connection which must exist between the conduct of a state's organs and its international responsibility." Genocide, para. 406.

38. Genocide, para. 392. For a critical analysis of this case, see Jorn Griebel and Milan Plucken, "New Developments Regarding the Rules of Attribution? The International Court of Justice's Decision in Bosnia v. Serbia," *Leiden Journal of International Law* 21, no. 3 (2008): 601, 612 et seq.

39. Nikolaos K. Tsagourias, "The Tallinn Manual on the International Law Applicable to Cyber Warfare: A Commentary on Chapter II—The Use of Force," *Yearbook of International Humanitarian Law* 15 (2012): 32–33. Hence, Tsagourias suggests that where "a state tolerates groups that go on to launch cyber attacks on another state, or is unwilling to suppress their activities, the attacks will be attributed to that state which will then become the target of self-defence action."

40. ICJ Tehran Hostages United States Diplomatic and Consular Staff in Tehran (US v. Iran), judgment, May 24, 1980, ICJ Reports (1980) 3, paras. 31–34.

41. Michael Stohl and George A. Lopez, *The State as Terrorist: The Dynamics of Governmental Violence and Repression* (Westport, CT: Greenwood, 1984), 6; Schmitt, *Tallinn Manual*, rule 6, para. 14.

42. *Nicaragua*, 38–39.

43. Scott J. Shackelford, *Managing Cyber Attacks in International Law, Business, and Relations: In Search of Cyber Peace* (New York: Cambridge University Press, 2014), 292.

44. Tor is software that enables online anonymity and protects users by routing traffic through a labyrinth of encrypted connections.

45. See Michael J. Schmitt, "Normative Voids and Asymmetry in Cyberspace," Just Security, December 29, 2014, http://justsecurity.org/. Schmitt has been analyzing in this context the 2014 allegedly North Korean cyber operation against Sony that resulted in a temporarily canceled film release and leaking of personal information. See Lori Grisham, "Timeline: North Korea and the Sony Pictures Hack," *USA Today*, January 5, 2015, http://www.usatoday.com/.

46. See articles 22, 49–54, of the ILC Articles. See also the discussion in Schmitt, *Tallinn Manual*, rule 9, paras. 1–13.

47. See ILC Draft Articles on Responsibility of States for Internationally Wrongful Acts, with Commentaries (2001), http://legal.un.org/, note 33.

48. ICJ Corfu Channel Case (merits), [1949] ICJ Reports 4, 22. See also ICJ Island of Palmas Case 2 R.I.A.A. (1928), 829, 839. See, generally, Malgosia Fitzmaurice, "The Corfu Channel Case and the Development of International Law," in *Liber Amicorum Judge Shigeru Oda*, ed. Nisuke Ado, Edward McWhinney, and Rudiger Wolfrum (The Hague, Netherlands: Kluwer Law International, 2002).

49. Robert Ago, "Fourth Report on State Responsibility," *International Law Commission Yearbook* 2 (1972): 71, 120 et seq.

50. "Every State has a duty to refrain from organizing, instigating, assisting, or participating in . . . terrorist acts in another State or acquiescing in organized activities within its territory directed towards the commission of such acts, when the acts referred to in the present paragraph involve a threat or use of force." UN GA Resolution 2625, UN GAOR, 25th Sess. Supp. No. 18, at 339, UN Doc. A/8018 (1970).

51. Martin Dixon, *Text on International Law* (London: Blackstone, 2000), 239.

52. Yoram Dinstein, *War, Aggression and Self-Defense* (Cambridge: Cambridge University Press, 2001), 214; Ian Brownlie, "International Law and the Activities of Armed Bands," *International and Comparative Law Quarterly* 7, no. 4 (1958): 734; J. E. S. Fawcett, "Intervention in International Law: A Study of Some Recent Cases," *Recueil des cours* 103 (1961): 363.

53. By reference to the obligation to prevent international terrorism in this context, see the discussion by Kimberley Trapp, *State Responsibility for International Terrorism: Problems and Prospects* (Oxford: Oxford University Press, 2011), 127 et seq. On the exercise of due diligence in the cyber context, see also UN GA Resolution 55/63, December 4, 2000, para. 1; "International Strategy for Cyberspace: Prosperity, Security, and Openness in a Networked World," White House, May 2011, http://www.whitehouse.gov/; U.S. Department of Defense, "Cyberspace Policy Report," 2011, http://www.defense.gov/, p. 8, para. 10; Council of Europe, International and Multi-stakeholder Co-operation on Cross-border Internet: Interim Report of the Ad-hoc Advisory Group on Cross-border Internet to the Steering Committee on the Media and New Communication Services (2010), para. 73.

54. PCIJ S.S. *Lotus* (Fr. v. Turk.) 1927 P.C.I.J. (ser. A) No. 10, at 4, 88 (Moore, J dissenting).

55. Vincent-Joël Proulx, "Babysitting Terrorists: Should States Be Strictly Liable for Failing to Prevent Transborder Attacks?" in *International Law: Contemporary Issues and Future Developments*, ed. Sanford Silverburg, 406–47 (Boulder, CO: Westview, 2011).

56. Hamadoun I. Touré, "The International Response to Cyberwar," in *The Quest for Cyber Peace*, by Hamadoun I. Touré and the Permanent Monitoring Panel on Information Security World Federation of Scientists, 86–103 (Geneva: International Telecommunication Union, 2011), 103, http://www.itu.int/.

57. See Christopher E. Lentz, "A State's Duty to Prevent and Respond to Cyberterrorist Acts," *Chicago Journal of International Law* 10, no. 2 (2010): 799–824; David Graham, "Cyber Threats and the Law of War," *Journal of National Security and Law* 4 (2010): 93 et seq.; Jeffrey Carr, *Inside Cyber Warfare—Mapping Cyber Underworld* (Sebastopol, CA: O'Reilly, 2012), 62 et seq.; Michael Gervais, "Cyber Attacks and the Laws of War," *Journal of Law and Cyberwarfare* 1, no. 1 (2012): 19 et seq.; and Jackson Maogoto, *Technology and the Law on the Use of Force* (New York: Routledge, 2015), 25 et seq. The duty to prevent cyber attack emanates from a number of UN resolutions that confirm this duty in a number of UN and regional conventions, for example, Council of Europe, Convention on Cybercrime (2001), 41 I.L.M. 41: 282: "The latter impose the obligation on state parties to criminalise cross-border hostile cyber activities." See also the Council of Europe, International and Multi-stakeholder, 10, 2919, para. 73.

58. See Schmitt, *Tallinn Manual*, rule 1, paras. 3, 9, 10.

59. Ibid., rules 5, 8. See also Draft Convention on International Information Security (2011), article 12, http://cryptome.org/.

60. See Schmitt, *Tallinn Manual*, rules 5, 8.

61. See also the discussion in the *Tallinn Manual*, rule 8, paras. 1–3.

62. See Draft Convention on International Information Security (2011); and Keir Giles, "Russia's Public Stance on Cyber Information Warfare," in *2012 4th International Conference on Cyber Conflict*, ed. Christian Czosseck, Rain Ottis, and Katharina Ziolkowski (Tallinn, Estonia: NATO CCD COE Publications, 2012), https://ccdcoe.org/.

63. On the subject, see Michael N. Schmitt, "The Use of Cyber Force and International Law," in *The Oxford Handbook of the Use of Force in International Law*, ed. Marc Weller (Oxford: Oxford University Press, 2015), 1110; Tsagourias, "Tallinn Manual," 19 et seq.; Wolff Heintschel von Heinegg, "The Tallinn Manual and International Cyber Security Law," *Yearbook of International Humanitarian Law* 3 (2012): 15–18; Matthew C. Waxman, "Cyber-Attacks and the Use of Force: Back to the Future of Article 2(4)," *Yale Journal of International Law* 36, no. 2 (2011): 421–59; Marco Benatar, "The Use of Cyber Force: Need for Legal Justification," *Gottingen Journal of International Law* 1, no. 3 (2009): 375–96.

64. Roscini, *Cyber Operations*, 88 et seq.

65. Rosalyn Higgins, *Problems and Processes: International Law and How We Use It* (Oxford: Oxford University Press, 1994), 248.

66. See Derek William Bowett, "The Use of Force for the Protection of Nationals Abroad," in *The Current Legal Regulation of Use of Force*, ed. Antonio Cassese (Dordrecht, Netherlands: Martinus Nijhoff, 1986), 41: "The two concepts serve different purposes and self-defence may well exist against delicts which cannot be characterised as aggression. In considering whether a situation affords a state the right of self-defence the only relevant concept is that of self-defence; the concept of aggression as it has been elaborated during the course of the last forty years has an entirely different purpose."

67. UN Definition of Aggression Resolution, Annex, GA Res. 3314 (XXIX) UN GAOR, 6th Comm 29th Sess. Supp. No. 31 at 142, UN Doc. A/9631 (1974). See, for example, articles 3 (b) (c) (f) and 3 (g) of resolution 3314.

68. Jean Combacau, "The Exception of Self-Defence in UN Practice," in *The Current Legal Regulation of Use of Force*, ed. Antonio Cassese (Dordrecht, Netherlands: Martinus Nijhoff, 1986), 22; Dino Kritsiotis, "Topographies of Force," in *International Law and Armed Conflict: Exploring the Faultlines*, ed. Michael Schmitt and Jelena Pejic (Leiden, Netherlands: Martinus Nijhoff, 2007), 29, 52 et seq.

69. Yoram Dinstein, "Cyber War and International Law: Concluding Remarks at the 2012 Naval War College International Law Conference," *International Law Studies* 89 (2013): 276, 279.

70. See also Schmitt, *Tallinn Manual*, rule 13, para. 2.

71. *Nicaragua*, 110.

72. See *Nicaragua*, 110; Case Concerning Oil Platforms (Iran v. US), merits, judgment, November 6, 2003, ICJ Reports (2003) (hereafter Oil Platforms), 187; Eritrea-Ethiopia Claims Commission, Partial Award: Jus Ad Bellum, Ethiopia's claims nos. 1–8, vol. XXVI, 433: "These relatively minor incidents were not of a magnitude to constitute an armed attack by either State against the other within the meaning of Article 51 of the UN Charter."

73. See *Nicaragua*, 103. Similarly, Albrecht Randelzhofer notes that "armed attacks" must be "military actions" that are on a certain scale and have a major effect (in Bruno Simma et al., *The Charter of the United Nations: A Commentary* [Oxford: Oxford University Press, 2002], 796). But see the Partial Award of the Eritrea-Ethiopia Commission where it was held that "localized border encounters between small infantry units, even those involving loss of life, do not constitute an armed attack for the purposes of the Charter." Eritrea-Ethiopia Claims Commission, Partial Award, 465.

74. Oil Platforms, para. 72.

75. M. Emmanuel Roucounas, "Tenth Commission: Present Problems of the Use of Armed Force in International Law; A. Self-Defence," Institut de Droit International, *AIDI* 72 (2007), article 5, 233, http://www.idi-iil.org/.

76. Yoram Dinstein, "Computer Network Attacks and Self-Defence," *International Law Studies* 76 (2002): 105; Nikolaos K. Tsagourias, "Cyber Attacks, Self-Defence and the Problem of Attribution," *Journal of Conflict and Security Law* 17, no. 2 (2012): 231; Schmitt, *Tallinn Manual*, rule 13; Draft Convention on International Information Security, art. 5 (11).

77. See, for example, U.S. Department of Defence, "Cyberspace Policy Report," 4; Tsagourias, "Tallinn Manual," 31.

78. Schmitt and other experts have suggested examining whether a hostile cyber operation reaches the threshold of an armed attack by considering factors such as severity, immediacy of effect, invasiveness, military character, and so forth. In the case of the alleged North Korean attack against Sony in 2014, this cyber operation did not qualify as an armed attack. See Michael J. Schmitt, "International Law and Cyber Attacks: Sony v. North Korea," Just Security, December 17, 2014, http://justsecurity.org/; Schmitt, *Tallinn Manual*, rule 13, paras. 5–7; Roscini, *Cyber Operations*, 74–76.

79. Schmitt, *Tallinn Manual*, rule 13, para. 13; Andrea Shalal-Esa, "Iran Strengthened Cyber Capabilities after Stuxnet," *Reuters*, January 17, 2013, http://www.reuters.com/.

80. See Schmitt, *Tallinn Manual*, rule 13, para. 8; Dinstein, *War, Aggression*, paras. 547–49; Christopher Greenwood, "Self-Defence," in *Max Planck Encyclopedia of Public International Law*, April 2012, para. 13, http://opil.ouplaw.com/; Derek William Bowett, *Self-Defence in International Law* (New York: Praeger, 1958), 184–93; Myers S. McDougal and Florentino P. Feliciano, *Law and Minimum World Public Order: The Legal Regulation and*

International Coercion (New Haven, CT: Yale University Press, 1961), 233–41; Julius Stone, *Aggression and World Order* (Berkeley: University of California Press, 1958), 92–101; and John Norton Moore, "The Secret War in Central America and the Future of World Order," *American Journal of International Law* 80, no. 1 (1986): 82–83. See also ICJ concurring to this view in the judgments of the Oil Platforms (191–92, para. 64 et seq.) and Armed Activities (174, paras. 146–47) cases, and *Nicaragua*, 120.

81. Schmitt, *Tallinn Manual*, rule 13, para. 8.

82. Schmitt, "Below the Threshold," 698.

83. Ian Brownlie, *International Law and the Use of Force by States* (Oxford, UK: Clarendon, 1963), 278.

84. Phillip Jessup, *A Modern Law of Nations* (Hamden, CT: Archon, 1968), 166; Dinstein, *War, Aggression*, 167.

85. See discussion regarding anticipatory and preemptive self-defense as well as reference to state practice in Kalliopi Chainoglou, *Reconceptualising the Law of Self-Defence* (Brussels: Bruyant, 2008), chap. 2.

86. William Michael Reisman and Andrea Armstrong, "Claims to Pre-emptive Uses of Force: Some Trends and Projections and Their Implication for World Order," in *International Law and Armed Conflict: Exploring the Faultlines*, ed. Michael Schmitt and Jelena Pejic, 79–112 (Leiden, Netherlands: Martinus Nijhoff, 2007); T. Gill, "The Temporal Dimension of Self-Defence: Anticipation, Pre-emption, Prevention and Immediacy," in *International Law and Armed Conflict: Exploring the Faultlines*, ed. Michael Schmitt and Jelena Pejic, 113–55 (Leiden, Netherlands: Martinus Nijhoff, 2007).

87. But for criticisms, see William Michael Reisman, "Expanding the UN Security Council: Much Ado," University of Pittsburgh, August 2005, http://jurist.law.pitt.edu/, where he comments, "After stating that there was no need to amend the Charter, the High Level Panel then reinterpreted it to find, *mirabile dictu*, that 'armed attack' included 'imminent attack.'" See also UN Human Rights Sub-Commission (2005) Joint Written Statement by CETIM and AAJ, Comment on the Secretary-General's Report on the Reform of the UN, E/CN.4/Sub.2/2005/NGO/7, http://www.cetim.ch/.

88. UN Secretary General's High-Level Panel on Threats, Challenges, and Change, A More Secure World: Our Shared Responsibility, UN Doc. A/59/565, December 2004, 63, para. 188, http://www.un.org/.

89. UN Secretary General's Report, In Larger Freedom: Towards Development, Security and Human Rights for All (2005) A/59/2005, para. 124, http://www.un.org/.

90. Chainoglou, *Reconceptualising*, chap. 6.

91. See Stone, *Aggression and World Order*, 99, where he observed, "Suppose military intelligence at the Pentagon received indisputable evidence that a hostile State was poised to launch intercontinental ballistic missiles, at a fixed zero hour only 24 hours ahead against New York, Boston and Washington, would it be an aggressor under the Charter if it refused to wait until those cities had received the missiles before it reacted by the use of force?"

92. See Rein Müllerson, "*Jus Ad Bellum* and International Terrorism," *Israel Yearbook of Human Rights* 32 (2002): 42; Higgins, *Problems and Process*, 250–55.

93. Dino Kritsiotis, "The Legality of the 1993 US Missile Strike on Iraq and the Right of Self-Defence in International Law," *International and Comparative Law Quarterly* 45, no. 1 (1996): 173–74.

94. Schmitt, *Tallinn Manual*, rule 15.

95. Roscini, *Cyber Operations*, 79.

96. Gerald Fitzmaurice, "The Definition of Aggression," *International and Comparative Law Quarterly* 1 (1952): 142–43.

97. ICJ Legal Consequences of the Construction of a Wall in the Occupied Palestinian Territory, Advisory Opinion, July 9, 2004, ICJ Reports (2005) (hereafter Wall Advisory Opinion), para. 139.

98. Sean D. Murphy, "Self-Defense and the Israeli *Wall Advisory Opinion*: An *Ipse Dixit* from the ICJ?" *American Journal of International Law* 99, no. 1 (2005): 62, 66 et seq.

99. See Wall Advisory Opinion, Judge Higgins Separate Opinion: "There is nothing in the text of Article 51 that thus stipulates that self-defence is available only when an armed attack is

made by a state" (215). See also Separate Opinion of Judge Kooijmans and the Declaration of Judge Buergenthal.

100. See UN High-Level Panel, More Secure World, para. 159, observing therein that "the norms governing the use of force by non-State actors have not kept pace with those pertaining to States."

101. Tsagourias, "Tallinn Manual," 32, correctly points out that "the question that remains is whether the non-state actor should have a degree of organization in order to be the author of the attack or whether even a single individual can be considered the author of the attack. Because neither the potential of non-state actors nor the level of technological development can be predicted, a case-by-case assessment may be more appropriate." See also Schmitt, *Tallinn Manual*, rule 13, paras. 16–17.

102. On the states' positions regarding cyber doctrines, see Kalliopi Chainoglou, "An Assessment of Jus in Bello Issues Concerning Computer Network Attacks: A Threat Reflected in National Security Agendas," *Romanian Journal of International Law* 12 (2010): 25–63; Roscini, *Cyber Operations*, 88 et seq.

103. Dinstein, "Cyber War," 280.

Bibliography

MONOGRAPHS AND EDITED VOLUMES

Abbate, Janet. (1999). *Inventing the Internet*. Cambridge, MA: MIT Press.

Akhgar, Babak, Staniforth, Andrew, and Bosco, Francesca. (2014). *Cyber Crime and Cyber Terrorism Investigator's Handbook*. Waltham, MA: Syngress.

Angillotti, D. (1955). *Corso di Diritto Internationale I*. Padua, Italy: CEDAM.

Arquilla, John, Ronfeldt, David, and Zanini, Michele. (1999). "Networks, Netwar, and Information-Age Terrorism." In *Countering the New Terrorism*, by Ian O. Lesser et al., 39–84. Santa Monica, CA: Rand, 1999.

Benedek, Wolfgang. (2008). "Internet Governance and Human Rights." In *Internet Governance and the Information Society: Global Perspectives and European Dimensions*, edited by Wolfgang Benedek, Veronika Bauer, and Matthias C. Kettemann. Utrecht, Netherlands: Eleven International.

Benedek, Wolfgang, and Kettemann, Matthias C. (2014). *Freedom of Expression and the Internet*. Strasbourg, France: Council of Europe.

Benkler, Yochai. (2006). *The Wealth of Networks: How Social Production Transforms Markets and Freedom*. New Haven, CT: Yale University Press.

Berkowitz, B. (2003). *The New Face of War: How War Will Be Fought in the 21st Century*. New York: Free Press.

Bjelopera, Jerome. (2012). "American Jihadist Terrorism: Combatting a Complex Threat." In *The Changing Nature of War*, edited by Kristen E. Boon, Aziz Huq, and Douglas C. Lovelace. Oxford: Oxford University Press.

Boås, Morten, and McNeill, D., eds. (2004). *Global Institutions and Development: Framing the World?* New York: Routledge.

Bobbitt, P. (2002). *The Shield of Achilles: War, Peace and the Course of History*. London: Penguin.

———. (2009). *Terror and Consent: The Wars of the Twenty First Century*. London: Penguin.

Bobbitt, Philip. (1982). *Constitutional Fate: Theory of the Constitution*. New York: Oxford University Press.

Boer-Buquicchio, Maud de. (2011). Foreword. In *Media Matters in the Cultural Contradictions of the "Information Society": Towards a Human-Rights-Based Governance*, by Divina Frau-Meigs. Strasbourg, France: Council of Europe Publishing.

Börzel, Tanja A., and Risse, Thomas. (2007). "Public-Private Partnerships: Effective and Legitimate Tools of International Governance?" In *Complex Sovereignty: On the Reconstitu-*

tion of Political Authority in the 21st Century, edited by Edgar Grande and Louis W. Pauly. Toronto: University of Toronto Press.

Bossuyt, Marc J. (1987). *Guide to the "travaux Préparatoires" of the International Covenant on Civil and Political Rights*. Boston: Martinus Nijhoff.

Bowett, Derek William. (1958). *Self-Defence in International Law*. New York: Praeger.

———. (1986). "The Use of Force for the Protection of Nationals Abroad." In *The Current Legal Regulation of Use of Force*, edited by Antonio Cassese. Dordrecht, Netherlands: Martinus Nijhoff.

Brownlie, I. (1983). *System of the Law of Nations: State Responsibility (Part I)*. Oxford, UK: Clarendon.

———. (1998a). *Principles of Public International Law*. Oxford, UK: Clarendon.

———. (1998b). *The Rule of Law in International Affairs: International Law at the Fifteenth Anniversary of the UN*. London: Martinus Nijhoff.

Brownlie, Ian. (1963). *International Law and the Use of Force by States*. Oxford, UK: Clarendon.

Brunton, F. (2013). *Spam: A Shadow History of the Internet*. Cambridge, MA: MIT Press.

Callon, M., Lascoumes, P., and Barthe, Y. (2001). *Agir dans un monde incertain. Essai sur la démocratie technique*. Paris: Seuil.

Caron, D. D. (1998). "The Basics of Responsibility: Attribution and Other Trans-Substance Rules." In *The Iran-United States Claims Tribunal: Its Contribution to the Law of State Responsibility*, edited by R. Lillich and D. Magraw. Irvington on Hudson, NY: Transnational.

Carr, Jeffrey. (2012). *Inside Cyber Warfare—Mapping Cyber Underworld*. Sebastopol, CA: O'Reilly.

Chainoglou, Kalliopi. (2008). *Reconceptualising the Law of Self-Defence*. Brussels: Bruyant.

———. (2013). "An Assessment of Cyberwarfare Issues in Light of International Humanitarian Law." In *The Liberal Way of War: Legal Perspectives*, edited by Robert P. Barnidge Jr. Farnham, UK: Ashgate.

Clapham, Andrew. 2007. *Human Rights: A Very Short Introduction*. Oxford: Oxford University Press.

Combacau, Jean. (1986). "The Exception of Self-Defence in UN Practice." In *The Current Legal Regulation of Use of Force*, edited by Antonio Cassese. Dordrecht, Netherlands: Martinus Nijhoff.

Conforti, B. (1995). *Diritto Internazionale*. Milan: Editiorale Scientifica.

Crawford, J. (2002). *The International Law Commission's Articles on State Responsibility*. Cambridge: Cambridge University Press.

Crawford, James. (2010). "The System of International Responsibility." in *The Law of International Responsibility*, edited by James Crawford, Alain Pellet, Simon Olleson, and Kate Parlett. Oxford: Oxford University Press.

———. (2013). *State Responsibility: The General Part*. Cambridge: Cambridge University Press.

Curien, N., and Maxwell, W. (2011). *La neutralité d'Internet*. Paris: La Découverte.

Dany, Charlotte. (2012). *Global Governance and NGO Participation Shaping the Information Society in the United Nations*. Hoboken, NJ: Taylor and Francis.

de Arechaga, E. J. (1968). "International Responsibility." In *Manual of Public International Law*. London: Macmillan.

Demchak, Chris. (2012). "Resilience, Disruption, and a 'Cyber Westphalia': Options for National Security in a Cybered Conflict World." In *Securing Cyberspace: A New Domain for National Security*, edited by Nicholas Burns and Jonathan Price. Washington, DC: Aspen Institute.

DeNardis, L. (2009). *Protocol Politics: The Globalization of Internet Governance*. Cambridge, MA: MIT Press.

Dinniss, Heather Harrison. (2012). *Cyber Warfare and the Laws of War*. New York: Cambridge University Press.

Dinstein, Yoram. (2005). "Sovereignty, the Security Council and the Use of Force." In *Redefining Sovereignty: The Use of Force after Cold War*, edited by Michael Bothe. Ardsley, NY: Transnational.

———. (2001). *War, Aggression and Self-Defense*. Cambridge: Cambridge University Press.

Dixon, Martin. (2000). *Text on International Law*. London: Blackstone.

Dodier, N. (1995). *Les Hommes et les Machines. La conscience collective dans les sociétés technicisées*. Paris: Métailié.

Dupuy, P. M. (1998). *Droit International Public*. Paris: Precis Dalloz.

Egyedi, T. M., and Mehos, D. C., eds. (2012). *Inverse Infrastructures: Disrupting Networks from Below*. Cheltenham, UK: Edward Elgar.

Elkin-Koren, N., and Salzberger, E. M. (2004). *Law, Economics and Cyberspace*. Cheltenham, UK: Edward Elgar.

Evans G., Sahnoun, Mohamed, and International Commission on Intervention and State Sovereignty. (2001). *The Responsibility to Protect*. Ottawa: International Development Research Centre. http://www.iciss.ca/.

Farchy, J. (2003). *Internet et le droit d'auteur: la culture Napster*. Paris: CNRS Editions.

Fitzmaurice, Malgosia. (2002). "The Corfu Channel Case and the Development of International Law." In *Liber Amicorum Judge Shigeru Oda*, edited by Nisuke Ado, Edward McWhinney, and Rudiger Wolfrum. The Hague, Netherlands: Kluwer Law International.

Flichy, P. (2001). *L'imaginaire d'internet*. Paris: La Découverte.

Flyverbom, Mikkel. (2011). *The Power of Networks: Organizing the Global Politics of the Internet*. Cheltenham, UK: Edward Elgar.

Franklin, Marianne. (2004). *Postcolonial Politics, the Internet, and Everyday Life: Pacific Traversals Online*. New York: Routledge.

———. (2005). *Internet and Postcolonial Politics of Representation*. London: Routledge.

———. (2013). *Digital Dilemmas: Power, Resistance, and the Internet*. Oxford: Oxford University Press.

Frau-Meigs, Divina, Nicey, Jérémie, Palmer, Michael, Pohle, Julia, and Tupper, Patricio, eds. (2012). *From NWICO to WSIS: 30 Years of Communication Geopolitics; Actors and Flows, Structures and Divides*. Bristol, UK: Intellect.

Fücks, Ralf, and Drossou, Olga. (2005). Preface. In *Visions in Process: World Summit on the Information Society, Geneva 2003—Tunis 2005*, edited by the Heinrich Böll Foundation. Berlin: Heinrich Böll Stiftung. http://worldsummit2003.de/.

Gerbner, George, Mowlana, Hamid, and Nordenstreng, Kaarle. (1993). *The Global Media Debate: Its Rise, Fall, and Renewal*. Norwood, NJ: Ablex.

Giblin, Rebecca. (2014). "Beyond Graduated Response." In *The Evolution and Equilibrium of Copyright in the Digital Age*, edited by Susy Frankel and Daniel J. Gervais. Cambridge: Cambridge University Press, 2014.

Giles, Keir. (2012). "Russia's Public Stance on Cyber Information Warfare." In *2012 4th International Conference on Cyber Conflict*, edited by Christian Czosseck, Rain Ottis, and Katharina Ziolkowski. Tallinn, Estonia: NATO CCD COE Publications. https://ccdcoe.org/.

Gill, T. (2007). "The Temporal Dimension of Self-Defence: Anticipation, Pre-emption, Prevention and Immediacy." In *International Law and Armed Conflict: Exploring the Faultlines*, edited by Michael Schmitt and Jelena Pejic, 113–55. Leiden, Netherlands: Martinus Nijhoff.

Goldsmith, Jack L., and Wu, Tim. (2006). *Who Controls the Internet? Illusions of a Borderless World*. New York: Oxford University Press.

Grote, George. (2004). *History of Greece*. Boston: Elibron Classics.

Grotius, Hugo. (1916). *The Freedom of the Seas; or, The Right Which Belongs to the Dutch to Take Part in the East Indian Trade*. Edited by James Brown Scott. New York: Oxford University Press.

———. (2007). *The Rights of War and Peace, including the Law of Nature and of Nations*. New York: Cosimo.

Guilhot, Nicolas. (2005). *The Democracy Makers: Human Rights and the Politics of Global Order*. New York: Columbia University Press.

Gurumurthy, Anita, and Singh, Parminder Jeet. (2012). "Reclaiming Development in the Information Society." In *Search of Economic Alternatives for Gender and Social Justice: Voices from India*, edited by C. Wichterich. Bangalore, India: WIDE/ITforChange.

Heintschel von Heinegg, Wolff. (2012). "Legal Implications of Territorial Sovereignty in Cyberspace." In *2012 4th International Conference on Cyber Conflict*, edited by Christian Czosseck, Rain Ottis, and Katharina Ziolkowski. Tallinn, Estonia: NATO CCD COE Publications. https://ccdcoe.org/.

Herman, Edward S., and Chomsky, Noam. (1988). *Manufacturing Consent: The Political Economy of the Mass Media*. New York: Random House.

Higgins, Rosalyn. (1994). *Problems and Process: International Law and How We Use It*. Oxford: Oxford University Press.

Horten, Monica. (2012). *The Copyright Enforcement Enigma: Internet Politics and the "Telecoms Package."* New York: Palgrave Macmillan.

———. (2013). *A Copyright Masquerade: How Copyright Lobbying Threatens Online Freedoms*. London: Zed.

Jenkins, Brian Michael. (2006). "Combating Global War on Terrorism." In *Countering Terrorism and WMD: Creating a Global Counter-Terrorist Network*, edited by P. Katona, M. B. Intriligator, and J. P. Sullivan, 181–98. New York: Routledge.

Jensen, Heike. (2005). "Gender and the WSIS Process: War of the Words." In *Visions in Process: World Summit on the Information Society, Geneva 2003—Tunis 2005*, edited by the Heinrich Böll Foundation. Berlin: Heinrich Böll Stiftung.

———. (2006). "Women's Human Rights in the Information Society." In *Human Rights in the Global Information Society*, edited by Rikke F. Jorgensen, 235–62. Cambridge MA: MIT Press.

Jessup, Phillip. (1968). *A Modern Law of Nations*. Hamden, CT: Archon.

John XXIII, Pope. (1963). *Pacem in Terris* (Peace on Earth). Boston: Daughters of St. Paul.

Jorgensen, Rikke Frank. (2006). *Human Rights in the Global Information Society*. Cambridge, MA: MIT Press.

———. (2013). *Framing the Net: The Internet and Human Rights*. Cheltenham, UK: Edward Elgar.

Joseph, Sarah, Schultz, Jenny, and Castan, Melissa. (2005). *The International Covenant on Civil and Political Rights: Cases, Materials, and Commentary*. 2nd ed. Oxford: Oxford University Press.

Kälin, Walter, and Künzli, Jörg. (2009). *The Law of International Human Rights Protection*. Oxford: Oxford University Press.

Kelsen, H. (1966). *Principles of International Law*. New York: Holt, Rinehart and Winston.

Knapp, Eric D., and Langill, Joel Thomas. (2015). *Industrial Network Security: Securing Critical Infrastructure Networks for Smart Grid, Scada, and Other Industrial Control Systems*. Waltham, MA: Elsevier.

Konstantinos, Komaitis. (2010). *The Current State of Domain Name Regulation: Domain Names as Second Class Citizens in a Mark-Dominated World*. London: Routledge.

Kritsiotis, Dino. (2007). "Topographies of Force." In *International Law and Armed Conflict: Exploring the Faultlines*, edited by Michael Schmitt and Jelena Pejic. Leiden, Netherlands: Martinus Nijhoff.

Krutz, Ronald L. (2005). *Securing SCADA Systems*. Indianapolis: Wiley.

Lasswell, Harold D., and McDougal, Myers S. (1992). *Jurisprudence for a Free Society*. New Haven, CT: Yale University Press.

Lauterpacht, H. (1955). *Oppenheim's International Law I*. London: Longmans.

Lessig, Lawrence. (1999). *Code: And Other Laws of Cyberspace*. New York: Ashgate.

Lessig, L. (2006). *Code: Version 2.0*. New York: Basic Books.

Lewis, James A. (2012). "Harnessing Leviathan: Internet Governance and Cybersecurity." In *Securing Cyberspace: A New Domain for National Security*, edited by Nicholas Burns and Jonathan Price. Washington, DC: Aspen Institute.

Lipschutz, Ronnie D., with James K. Rowe. (2005). *Globalization, Governmentality and Global Politics: Regulation for the Rest of Us?* London: Routledge.

Liptak, Deborah A. (2012). "Information Warfare and Cybersecurity." In *Web of Deceit: Misinformation and Manipulation in the Age of Social Media*, edited by Anne P. Mintz. Medford, NJ: CyberAge Books.

Mandiberg, Michael, ed. (2012). *The Social Media Reader*. New York: New York University Press.

Mansell, Robin, and Silverstone, Roger, eds. (1996). *Communication by Design: The Politics of Information and Communication Technologies*. New York: Oxford University Press.

Maogoto, Jackson. (2015). *Technology and the Law on the Use of Force*. New York: Routledge.

Marsden, C. (2010). *Net Neutrality: Towards a Co-Regulatory Solution*. New York: Bloomsbury Academic.

McDougal, Myers S., and Feliciano, Florentino P. (1961). *Law and Minimum World Public Order: The Legal Regulation and International Coercion*. New Haven, CT: Yale University Press.

McDougal, Myers S., Lasswell, Harold D., and Chen, Lung-chu, eds. (1980). *Human Rights and the World Public Order: The Basic Policies of an International Law of Human Dignity*. New Haven, CT: Yale University Press.

McDougal, Myers S., Lasswell, Harold D., and Miller, James C. (1967). *The Interpretation of Agreements and World Public Order: Principles of Content and Procedure*. New Haven, CT: Yale University Press.

Midson, David. (2014). "Geography, Territory and Sovereignty in Cyber Warfare." In *New Technologies and the Law of Armed Conflict*, edited by Hitoshi Nasu and Robert McLaughlin, 75–94. The Hague, Netherlands: TMC ASSER.

Minar, N., and Hedlund, M. (2001). "A Network of Peers: Peer-to-Peer Models through the History of the Internet." In *Peer-to-Peer: Harnessing the Power of Disruptive Technologies*, edited by A. Oram, 9–20. Sebastopol, CA: O'Reilly.

Morgan, C. H. (2001). *Cyber Attacks and Computer Intrusion Investigations*. Colorado Springs, CO: Air Force Office of Special Investigations.

Morozov, Evgeny. (2011). *Net Delusion: The Dark Side of Internet Freedom*. Philadelphia: Perseus.

Mounier, P. (2002). *Les maîtres du réseau. Les enjeux politiques d'Internet*. Paris: La Découverte.

Mueller, M. (2012). "Property and Commons in Internet Governance." In *Governance, Regulation and Powers on the Internet*, edited by E. Brousseau, M. Marzouki, and C. Méadel. Cambridge: Cambridge University Press.

Mueller, Milton. (2010). *Networks and States: The Global Politics of Internet Governance*. Boston: MIT Press.

Musiani, F. (2013). *Nains sans géants. Architecture décentralisée et services internet*. Paris: Presses des Mines.

Napoleoni, L. (2003). *Terror Incorporated: Tracing the Money behind Global Terrorism*. New York: Penguin.

Orakhelashvili, Alexander. (2007). "Natural Law and Justice." In *Max Planck Encyclopedia of Public International Law*. New York: Oxford University Press.

Oram, A., ed. (2001). *Peer-to-Peer: Harnessing the Power of Disruptive Technologies*. Sebastopol, CA: O'Reilly.

Ostrom, E. (1990). *Governing the Commons: The Evolution of Institutions for Collective Action*. Cambridge: Cambridge University Press.

Proulx, Vincent-Joël. (2011). "Babysitting Terrorists: Should States Be Strictly Liable for Failing to Prevent Transborder Attacks?" In *International Law: Contemporary Issues and Future Developments*, edited by Sanford Silverburg, 406–47. Boulder, CO: Westview.

Quintas, Paul. (1996). "Software by Design." In *Communication by Design: The Politics of Information and Communication Technologies*, edited by Robin Mansell and Robert Silverstone, 75–102. New York: Oxford University Press.

Rauhofer, Judith. (2014). "Round and Round the Garden? Big Data, Small Government and the Balance of Power in the Information Age." In *Proceedings of the 17th International Legal*

Informatics Symposium (IRIS) 2014, edited by E. Schweighofer, F. Krummer, and W. Hötzendorfer. Vienna: OCG.

Raymond, E. (1997). *The Cathedral and the Bazaar: Musings on Linux and Open Source by an Accidental Revolutionary*. Sebastopol, CA: O'Reilly.

Reisman, William Michael, and Armstrong, Andrea. (2007). "Claims to Pre-emptive Uses of Force: Some Trends and Projections and Their Implication for World Order." In *International Law and Armed Conflict: Exploring the Faultlines*, edited by Michael Schmitt and Jelena Pejic, 79–112. Leiden, Netherlands: Martinus Nijhoff.

Rengel, Alexandra. (2013). *Privacy in the 21st Century*. Studies in Intercultural Human Rights. Leiden, Netherlands: Martinus Nijhoff.

Roscini, Marco. (2014). *Cyber Operations and the Use of Force in International Law*. Oxford: Oxford University Press.

Rousseau, Jean-Jacques. (2003). *On the Social Contract*. Mineola, NY: Dover.

Rozenweig, Paul. (2013). *Cyber Warfare: How Conflicts in Cyberspace Are Challenging America and Changing the World*. Santa Barbara, CA: Praeger.

Rundle, M., and Birding, M. (2008). "Filtering and the International System." In *Access Denied: The Practice and Policy of Global Internet Filtering*, edited by R. Deibert , J. Palfrey, R. Rohozinski, and J. Zittrain, 73–102. Cambridge, MA: MIT Press.

Schachter, Oscar. (1982). *International Law in Theory and Practice: General Course in Public International Law*. Collected Courses of the Hague Academy of International Law 178. Leiden, Netherlands: Martinus Nijhoff.

Schafer, V., Le Crosnier, H., and Musiani, F. (2011). *La neutralité de l'Internet, un enjeu de communication*. Paris: CNRS Editions/Les Essentiels d'Hermès.

Schafer, V., and Thierry, B. G. (2012). *Le Minitel. L'enfance numérique de la France*. Paris: Nuvis.

Schmitt, Michael N., ed. (2013). *Tallinn Manual on the International Law Applicable to Cyberwarfare*. Cambridge: Cambridge University Press.

———. (2015). "The Use of Cyber Force and International Law." In *The Oxford Handbook of the Use of Force in International Law*, edited by Marc Weller. Oxford: Oxford University Press.

Sears, Kathleen. (2014). *Mythology 101: From Gods and Goddesses to Monsters and Mortals; Your Guide to Ancient Mythology*. Avon, MA: Adams.

Shackelford, Scott J. (2014). *Managing Cyber Attacks in International Law, Business, and Relations: In Search of Cyber Peace*. New York: Cambridge University Press.

Shawcross, W. (2005). *Allies: The US, Britain, Europe and the War in Iraq*. New York: Public Affairs.

Simma, Bruno, et al. (2002). *The Charter of the United Nations: A Commentary*. Oxford: Oxford University Press.

Stalder, Felix. (2012). "Between Democracy and Spectacle: The Front-End and Back-End of the Social Web." In *The Social Media Reader*, edited by Michael Mandiberg, 242–56. New York: New York University Press.

Stohl, Michael, and Lopez, George A. (1984). *The State as Terrorist: The Dynamics of Governmental Violence and Repression*. Westport, CT: Greenwood.

Stone, Julius. (1958). *Aggression and World Order*. Berkeley: University of California Press.

Taylor, I., and Harrison, A. (2009). *From P2P to Web Services and Grids: Evolving Distributed Communities*. 2nd exp. ed. London: Springer-Verlag.

Thompson, John. (1984). *Studies in the Theory of Ideology*. Cambridge: Polity.

Trapp, Kimberley. (2011). *State Responsibility for International Terrorism: Problems and Prospects*. Oxford: Oxford University Press.

Tunkin, G. I. (1970). *Teoria Mezhdunarodnogo Prava*. Moscow: Mezdhuranodye Otnoshenia.

U.S. National Science and Technology Council, Interagency Working Group (IWG) on Cyber Security and Information Assurance (CSIA). (2006). *Federal Plan for Cyber Security and Information Assurance Research and Development: A Report*. Washington, DC: National Coordination Office for Networking and Information Technology Research and Development.

Vaidyanathan, Siva. (2012). *The Googlization of Everything (and Why We Should Worry)*. Berkeley: University of California Press.

van Schewick, B. (2010). *Internet Architecture and Innovation*. Cambridge, MA: MIT Press.

Vincent, Andrew. (2010). *The Politics of Human Rights*. Oxford: Oxford University Press.

Weber, Rolf H., and Heinrich, Ulrike I. (2012). *Anonymization*. Springer Briefs in Cybersecurity. London: Springer.

Weller, Marc, ed. (2015). *Oxford Hand of the Use of Force in International Law*. Oxford: Oxford University Press.

Wengler, W. (1964). *Volkerrecht I*. Berlin: Springer.

Wolfrum, R. (1995). "Internationally Wrongful Acts." In *Encyclopedia of Public International Law*. Amsterdam: North Holland.

Zetter, Kim. (2014). *Countdown to Zero Day: Stuxnet and the Launch of the World's First Digital Weapon*. New York: Crown.

Zittrain, Jonathan, and Palfrey, John. (2008). "Internet Filtering: The Politics and Mechanisms of Control." In *Access Denied: The Practice and Policy of Global Internet Filtering*, edited by R. Deibert, J. Palfrey, R. Rohozinski, and J. Zittrain. Cambridge, MA: MIT Press.

ARTICLES

Ago, Robert. (1972). "Fourth Report on State Responsibility." *International Law Commission Yearbook* 2:71–121.

Aigrain, P. (2011). "Another Narrative: Addressing Research Challenges and Other Open Issues." Presentation at the PARADISO Conference, Brussels, September 7–9.

Angelopoulos, Christina. (2014). "Are Blocking Injunctions against ISPs Allowed in Europe? Copyright Enforcement in the Post-Telekabel EU Legal Landscape." *Journal of Intellectual Property Law and Practice* 9 (10): 812–21. http://dx.doi.org/10.1093/jiplp/jpu136.

Bäckstrand, K. (2008). "Accountability of Networked Climate Governance: The Rise of Transnational Climate Partnerships." *Global Environmental Politics* 8 (3): 74–102.

Balleste, Roy. (2008). "The Earth Alliance Constitution: International Human Rights Law and Babylon." *Florida Coastal Law Review* 10 (1): 33–66.

Banks, Williams C. (2013). "The Role of Counterterrorism Law in Shaping Ad Bellum Norms for Cyber Warfare." *Israel Yearbook on Human Rights* 43:45–80.

Barron, Anne. (2010). "'Graduated Response' à l'Anglaise: Online Copyright Infringement and the Digital Economy Act 2010." *Journal of Media Law* 3 (2): 305–47.

Becker, Sven, and Niggemeier, Stefan. (2012). "Google's Lobby Offensive: Internet Giant Builds Web of Influence in Berlin." *Spiegel Online International*, September 25. http://www.spiegel.de/international/.

Benatar, Marco. (2009). "The Use of Cyber Force: Need for Legal Justification." *Gottingen Journal of International Law* 1 (3): 375–96.

Bendrath, Ralf, and Milton Mueller. (2011). "The End of the Net as We Know It? Deep Packet Inspection and Internet Governance." *New Media and Society* 13 (7): 1142–60.

Beuscart, J.-S. (2002). "Les usagers de Napster, entre communauté et clientèle. Construction et régulation d'un collectif sociotechnique." *Sociologie du Travail* 44 (4): 461–80.

Boyle, J. (2003). "The Second Enclosure Movement and the Construction of the Public Domain." *Law and Contemporary Problems* 33. http://www.law.duke.edu/.

Braman, S. (2011). "Designing for Instability: Internet Architecture and Constant Change." Presentation at the Media in Transition 7 (MiT7): Unstable Platforms; The Promise and Peril of Transition conference, Cambridge, MA, May 13–15.

Bridy, Annemarie. (2011). "Acta and the Specter of Graduated Response." *American University International Law Review* 26 (3): 558–77.

———. (2013). "Six Strikes Measured against Five Norms." *Fordham Intellectual Property Media and Entertainment Law Journal* 23 (1): 1–67.

Brownlie, Ian. (1958). "International Law and the Activities of Armed Bands." *International and Comparative Law Quarterly* 7 (4): 712–35.

Campbell, James K. (1997). "Excerpts from Research Study 'Weapons of Mass Destruction and Terrorism: Proliferation by Non State Actors.'" *Terrorism and Political Violence* 9 (2): 24–50.

Chainoglou, Kalliopi. (2010). "An Assessment of Jus in Bello Issues Concerning Computer Network Attacks: A Threat Reflected in National Security Agendas." *Romanian Journal of International Law* 12:25–63.

Coudert, Fanny. (2010). "When Video Cameras Watch and Screen: Privacy Implications of Pattern Recognition Technologies." *Computer Law and Security Review* 26 (4): 377–84.

Council of Europe. (2009). "A New Notion of Media?" 1st Council of Europe Conference of Ministers Responsible for Media and New Communication Services. Reykjavik, Iceland, May 28–29, 2009.

Cronin, A. K. (2002). "Rethinking Sovereignty: American Strategy in the Age of Terrorism." *Survival* 44 (2): 119–39.

Dauphin, F., and Dagiral, E. (2005). "P2P: From File Sharing to Meta-information Pooling?" *Communications and Strategies* 59 (3): 35–51.

Deibert, Ronald J. (2000). "International Plug 'n Play? Citizen Activism, the Internet, and Global Public Policy." *International Studies Perspectives* 1 (3): 255–72.

———. (2015). "The Geopolitics of Cyberspace after Snowden." *Current History: A Journal of Contemporary World Affairs* 114 (768): 9–15. http://www.currenthistory.com/.

Dinstein, Yoram. (2002). "Computer Network Attacks and Self-Defence." *International Law Studies* 76:99–119.

———. (2013). "Cyber War and International Law: Concluding Remarks at the 2012 Naval War College International Law Conference." *International Law Studies* 89:276–87.

Döge, Jenny. (2010). "Cyber Warfare: Challenges for the Applicability of the Traditional Laws of War Regime." *Archiv des Volkerrechts* 48 (4): 486–501.

EDPS. (2014). "Urgent Reform of EU Data Protection Framework Is Essential for a Connected Continent." Press release, January 16, 2014.

Elkin-Koren, N. (2006). "Making Technology Visible: Liability of Internet Service Providers for Peer-to-Peer Traffic." *New York University Journal of Legislation and Public Policy* 9 (15): 15–76.

Eriksson J., and Giacomello, G. (2009). "Who Controls the Internet? Beyond the Obstinacy or Obsolescence of the State." *International Studies Review* 11 (1): 205–30.

Evans, G., and Sahnoun, M. (2002). "The Responsibility to Protect." *Foreign Affairs* 81 (6): 99–110.

Fawcett, J. E. S. (1961). "Intervention in International Law: A Study of Some Recent Cases." *Recueil des cours* 103:343–421.

Feinstein, L., and Slaughter, A. M. (2004). "A Duty to Prevent." *Foreign Affairs* 83 (1): 136–50.

Fitzmaurice, Gerald. (1952). "The Definition of Aggression." *International and Comparative Law Quarterly* 1:137–44.

Foster, John Bellamy, and McChesney, Robert W. (2011). "The Internet's Unholy Marriage to Capitalism." *Monthly Review* 62 (10): 1–30.

Fovino, I. N., Coletta, A., Carcano, A., and Masera, M. (2012). "Critical State-Based Filtering System for Securing SCADA Network Protocols." *IEEE Transactions on Industrial Electronics* 59 (10): 3943–50.

Franklin, M. I. (2007). "NGO's and the 'Information Society': Grassroots Advocacy at the UN—a Cautionary Tale." *Review of Policy Research* 24 (4): 309–30.

———. (2010). "Digital Dilemmas: Transnational Politics in the 21st Century." *Brown Journal of World Affairs* 16 (11): 67–85.

Geiss, Robin. (2013). "Cyber Warfare and Non-international Armed Conflicts." *Israel Yearbook on Human Rights* 43:141–58.

Gervais, Michael. (2012a). "Cyber Attacks and the Laws of War." *Emory International Law Review* 26:825–90.

———. (2012b). "Cyber Attacks and the Laws of War." *Journal of Law and Cyberwarfare* 1 (1): 7–98.

Glennon, Michael J. (2013). "The Road Ahead: Gaps, Drips, and Cyber-Conflict." *Israel Yearbook on Human Rights* 43:1–22.

Graham, David. (2010). "Cyber Threats and the Law of War." *Journal of National Security and Law* 4:87–102.

Griebel, Jorn, and Plucken, Milan. (2008). "New Developments Regarding the Rules of Attribution? The International Court of Justice's Decision in Bosnia v. Serbia." *Leiden Journal of International Law* 21 (3): 601–22.

Gymrek, Melissa, McGuire, Amy L., Golan, David, Halperin, Eran, and Erlich, Yaniv. (2013). "Identifying Personal Genomes by Surname Inference." *Science* 339 (6117): 321–24.

Hales, D. (2006). "Emergent Group-Level Selection in a Peer-to-Peer Network." *Complexus* 3 (1–3): 108–18.

Hamelink, C. J. (1998). "International Communication: Global Market and Morality." *Communication Abstracts* 21 (4).

Hayes, Ben. (2010). "Spying on a See Through World: The 'Open Source' Intelligence Industry." *Statewatch Bulletin* 20 (1). http://database.statewatch.org/.

Healy, Hazel. (2012). "Internet Showdown: Why Digital Freedom Matters—to Us All." *New Internationalist* 458. http://newint.org/.

Hegland, C. (2004). "Global Jihad." *National Journal* 36:1400–401.

Heintschel von Heinegg, Wolff. (2012). "The Tallinn Manual and International Cyber Security Law." *Yearbook of International Humanitarian Law* 3:15–18.

Hmoud, Mahmoud. (2004). "The Use of Force against Iraq: Occupation and Security Council Resolution 1483." *Cornell International Law Journal* 36 (3): 435–53.

Hoeren, Thomas. (2009). "The European Liability and Responsibility of Providers of Online Platforms such as 'Second Life.'" *Journal of Information Law and Technology* 1. http://www2.warwick.ac.uk/.

Jenkins, Brian Michael. (2001). "Terrorism: Current and Long Term Threats." Statement to the Senate Armed Services Subcommittee on Emerging Threats, November 15. http://www.rand.org/.

Jenkins, Brian Michael. (1987). "The Future Course of International Terrorism." *Futurist*, July–August.

Joseph, Paul, and Carton, Sharon. (1992). "The Law of the Federation: Images of Law, Lawyers, and the Legal System in 'Star Trek: The Next Generation.'" *University of Toledo Law Review* 24:43–85.

Kaminsky, Margot. (2011). "An Overview and the Evolution of the Anti-Counterfeiting Trade Agreement (ACTA)." PIJIP Research Paper 19. American University Washington College of Law, Washington, DC.

Kaspar, Lea, Brown, Deborah, and Varon, Joana. (2013). "Internet Governance Processes: Visualising the Playing Field." Global Partners Digital, November 5. http://www.gp-digital.org/.

Kitfield, James. (2001). "Anti-Terror Alliance." *Government Executive* 33 (2): 51.

Kritsiotis, Dino. (1996). "The Legality of the 1993 US Missile Strike on Iraq and the Right of Self-Defence in International Law." *International and Comparative Law Quarterly* 45 (1): 162–77.

Kuczerawy, A. (2015). "Intermediary Liability and Freedom of Expression: Recent Developments in the EU Notice and Action Initiative." *Computer Law and Security Review: The International Journal of Technology* 31 (1): 46–56.

Kulesza, Joanna. (2009). "State Responsibility for Cyber Attacks on International Peace and Security." *Polish Yearbook of International Law* 29:139–52.

Kulesza, Joanna, and Balleste, Roy. (2013). "Signs and Portents in Cyberspace: The Rise of Jus Internet as a New Order in International Law." *Fordham Intellectual Property, Media, and Entertainment Law Journal* 23:1311–49.

Lentz, Christopher E. (2010). "A State's Duty to Prevent and Respond to Cyberterrorist Acts." *Chicago Journal of International Law* 10 (2): 799–824.

Libicki, Martin C. (2012). "The Specter of Non-Obvious Warfare." *Strategic Studies Quarterly* 6 (3): 88–101.

Lin, Herbert S. (2010). "Offensive Cyber Operations and the Use of Force." *Journal of National Security Law and Policy* 4:63–86.

Lung-chu Chen. (1999). "In Affectionate Memory of Professor Myres McDougal: Champion for an International Law of Human Dignity." *Yale Law Journal* 108 (5): 953–56.

Lyon, David. (2010). "National ID's in a Global World: Surveillance, Security, and Citizenship." *Case Western Reserve Journal of International Law* 42 (3): 607–23.

Margulies, Peter. (2013). "Sovereignty and Cyber Attacks: Technology's Challenge to the Law of State Responsibility." *Melbourne Journal of International Law* 14 (2): 496–519.

Moore, John Norton. (1986). "The Secret War in Central America and the Future of World Order." *American Journal of International Law* 80 (1): 43–127.

Moore, Stephen. (2013). "Cyber Attacks and the Beginnings of an International Cyber Treaty." *North Carolina Journal of International Law and Commercial Regulation* 39 (1): 223–57.

Mowbray, M. (2009). "The Fog over the Grimpen Mire: Cloud Computing and the Law." *Scripted Journal of Law, Technology and Society* 6 (1): 132–46.

Mudrinich, E. M. (2012). "Cyber 3.0: The Department of Defense Strategy for Operating in Cyberspace and the Attribution Problem." *Air Force Law Review* 68:167–206.

Mueller, Milton, Kuehn, Andreas, and Santoso, Stephanie. (2012). "Policing the Network: Using DPI for Copyright Enforcement." Surveillance and Society 9 (4): 348–64.

Müllerson, Rein A. (2002). "*Jus Ad Bellum* and International Terrorism." *Israel Yearbook of Human Rights* 32:1–52.

Murphy, Sean D. (2005). "Self-Defense and the Israeli *Wall Advisory Opinion*: An *Ipse Dixit* from the ICJ?" *American Journal of International Law* 99 (1): 62–76.

Musiani, F., and Méadel, C. (2014). "Asymétrisation et barrières: évolutions d'architecture et reconfigurations de la « coopération » dans l'internet des origines." Paper prepared for the annual symposium of the Société Française des Sciences de l'Information et de la Communication (SFSIC), Toulon, France, June 4–6.

Musiani, F., and Schafer, V. (2011). "Le modèle Internet en question (années 1970–2010)." *Flux* 85–86 (3–4): 62–71.

Neumann, P. N. (2006). "Europe's Jihadist Dilemma." *Survival* 48 (2): 77–84.

O'Connell, Mary Ellen. (2012). "Cyber Security without Cyber War." *Journal of Conflict and Security Law* 17 (2): 187–209.

Ofcom. (2011). "'Site Blocking' to Reduce Online Copyright Infringement: A Review of Sections 17 and 18 of the Digital Economy Act." May 27, 2011. http://stakeholders.ofcom.org.uk/.

Pacht, Laurence T. (2014). "The Case for a Convention on State Responsibility." *Nordic Journal of International Law* 83 (4): 439–75.

Peguera, Miquel. (2010). "Internet Service Providers' Liability in Spain: Recent Case Law and Future Perspectives." *Journal of Intellectual Property, Information Technology and Electronic Commerce Law* 1 (3): 151–64.

Peha, Jon, and Mateus, Alexandre. (2014). "Policy Implications of Technology for Detecting P2P and Copyright Violations." *Telecommunications Policy* 38:66–85.

Pfaffenberger, B. (1996). "If I Want It, It's OK: Usenet and the (Outer) Limits of Free Speech." *Information Society* 4 (12): 365–73. http://pfaff.sts.virginia.edu/.

Pisillo Mazzeschi, Riccardo. (1992). "The Due Diligence Rule and the Nature of the International Responsibility of States." *German Yearbook of International Law* 35:9–51.

Reisman, W. Michael. (1990). "Sovereignty and Human Rights in Contemporary International Law." *American Journal of International Law* 84 (4): 866–76.

———. (2008). "Development and Nation-Building: A Framework for Policy-Oriented Inquiry." *Maine Law Review* 60 (2): 309–16.

Roscini, Marco. (2010). "World Wider Warfare: Jus Ad Bellum and the Use of Cyber Force." *Max Planck Yearbook of United Nations Law* 14:85–130.

Roseme, S. (1997–1998). "State Responsibility and International Crimes: Further Reflections on Article 19 of the Draft Articles on State Responsibility." *New York University Journal of International Law and Politics* 30 (1–2): 145–66.

Scheffer, D. J. (2003). "Agora: Future Implications of the Iraq Conflict." *American Journal of International Law* 97:844–47.

Schmitt, Michael N. (2014). "'Below the Threshold' Cyber Operations: The Countermeasures Response Option and International Law." *Virginia Journal of International Law* 54 (3): 697–732.

———. (2011). "Cyber Operations and the *Jus in Bello*: Key Issues." *Israel Yearbook on Human Rights* 41:113–35.

Schollmeier, R. (2001). "A Definition of Peer-to-Peer Networking for the Classification of Peer-to-Peer Architectures and Applications." *Proceedings of the First International Conference on Peer-to-Peer Computing*, Linköping, Sweden, August 27–29.

Schroeder, Joshua. (2013). "Choosing an Internet Shaped by Freedom: A Legal Rationale to Rein in Copyright Gatekeeping." *Berkeley Journal of Entertainment and Sports Law* 2 (1): 48–88.

Segura-Serrano, Antonio. (2006). "Internet Regulation: A Hard-Law Proposal." New York University School of Law, Jean Monnet Working Paper 10.

Shackelford, Scott J. (2009). "From Nuclear War to Net War: Analogizing Cyber Attacks in International Law." *Berkeley Journal of International Law* 27 (1): 192–251.

Shackelford, Scott J., and Andres, Richard B. (2011). "State Responsibility for Cyber Attacks: Competing Standards for a Growing Problem." *Georgetown Journal of International Law* 42 (4): 971–1016.

Shackelford, Scott J., Richards, Eric L., Raymond, Anjanette H., and Craig, Amanda N. (2015). "Using BITs to Protect Bytes: Promoting Cyber Peace by Safeguarding Trade Secrets through Bilateral Investment Treaties." *American Business Law Journal* 52 (1): 1–74.

Simon, Steven, and Benjamin, Daniel. (2000). "America and the New Terrorism." *Survival* 42 (1): 59–75.

———. (2001). "The Terror." *Survival* 43 (4): 5–87.

Sklerov, Matthew J. (2009). "Solving the Dilemma of State Responses to Cyberattacks: A Justification for the Use of Active Defenses against States Who Neglect Their Duty to Prevent." *Military Law Review* 202:1–85.

Snijders, Chris, Matzat, Uwe, and Reips, Ulf-Dietrich. (2012). "'Big Data': Big Gaps of Knowledge in the Field of Internet." *International Journal of Internet Science* 7 (1): 1–5. http://www.ijis.net/.

Solce, Natasha. (2008). "The Battlefield of Cyberspace: The Inevitable New Military Branch—The Cyber Force." *Albany Law Journal of Science and Technology* 18 (1): 293–324.

Stalla-Bourdillon, Sophie. (2013). "Online Monitoring, Filtering, Blocking . . . What Is the Difference? Where to Draw the Line?" *Computer Law and Security Review* 29 (6): 702–12.

Stalla-Bourdillon, Sophie, Papadakia, Evangelia, and Chown, Tim. (2014). "From Porn to Cybersecurity Passing by Copyright: How Mass Surveillance Technologies Are Gaining Legitimacy . . . The Case of Deep Packet Inspection Technologies." *Computer Law and Security Review* 30 (6): 670–86.

Talbot, David. (2005). "Terror's Server: Fraud, Gruesome Propaganda, Terror Planning; The Net Enables It All; The Online Industry Can Help Fix It." *Technology Review* 108 (2): 46–53.

Taylor, Bonnie L. (2003). "Storing DNA Samples of Non-Convicted Persons and the Debate over DNA Database Expansion." *Thomas M. Cooley Law Review* 20 (3): 509–46.

Tsagourias, Nikolaos K. (2012a). "Cyber Attacks, Self-Defence and the Problem of Attribution." *Journal of Conflict and Security Law* 17 (2): 229–44.

———. (2012b). "The Tallinn Manual on the International Law Applicable to Cyber Warfare: A Commentary on Chapter II—The Use of Force." *Yearbook of International Humanitarian Law* 15:19–43.

U.S. Department of Immigration and Customs Enforcement (ICE). (2010). "ICE Seizes 82 Website Domains Involved in Selling Counterfeit Goods as Part of Cyber Monday Crackdown." Press release, November 29, 2010.

Vermeulen, Mathias, and Bellanova, Rocco. (2013). "European 'Smart' Surveillance: What's at Stake for Data Protection, Privacy and Non-discrimination?" *Security and Human Rights* 23 (4): 297–311.

Vogel, Joachim. (2008). "Towards a Global Convention against Cybercrime." *ReAIDP/e-RIAPL* C-07: 1–10.

Warren, Samuel D., and Brandeis, Louis Dembitz. (1890, December 15). "The Right to Privacy." *Harvard Law Review* 4 (5): 193–220.
Waxman, Matthew C. (2011). "Cyber-Attacks and the Use of Force: Back to the Future of Article 2(4)." *Yale Journal of International Law* 36 (2): 421–59.
Weber, Rolf H., and Staiger, Dominic N. (2014). "Bridging the Gap between Individual Privacy and Public Security." *Groningen Journal of International Law* 2 (2): 14–32.
———. (2014, May 15). "Spannungsfelder von Datenschutz und Datenüberwachung in der Schweiz und in den USA." *Jusletter IT* 9. http://richterzeitung.weblaw.ch/.
Weimann, Gabriel. (2012). "Lone Wolves in Cyberspace." *Journal of Terrorism Research* 3 (2). http://ojs.st-andrews.ac.uk/.
Wood, J. A. (2010). "The Darknet: A Digital Copyright Revolution." *Richmond Journal of Law and Technology* 16 (4). http://jolt.richmond.edu/.
Wright, Philip Quincy. (1953). "The Outlawry of War and the Law of War." *American Journal of International Law* 47 (3): 365–76.

CASE LAW

Bundesverfassungsgericht (1 BvR 2074/05). Unreported March 11, 2008.
California v. Ciraolo, 476 U.S. 207 (1986).
Cartier International v. British Sky Broadcasting, October 17, 2014, no. HC14C01382, High Court of Justice, judgment.
Case Concerning Oil Platforms (Iran v. US), merits, judgment, November 6, 2003, ICJ Reports (2003).
Chattin Case (1927) RIAA IV 282, 285–86.
Claims of Italian Nationals Resident in Peru, RIAA XV, 395, 399, 401, 404, 407–11.
Conseil Constitutionnel. (2009). Decision n° 2009-580 of June 10th 2009, Loi favorisant la diffusion et la protection de la création sur internet.
Consejo Fiscal. (2010). Informe Del Consejo Fiscal Anteproyecto De Ley De Economia Sostenible y Anteproyecto De Ley Orgánica Complementaria De La Ley De Economia Sostenible, February 12, 2010.
Dispute concerning the Interpretation of Article 79 of the Treaty of Peace (1955) RIAA XIII 389, 438.
Doe v. Attorney General of U.S., 941 F.2d at 796.
Eagle v. Morgan, 88 F.3d at 625 C.A.8 (Ark.) (1996).
ECHR Concurring Opinion of Judge Pinto De Albuquerque, Case of Ahmet Yildirim v. Turkey (Application no. 3111/10), Strasbourg, December 18, 2012, final March 18, 2013.
ECHR Herbecq and the association Ligue des droits de l'homme v. Belgium, January 14, 1998, Case-Nr. 32200/96 and 32201/96.
ECHR Neij and Sunde Kolmisoppi against Sweden in the European Court of Human Rights Application no. 40397/12 (2013).
ECHR Von Hannover v. Germany, June 24, 2004, Case-Nr. 59320/00. http://hudoc.echr.coe.int/.
ECHR, Yildirim v. Turkey, Application No. 3111/10, December 18, 2012, final March 18, 2013.
ECJ case number C-70/10 in the European Court of Justice, Scarlet Extended v. Societe Belge des auteurs, compositeur, et editeurs (SABAM), sections 52, 55.
ECJ case of Promusicae v. Telefonica in the European Court of Justice (2008), case C-275/06.
ECJ judgment in joint cases C-293/12 and C-594/12 Digital Rights Ireland and Seitlinger and Others. http://curia.europa.eu/.
ECJ judgment in joint cases C-293/12 and C-594/12, press statement 54/14, Luxemburg, April 8, 2014. http://curia.europa.eu/.
ECJ judgment of February 27, 2008, 1 BvR 370/07; 1 BvR 595/07.
Entick v. Carrington, 19 State Trials 1029 (1765).
Eritrea-Ethiopia Claims Commission, Partial Award: Jus Ad Bellum, Ethiopia's claims nos. 1–8, vol. XXVI, 433, 465, December 19, 2005.

European Parliament, Del Castillo report, March 26, 2014, amendment 241.

Finnish Ship-owners, RIAA III, 1479, 1501.

Gauthier v. Canada, Human Rights Committee, Communication no. 633 (1995), CCPR/C/65/D/633 (1995), April 7, 1999.

GoldenEye International Ltd v. Telefonica, no. A3/2012/1477, Court of Appeal, S.117.

Houchins v. KQED, Inc., 438 U.S. 1, 98 S. Ct. 2588, 57 L. Ed. 2d 553 (1978).

House of Lords, House of Commons. (2010). Joint Committee on Human Rights, Legislative Scrutiny: Digital Economy Bill, Fifth Report of session 2009–2010, February 5, 2010.

———. (2011). Joint Committee on the Draft Defamation Bill, First Report Draft Defamation Bill, October 12.

ICJ Accordance with International Law of the Unilateral Declaration of Independence in Respect of Kosovo (Advisory Opinion), ICJ Reports (2010) 403, para. 84. http://www.icj-cij.org/.

ICJ Accordance with International Law of the Unilateral Declaration of Independence in Respect of Kosovo (Request for Advisory Opinion), July 22, 2010, General List No. 141.

ICJ Advisory Opinion on the Legal Consequences of the Construction of a Wall in the Occupied Palestinian Territory, [2004] ICJ Reports 131, paras. 3–4, 145.

ICJ Advisory Opinion on the Legality of the Threat or Use of Nuclear Weapons, [1996] ICJ Reports 226, para. 83.

ICJ Application of the Convention on the Prevention and Punishment of the Crime of Genocide (Bosnia and Herzegovina v. Serbia and Montenegro), merits, judgment, February 26, 2007, ICJ Reports (2007).

ICJ Application of the Convention on the Prevention and Punishment of the Crime of Genocide (Preliminary Objections), [1996] ICJ Reports 505, paras. 31–32.

ICJ Armed Activities on the Territory of the Congo (DRV v. Uganda), judgment, December 19, 2005, ICJ Reports (2005).

ICJ Barcelona Traction Light and Power Company Limited (Second Phase), [1970] ICJ Reports 3, paras. 32–33.

ICJ Case concerning Application of the Convention of the Prevention and Punishment of the Crime of Genocide: Bosnia and Herzegovina v. Serbia and Montenegro (judgment), ICJ Reports (2007), paras. 399–401. http://www.icj-cij.org/.

ICJ Case concerning the Factory at Chorzow (merits), [1928] PCIJ Series A17 at 47.

ICJ Case concerning United States Diplomatic and Consular Staff in Tehran (judgment), ICJ Reports (1980) 3, para. 74. http://www.icj-cij.org/.

ICJ Case on Military and Paramilitary Activities in and against Nicaragua (merits), ICJ Reports (1986) 14.

ICJ Case on Military and Paramilitary Activities in and against Nicaragua (Nicaragua v. US), jurisdiction, judgment, November 26, 1984, ICJ Reports (1984).

ICJ Corfu Channel Case (merits), [1949] ICJ Reports 4.

ICJ East Timor, [1995] ICJ Reports 90, para. 29.

ICJ Gabcikovo-Nagymaros Project (Hungary v. Slovakia), [1997] ICJ Reports 7.

ICJ German Settlers in Poland, [1923] PCIJ Series B 6, para. 22.

ICJ Island of Palmas Case 2 R.I.A.A. (1928).

ICJ Legal Consequences of the Construction of a Wall in the Occupied Palestinian Territory, Advisory Opinion, July 9, 2004, ICJ Reports (2005).

ICJ Oil Platforms Case: Iran v. United States, judgment (2003) ICJ 161 (November 6), paras. 12–13 (separate opinion of Judge Simma).

ICJ Tadic Case (judgment of the Appeals Chamber), IT-94-1 (1999) 4, para. 145. http://www.icty.org/.

ICJ Tehran Hostages United States Diplomatic and Consular Staff in Tehran (US v. Iran), judgment, May 24, 1980, ICJ Reports (1980) 3, paras. 31–34.

ICJ United States Diplomatic and Consular Staff in Tehran, [1980] ICJ Reports 3, paras. 56, 63–67.

ICJ Wall Advisory Opinion, Judge Higgins Separate Opinion.

ICTY, Prosecutor v. Tadic, IT-94-1-A, Appeals Chamber judgment, July 15, 1999.

Interpretation of Peace Treaties with Bulgaria, Hungary and Romania (Second Phase), [1950] ICJ Reports paras. 221, 228.

JB Pictures, Inc., v. Department of Defense, 86 F.3d 236 (D.C. Cir. 1996).

Katz v. United States, 389 U.S. 347 (1967).

Kivenmaa v. Finland, Human Rights Committee, Communication No. 412/1990, CCPR/C/50/D/412/1990, March 31, 1994.

Krone Verlag GmbH and Co. KG v. Austria, judgment, February 26, 2002, No. 34315/96, section 34.

"Moses Case." In Moore, International Arbitrations, III, 3127–29 (1871).

Nixon v. Warner Communications, Inc., 435 U.S. 589, 98 S. Ct. 1306, 55 L. Ed. 2d 570 (1978).

OGH, 24. 6. (2014) 4 Ob 71/14s.

Oil Platforms and Armed Activities in the Congo (Congo v. Uganda).

Olsmtead v. United States, 277 U.S. 438, 478 (1928) (Brandeis, J dissenting).

Ople v. Torres, G.R. No. 127685, July 23, 1998.

PCIJ Case concerning the Factory at Chorzow (Jurisdiction), [1927] PCIJ Series A9 at 21.

PCIJ S.S. *Lotus* (Fr. v. Turk.) 1927 P.C.I.J. (ser. A) No. 10, at 4, 88 (Moore, J dissenting).

PCIJ The Case of the S.S. Lotus (France v. Turkey), 1927 PCIJ (ser. A) no. 10 (September 7) at 18. http://www.worldcourts.com/.

Peck v. the United Kingdom, 36 EHRR 41 (2003).

Perry v. United Kingdom, [2003] ECHR 375, (2004) 39 EHRR 3, § 38.

Phosphates in Morocco (Preliminary Objections), [1938] PCIJ Series A/B no. 74, paras. 10, 28.

Reno v. ACLU, 521 US 844, 850–51 (1997).

RIAA Lehigh Valley Railroad Company and Others (Sabotage Cases: Black Tom and Kings Land Incidents), [1930] RIAA VIII 84. [1939] RIAA VIII 225, 458.

RIAA Responsibility of Germany for Damage Caused in the Portuguese Colonies in the South Africa (Naulilaa Arbitration) (Portugal v. Germany), July 31, 1928, 2 RIAA 1011 at 1028.

RIAA Stephens Case, [1927] RIAA IV 265–67.

RIAA The Zafiro Case, [1925] RIAA VI 160.

RIAA XV (1901) at 395, 399, 401, 404, 407, 408, 409; RIAA II (1925) at 615, 641; RIAA XIV (1953) at 159, 163; RIAA XX (1990) at 217.

Ritchie v. Coldwater Community Schools, 947 F. Supp. 2d 791 (W.D. Mich. 2013).

Roger Deplanche v. Joseph A. Califano, Secretary of Health, Education and Welfare, individually and in his official capacity as secretary, 549 F.Supp. 685.

Salvador Commercial Company Case, (1902) RIAA XV 455, 477 (1902).

Smith v. Maryland, 442 U.S. 735 (1979).

Stoianoff v. Commissioner of Motor Vehicles, 107 F.Supp.2d 439 (S.D.N.Y. 2000).

Twentieth Century Fox v. BT, no. HC10C04385, High Court of Justice, S.119.

Twentieth Century Fox v. Newzbin, no. H C08C03346, judgment of Kitchin J, March 29, 2010, S.135.

Whalen v. Roe, 429 U.S. at 598–99, 97 S.Ct. 869, 51 L.Ed.2d 64 (1977).

UNITED NATIONS AND INTERNATIONAL DOCUMENTS

Annan, K. (2003). "Secretary General's Address to the General Assembly," United Nations, New York, September 23. http://www.un.org/.

Convention on the Elimination of All Forms of Discrimination against Women, article 10, December 18, 1979, 1249 U.N.T.S. 13; 19 I.L.M. 33 (1980).

Convention on the Rights of the Child, article 29(b), November 20, 1989, 1577 U.N.T.S. 3; 28 I.L.M. 1456 (1989).

Council of Europe, Convention on Cybercrime (2001), ETS No. 185.

Council of Europe, Convention on Cybercrime (2001), 41 I.L.M. 41.

Council of Europe, International and Multi-stakeholder Co-operation on Cross-border Internet: Interim Report of the Ad-hoc Advisory Group on Cross-border Internet to the Steering Committee on the Media and New Communication Services (2010).

Council of Europe, Committee of Ministers. (2012). Internet Governance: Council of Europe Strategy 2012–2015, CM Documents, CM(2011)175 final, March 15, 2012. https://wcd.coe.int/.

Council of Europe. (2014a). Recommendation CM/Rec(2014)6 of the Committee of Ministers to Member States on a Guide to Human Rights for Internet Users, Adopted by the Committee of Ministers on April 16, 2014, at the 1197th meeting of the Ministers' Deputies. https://wcd.coe.int/.

———. (2014b). The Rule of Law on the Internet and in the Wider Digital World: Issue Paper Published by the Council of Europe Commissioner for Human Rights, CommDH/Issue Paper (2014)1/8 December 2014. Strasbourg: Council of Europe. https://wcd.coe.int/.

Directive 2000/31/EC of the European Parliament and of the Council of June 8, 2000, on Certain Legal Aspects of Information Society Services, in Particular Electronic Commerce, in the Internal Market (Directive on electronic commerce, OJ L 178, 17.7.2000), articles 12–15.

Directive 2001/29/EC on Copyright in the Information Society.

Directive 2004/48/ec; Directive 2000/31/EC; Copyright, Designs and Patents Act 1988.

Directive 2006/24/EC of the European Parliament and of the Council of March 15, 2006, on the Retention of Data Generated or Processed in Connection with the Provision of Publicly Available Electronic Communications Services or of Public Communications Networks and Amending Directive 2002/58/EC. http://eur-lex.europa.eu/; 25.01.2012. COM(2012) 10.

Directive 2009/140/EC, article 1.3a.

Directive 95/46/EC of the European Parliament and of the Council of October 24, 1995, on the Protection of Individuals with Regard to the Processing of Personal Data and on the Free Movement of Such Data. http://eur-lex.europa.eu/.

EU Parliament, Proposal for a Regulation of the European Parliament and of the Council on the Protection of Individuals with Regard to the Processing of Personal Data and on the Free Movement of Such Data (General Data Protection Regulation) (2012).

European Commission. (2011a). P-0805/11FR, Réponse donnée par M.Barnier au nom de la Commission, March 7, 2011.

———. (2011b). Ref. Ares(2011)367168, Synthesis Report on the Stakeholders' Dialogue on Illegal Up- and Downloading 2009–2010, April 4, 2011.

———. (2011c). Communication from the Commission to the European Parliament, the Council, the European Economic and Social Committee and the Committee of the Regions, a Single Market for Intellectual Property Rights Boosting Creativity and Innovation to Provide Economic Growth, High-Quality Jobs and First-Class Products and Services in Europe Com, 287 Final, May 24.

———. (2011d). COM(2011) 942, Commission Communication to the European Parliament, the Council, the Economic and Social Committee and the Committee of the Regions, a Coherent Framework for Building Trust in the Digital Single Market for E-commerce and Online Services.

European Commission, Commission Staff Working Document on the Review of the European Programme for Critical Infrastructure Protection (EPCIP) (2012).

European Commission, Communication from the Commission on a European Programme for Critical Infrastructure Protection (2006).

European Commission, Communication from the Commission on the Global Approach to Transfers of Passenger Name Record Data to Third Countries, European Commission, Brussels (2010), 3.

European Commission, Council Directive 2008/114/EC of December 8, 2008, on the Identification and Designation of European Critical Infrastructures and the Assessment of the Need to Improve Their Protection, OJ L 345, 23.12 (2008), 75–82.

European Commission, Critical Infrastructure, Migration and Home Affairs. Last updated June 23, 2015. http://ec.europa.eu/.

European Commission, Critical Infrastructure Protection (2004). http://europa.eu/.

European Commission, DG Enterprise and Industry, Towards a More Secure Society and Increased Industrial Competitiveness: Security Research Projects under the 7th Framework Programme for Research, Security, European Commission, Brussels (2009), 6.

European Commission Directive 2002/58/EC of the European Parliament and of the Council of July 12, 2002, concerning the Processing of Personal Data and the Protection of Privacy in the Electronic Communications Sector (Directive on Privacy and Electronic Communications, OJ L 201, 2002), article 13.

European Commission Proposal for a Directive of the European Parliament and of the Council concerning Measures to Ensure a High Common Level of Network and Information Security across the Union, COM (2013).

ILC Draft Articles on Responsibility of States for Internationally Wrongful Acts, with Commentaries (2001). http://legal.un.org/.

ILC Report of the International Law Commission, 32nd Session, [1980] II (2) ILC Ybk 1, 53–54.

ILC UN GAOR 56th Sess. Supp. No. 10, 43, "Draft Articles on Responsibility of States for Internationally Wrongful Acts." In Report of the International Law Commission on the Work of Its Fifty-Third Session, UN Doc. A/56/10 (2001). http://www.un.org/law/ilc.

International Convention on the Elimination of All Forms of Racial Discrimination, article 7, G.A. res. 2106 (XX), Annex, 20 U.N. GAOR Supp. No. 14 at 47, U.N. Doc. A/6014 (1966), 660 U.N.T.S. 195, entered into force January 4, 1969.

International Covenant on Economic, Social and Cultural Rights, GA res. 2200A (XXI).

IRP Coalition. ([2011] 2015). The Charter of Human Rights and Principles for the Internet Booklet, 4th ed. Internet Rights and Principles Coalition. http://internetrightsandprinciples.org/.

MacBride, Seán. (1980). Many Voices One World (MacBride Report), UNESCO, International Commission for the Study of Communication Problems.

Organisation for Economic Cooperation and Development (OECD). (1988). Recommendation of the Council concerning Chemical Accident Prevention, Preparedness and Response.

———. (2002). Recommendation of the Council concerning Guidelines for the Security of Information Systems and Networks: Towards a Culture of Security.

———. (2008). Recommendation on the Protection of Critical Information Infrastructures.

———. (2014). Recommendation of the Council on the Governance of Critical Risks.

Proposal for a Directive of the European Parliament and of the Council on the Protection of Individuals with Regard to the Processing of Personal Data by Competent Authorities for the Purposes of Prevention, Investigation, Detection or Prosecution of Criminal Offences or the Execution of Criminal Penalties, and the Free Movement of Such Data. http://eur-lex.europa.eu/.

Telecommunications Technology Association (TTA). (2012). "NGN: Requirements for Deep Packet Inspection in Next Generation Networks." Telecommunications Technology Association Standard, 2012-1357.Y.2770.

UN CCPR General Comment No. 03: Implementation at the National Level, article 2, Thirteenth session, July 29, 1981.

UN CCPR General Comment No. 10: Freedom of Expression, article 19, Nineteenth session, June 29, 1983.

UN Declaration on Principles of International Law concerning Friendly Relations and Cooperation among States in Accordance with the Charter of the United Nations, GA Res 2625, December 17, 1970.

UN Definition of Aggression Resolution, Annex, GA Res. 3314 (XXIX) UN GAOR, 6th Comm 29th Sess. Supp. No. 31 at 142, UN Doc. A/9631 (1974).

UN Doc A/56/10, 2001, chap. 4, commentary to article 8 (3).

UN Doc A/66/152, July 15, 2001.

UN Doc A/68/98, July 24, 2013.

UNESCO. (2015). Outcome Document: "CONNECTing the Dots: Options for Future Action" Conference, held at the UNESCO Headquarters, Paris, March 3–4. http://www.unesco.org/.

UN GA Resolution 55/63, December 4, 2000.

UN GA Resolution 2625, UN GAOR, 25th Sess. Supp. No. 18, at 339, UN Doc. A/8018 (1970).

UN General Assembly. (2000). Millennium Development Goals. http://www.un.org/millenniumgoals/

UN General Assembly, "2005 World Summit Outcome." UN Doc. A/Res/60/I, September 16, 2005, 30. http://www.un.org/.

UN Human Rights Commission [CCPR], General Comment No. 29, State of Emergency, article 4, section 2, UN Doc. CCPR/C/21/Rev.1/Add 11 (August 31, 2001).

UN Human Rights Council (2012), A/HRC/RES/20/8.

UN Human Rights Sub-Commission (2005) Joint Written Statement by CETIM and AAJ, Comment on the Secretary-General's Report on the Reform of the UN, E/CN.4/Sub.2/2005/NGO/7. http://www.cetim.ch/.

UN International Law Commission, Report of the International Law Commission, Draft Articles of State Responsibility, UN GAOR, 53rd Sess. Supp. No. 10, UN Doc. A/56/10 (2001). http://www.un.org/law/ilc/.

UN Frank La Rue Report of the Special Rapporteur on the Promotion and Protection of the Right to Freedom of Opinion and Expression, para. 60, Human Rights Council, Seventeenth Session, A/HRC/17/27, May 16, 2011.

UN League of Nations Conference for the Codification of International Law, Bases of Discussion for the Conference Drawn up by the Preparatory Committee III: Responsibility of States for Damage Caused in their Territory to the Person or Property of Foreigners (Doc. C.75 M.69 1929 V.) 25, 41, 52.

UN Materials on the Responsibility of States for International Wrongful Acts, UN Legislative Series (New York: UN, 2012), ST/LEG/SER B/25, pp. 27–28, paras. 3–5. http://legal.un.org/.

UN Secretary General's High-Level Panel on Threats, Challenges, and Change, A More Secure World: Our Shared Responsibility, UN Doc. A/59/565, December 2004.http://www.un.org/.

UN Secretary General's Report, In Larger Freedom: Towards Development, Security and Human Rights for All (2005) A/59/2005, para. 124. http://www.un.org/.

UN (2011), I.B.3 and B.5, II.B.21. UN Security Council Resolution 1244, June 10, 1999 (4011th meeting).

UN Security Council Resolution 1483, May 22, 2003 (4761st meeting).

UN Security Council Resolution 1511, October 16, 2003 (4844th meeting).

UN Security Council Resolution 1546, June 8, 2004 (4987th meeting).

UNTS "Geneva Convention Relative to the Treatment of Prisoners of War," August 12, 1949, United Nations Treaty Series 75, no. 972 (1950).

U.S. v. Kincade, 379 F.3d 813, 818–19 (9th Cir. 2004).

WSIS Civil Society Caucus. (2003). "Shaping Information Societies for Human Needs." Civil Society Declaration Unanimously Adopted by the WSIS Civil Society Plenary on December 8. http://www.itu.int/.

———. (2005). "Civil Society Declaration: Much More Could Have Been Achieved." Document WSIS-05/TUNIS/CONTR/13-E, December 18. http://www.itu.int/.

Zalnieriute, Monika, and Schneider, Thomas. (2014). "ICANN's Procedures and Policies in the Light of Human Rights, Fundamental Freedoms and Democratic Values." Report for the Council of Europe DG1(2014)12, October 8. http://www.coe.int/.

INTERNATIONAL TREATIES

Anti-Counterfeiting Trade Agreement (ACTA), December 2010 version.

Charter of Fundamental Rights of the European Union (2000/C 364/01), article 17.2.

Convention on International Civil Aviation, Document 7300. http://www.icao.int/.

Draft Convention on International Information Security (2011). http://cryptome.org/.

Hague Convention IV Respecting the Laws and Customs of War on Land, 1907 Hague Conventions 100, 103.

Human Rights Committee, International Covenant on Civil and Political Rights, 102nd session, September 12, 2011, CCPR-C-GC/34, no. 23.

Protocol Additional to the Geneva Conventions of August 12, 1949, Relating to the Protection of Victims of International Armed Conflicts (Protocol I), [1977] UNJY 95 at 132.

Universal Declaration of Human Rights (UN 1948, article 30).

Versailles Treaty of Peace with Germany, Peace Treaties Series II (1919) 1265, 1934.

U.S. STATUTES AND OTHER NATIONAL LAWS

18 U.S. Code § 2518(4).
42 U.S. Code § 14135a.
429 U.S. at 598–99, 97 S.Ct. 869, 51 L.Ed.2d 64 (1977).
442 U.S. 735 (1979).
476 U.S. 207 (1986).
Defamation Act (2013).
Ley 2/2011, de 4 de Marzo de Economia Sostenible, Annex 43 (Ley Sinde, or Sinde's law).
Loi no. 2009-669 du 12 juin 2009 favorisant la diffusion et la protection de la Création sur Internet (Creation and Internet Law) (2009).
Privacy Act of 1974, 5 U.S.C. § 552a. http://www.gpo.gov/.
Uniting and Strengthening America by Providing Appropriate Tools Required to Intercept and Obstruct Terrorism (USA Patriot Act) Act of 2001. http://www.gpo.gov/.

GOVERNMENT DOCUMENTS

Anderson, Robert, Jr. (2014). "Cyber Security, Terrorism, and Beyond: Addressing Evolving Threats to the Homeland," Statement before the Senate Committee on Homeland Security and Governmental Affairs, September 10. http://www.fbi.gov/.
Article 29 Data Protection Working Party, Opinion 4/2004 on the Processing of Personal Data by Means of Video Surveillance, Brussels, 15.
Article 29 Working Party, European Data Protection Authorities Clarify Principle of Purpose Limitation, Brussels, April 8, 2013. http://ec.europa.eu/.
"Big Data: Seizing Opportunities, Preserving Values," Executive Office of the President, May 2014. http://www.whitehouse.gov/.
Clinton, Hillary. (2010). "Secretary of State." Remarks on Internet Freedom from US Department of State, Washington, DC, January 21.
Defense Science Board. (2013). "Task Force Report: Resilient Military Systems and the Advanced Cyber Threat." U.S. Department of Defense, January.
"DNA: Federal DNA Database Unit (FDDU)." FBI. Accessed September 3, 2015. http://www.fbi.gov/.
Hason, Fergus. (2012). "Internet Freedom: The Role of the U.S. State Department." Accessed June 29, 2014. http://www.brookings.edu/.
Lynn, W. J. (2011). "Remarks on the Department of Defense Cyber Strategy" (speech). National Defense University, Washington, DC, July 14. http://www.defense.gov/.
Obama, Barack. (2009). "Remarks by the President on Securing Our Nation's Cyber Infrastructure" (speech). White House East Room, May 29. http://www.whitehouse.gov/.
———. (2012). "Taking the Cyberattack Threat Seriously." *Wall Street Journal*, July 19. http://www.wsj.com/.
———. (2014). "Remarks by the President in Year-End Conference." December 19. http://www.whitehouse.gov/.
Office of the National Counterintelligence Executive. (2011). "Foreign Spies Stealing US Economic Secrets in Cyberspace: Report to Congress on Foreign Economic Collection and Industrial Espionage, 2009–2011." National Counterintelligence and Security Center, October. http://www.ncix.gov/.
Panetta, Leon E. (2012). "Remarks by Secretary Panetta on Cybersecurity to the Business Executives for National Security, New York City" (speech), October 11. http://www.defense.gov/.
Public Safety Canada. (2010). "Cyber Security: A Shared Responsibility." Last updated March 4, 2014. http://www.publicsafety.gc.ca/cyber.

————. (2014). "Canadian Cyber Incident Response Centre (CCIRC)." Last updated December 12. http://www.publicsafety.gc.ca/.

Public Safety Canada and Department of Homeland Security. (2012). "Cybersecurity Action Plan between Public Safety Canada and the Department of Homeland Security." Last updated March 4, 2014. http://www.publicsafety.gc.ca/.

Rumsfeld, D. (2002). "Status of Taliban and Al Qaeda." Memorandum for Chairman of the Joint Chiefs of Staff, January 19. http://www.defenselink.mil/.

Stop Online Piracy Act (SOPA), 12th congress, 1st session, HR 3261, A Bill to Promote Prosperity, Creativity, Entrepreneurship, and Innovation by Combating the Theft of U.S. Property, and for Other Purposes.

U.S. Department of Defense. (2011). "Cyberspace Policy Report." http://www.defense.gov/.

U.S. Department of Homeland Security, National Cyber Division, U.S. Computer Emergency Readiness Team. (2004). "Privacy Impact Assessment: Einstein Program; Collecting, Analyzing, and Sharing Computer Security Information across the Federal Civilian Government." September. http://www.dhs.gov/.

U.S. Office of Homeland Security. (2013). "What Is Critical Infrastructure?" Last updated August 26, 2015. http://www.dhs.gov/.

White House. (2011). "International Strategy for Cyberspace: Prosperity, Security, and Openness in a Networked World." May. http://www.whitehouse.gov/.

White House, Office of the Press Secretary. (2013). "Presidential Policy Directive: Critical Infrastructure Security and Resilience." February 12. http://www.whitehouse.gov/.

WEBSITES AND OTHER ONLINE RESOURCES

Aigrain, P. (2010). "Declouding Freedom: Reclaiming Servers, Services, and Data." 2020 FLOSS Roadmap (2010 version, 3rd ed.). Accessed August 28, 2015. https://flossroadmap.co-ment.com/.

Alvestrand, H. (2004). "Request for Comments: 3935; A Mission Statement for the IETF." Cisco Systems, October. http://www.ietf.org/.

America's Navy. (2009). "Eternal Father: The Navy Hymn." Last updated August 17. http://www.navy.mil/.

Banisar, David, and Davies, Simon. (2015). "Privacy and Human Rights: An International Survey of Privacy Laws and Practice." Global Internet Liberty Campaign, Privacy International. Accessed August 28. http://www.gilc.org/.

Baker, Stewart Abercrombie, Filipiak, Natalia, and Timlin, Katrina. (2011). "In the Dark: Crucial Industries Confront Cyber Attacks." McAfee. http://www.mcafee.com/.

Best, Richard A., and Cumming, Alfred. (2007). "Open Source Intelligence (OSINT): Issues for Congress." Congressional Research Service, December 5. http://www.au.af.mil/.

Boyd, Dana. (2010). "Privacy and Publicity in the Context of Big Data." WWW2010, April 29. http://www.danah.org/.

Burgess, M. (2003). "A Brief History of Terrorism." Center for Defense Information, July 2. http://www.cdi.org/.

Center for Church Music. (2015). "Eternal Father, Strong to Save." Accessed September 2. http://songsandhymns.org/.

Center for Strategic and International Studies. (2014). "Significant Cyber Incidents Since 2006." Last updated August 7. http://csis.org/.

Cloud Computing Journal. (2008). "Twenty-One Experts Define Cloud Computing." Accessed August 28, 2015. http://cloudcomputing.sys-con.com/.

Corwin, Philip S. (2014). "If the Stakeholders Already Control the Internet, Why NETmundial and the IANA Transition?" CircleID, March 16. http://www.circleid.com/.

Couts, Andrew. (2012). "CISPA Supporters List: 800+ Companies That Could Help Uncle Sam Snag Your Data." *Digital Trends*, April 12. http://www.digitaltrends.com/.

Donilon, Tom. (2013). "Remarks by Tom Donilon, National Security Advisor to the President: 'The United States and the Asia-Pacific in 2013'" (speech). White House, Office of the Press Secretary, March 11. http://www.whitehouse.gov/.

Drummond, David. (2010). "A New Approach to China." Google: Official Blog, January 12. http://googleblog.blogspot.co.uk/.

Ermert, Monika. (2010). "ICANN Boss Creates a Stir with DNS Security Warning." H-Security Online, March 12. http://www.h-online.com/.

Federal Business Opportunities. (2014). "Malware, Solicitation Number: RFQ1307A." February 3. https://www.fbo.gov/.

Find Biometrics. (2015). "Vein Recognition." Accessed August 30. http://www.findbiometrics.com/.

GeneWatch UK. (2015). "The UK Police National DNA Database." Accessed August 28. http://www.genewatch.org/.

Greenwood, Christopher. (2012). "Self-Defence." In *Max Planck Encyclopedia of Public International Law*. April. http://opil.ouplaw.com/.

Information Commissioner's Office. (2008). "In the Picture: A Data Protection Code of Practice for Surveillance Cameras and Personal Information." http://ico.org.uk/.

International Telecommunication Union (ITU). (2015). "ITU-T Recommendations." Accessed September 1. http://www.itu.int/.

Internet Governance Forum (IGF). (2008). "Chairman's Summary." Third Meeting of the United Nations Internet Governance Forum, Hyderabad, India, December 3–6. http://www.intgovforum.org/.

———. (2011). "What Is the Internet Governance Forum?" Background Note: Internet Governance Forum, Nairobi, September 23–27. http://www.intgovforum.org/.

ITU/WSIS (2003a). "Declaration of Principles: Building the Information Society: A Global Challenge in the New Millennium." Document WSIS-03/GENEVA/DOC/4-E. http://www.itu.int/.

———. (2003b). "Plan of Action." Document WSIS-03/GENEVA/DOC/5-E, December. http://www.itu.int/.

———. (2005). "Tunis Agenda for the Information Society." WSIS-05/TUNIS/DOC/6 (Rev. 1)-E, November 18. http://www.itu.int/.

Internet Society. (2015). "What Is the Internet?" Accessed September 7. http://www.internetsociety.org/.

Jakubowicz, Karol. (2009). "A New Notion of Media? Media and Media-Like Content and Activities on New Communication Services." Media and Information Society Division, Directorate General of Human Rights and Legal Affairs, Council of Europe. April. http://www.coe.int/.

Kaspersky Lab. (2015). "Spam and Phishing Statistics Report Q1-2014." Accessed August 31. http://usa.kaspersky.com/.

Liberty. (2014). "No Snoopers' Charter: Campaigning for an End to Blanket Surveillance of the Entire Population." Accessed September 22, 2015. https://www.liberty-human-rights.org.uk/.

Macdonald, K. (2013a). "A Human Rights Audit of the Internet Watch Foundation." IWF, November 2013. https://www.iwf.org.uk/.

———. (2013b). "Review of .uk Registration Policy." Nominet, December 2013. http://www.nominet.uk/.

MacKinnon, Rebecca, Hickok, Elonnai, Bar, Allon, and Lim, Hae-in. (2014). "Fostering Freedom Online: The Role of Internet Intermediaries." A report prepared for UNESCO's Division for Freedom of Expression and Media Development, UNESCO/Internet Society, Paris. http://unesdoc.unesco.org/.

Madden, Mary. (2014). "Public Perceptions of Privacy and Security in the Post-Snowden Era." Pew Research Internet Project, November 12. http://www.pewinternet.org/.

Matthews, Duncan. (2008). "The Fight against Counterfeiting and Piracy in the Bilateral Trade Agreements of the EU." Directorate General External Policies of the Union, June. http://www.europarl.europa.eu/.

McCormick, N. (1992). "Beyond the Sovereign State." Chorley Lecture 21, London School of Economics, *Modern Law Review*, June 3. http://www.modernlawreview.co.uk/.

McNair-Wilson, Laura. (2011). "Defamation and Twitter: First Love." *Inforrm's Blog*, January 29. https://inforrm.wordpress.com/.

MIPT Terrorism Knowledge Base. (2006). "TKB Incident Analysis Wizard." Accessed November 22. http://www.tkb.org/.

Moglen, E. (2010). "Freedom in the Cloud: Software Freedom, Privacy, and Security for Web 2.0 and Cloud Computing." ISOC Meeting, New York, February 5. Software Freedom Law Center. https://www.softwarefreedom.org/.

Necessary and Proportionate. (2013). "International Principles on the Application of Human Rights to Communications Surveillance." July. https://en.necessaryandproportionate.org/.

NETmundial. (2014). "Global Multistakeholder Meeting on the Future of Internet Governance." NETmundial Multistakeholder Statement of Sao Paulo, April 24. http://netmundial. br/.

———. (2015). "NETmundial: The Beginning of a Process." Accessed September 7. http:// netmundial.br/.

Nye, Joseph S., Jr. (2015). "Cyber Power." Massachusetts Institute of Technology, Accessed August 28. http://web.mit.edu/.

Open Net Initiative. (2013). "YouTube Censored: A Recent History." OpenNet Initiative. Accessed August 26. https://opennet.net/

Oram, A. (2004). "From P2P to Web Services: Addressing and Coordination." O'Reilly XML.com, April 7. http://www.xml.com/.

Ouzounis, Vangelis. (2015). "Resilience of Networks and Services and Critical Information Infrastructure Protection." European Union Agency for Network and Information Security (ENISA). Accessed August 28. https://www.enisa.europa.eu/.

Philpott, Dan. (2003). "Sovereignty." In *Stanford Encyclopedia of Philosophy*, edited by E. N. Zalta. http://plato.stanford.edu/.

Postel, Jon. (1994). "Domain Name System Structure and Delegation." Information Sciences Institute, March. https://www.ietf.org/.

Pouchard, Line C., Dobson, Jonathan M., and Trien, Joseph P. (2009). "A Framework for the Systematic Collection of Open Source Intelligence." Association for the Advancement of Artificial Intelligence. Accessed August 28, 2015. http://www.aaai.org/.

Reisman, William Michael. (2005). "Expanding the UN Security Council: Much Ado." University of Pittsburgh, August. http://jurist.law.pitt.edu/.

Reporters without Borders. (2014). "World Press Freedom Index 2014." Accessed August 29, 2015. http://rsf.org/.

Roucounas, M. Emmanuel. (2007). "Tenth Commission: Present Problems of the Use of Armed Force in International Law; A. Self-Defence." Institut de Droit International, *AIDI* 72, article 5. http://www.idi-iil.org/.

Royal Naval Association. (2015). "Frequently Asked Questions." Accessed August 29. http:// www.royal-naval-association.co.uk/.

Schmitt, Michael J. (2014a). "International Law and Cyber Attacks: Sony v. North Korea." Just Security, December 17. http://justsecurity.org/.

———. (2014b). "Normative Voids and Asymmetry in Cyberspace." Just Security, December 29. http://justsecurity.org/.

Schultz, Susanne. (2015). "'Stop the DNA Collection Frenzy!' Expansion of Germany's DNA Database." Forensic Genetics Policy Initiative. Accessed September 3. http:// dnapolicyinitiative.org/.

Shackleford, Scott J. (2010). "State Responsibility for Cyber Attacks: Competing Standards for a Growing Problem." In *Conference on Cyber Conflict Proceedings 2010*, edited by Christian Czosseck and Karlin Podins, 197–208. Tallinn, Estonia: CCD COE Publications. https:/ /ccdcoe.org/.

Shannon, Greg. (2010). "CERT Research Report." Software Engineering Institute, Carnegie Mellon University. Accessed August 29, 2015. https://resources.sei.cmu.edu/.

Statewatch. (2015). "Statewatch Briefing: ID Cards in the EU; Current State of Play." Accessed August 29. http://statewatch.org/.

Sullivan, Laurie. (2006). "Iris Scanning for New Jersey Grade School." *Information Week*, January 23. http://www.informationweek.com/.

Theohary, Catherine A., and Rollins, John. (2011). "Terrorist Use of the Internet: Information Operations in Cyberspace." Congressional Research Service, March 8. http://www.fas.org/.

Tor. (2015). "Inception." Accessed September 3. http://www.torproject.org/.

Touré, Hamadoun I. (2011). "The International Response to Cyberwar." In *The Quest for Cyber Peace*, by Hamadoun I. Touré and the Permanent Monitoring Panel on Information Security World Federation of Scientists, 86–103. Geneva: International Telecommunication Union. http://www.itu.int/.

U.S. Computer Emergency Readiness Team (US-CERT). (2015). "About Us." Accessed September 2. https://www.us-cert.gov/.

Wikipedia. (2015a). "List of Organizations with Official Stances on the SOPA and PIPA." Last updated May 9. http://en.wikipedia.org/.

———. (2015b). "Network Address Translation." Last updated September 5. http://en.wikipedia.org/.

Wilson, Clay. (2012). "Industrial and SCADA Systems May Be Increasingly Targeted for Cyberattack." University of Maryland University College, December 22. http://www.pesolutions-it.com/.

WinFuture. (2015). "Finanzämter fahnden per Street View nach Tricksern." Accessed September 3. http://winfuture.de/.

Working Group on Internet Governance (WGIG). (2005). "Report of the Working Group on Internet Governance." Château de Bossey, June. http://www.wgig.org/.

World Conference on International Telecommunications (WCIT). (2012). "Cybersecurity." Background Brief 6. Accessed September 2, 2015. http://www.itu.int/.

WorldLII. (2013a). "Resolution on Profiling." Thirty-Fifth International Conference of Data Protection and Privacy Commissioners Resolutions and Declarations 3. September 26. http://www.worldlii.org/.

———. (2013b). "Resolution on Web Tracking and Privacy." Thirty-Fifth International Conference of Data Protection and Privacy Commissioners Resolutions and Declarations 9. September 26. http://www.worldlii.org/.

World Summit on the Information Society (WSIS). (2005). "Tunis Agenda for the Information Society." November 18. http://www.itu.int/.

NEWSPAPER ARTICLES

Anthony, Sebastian. (2013). "China Continues Cyberwar Campaign, Hacks the New York Times." ExtremeTech, January 31. http://www.extremetech.com/.

Bartlett, Jamie. (2014). "Why Terrorists and Far-Right Extremists Will Be Early Adopters." *Telegraph*, November 4. http://www.telegraph.co.uk/.

———. (2015). "The March of the Armchair Jihadis." *Financial Times*, January 13. http://www.ft.com/.

BBC News. (2011). "Egypt: Mubarak Sacks Cabinet and Defends Security Role." January 29. http://www.bbc.co.uk/.

———. (2012). "Cyber-Security Bill Cispa Passes US House." April 26. http://www.bbc.com/.

Berners-Lee, T. (2010). "Long Live the Web: A Call for Continued Open Standards and Neutrality." *Scientific American*, December. http://www.scientificamerican.com/.

Branigan, Tania. (2010). "China Responds to Google Hacking Claims." *Guardian*, January 14. http://www.theguardian.com/.

Cerf, Vint. (2012). "Internet Access Is Not a Human Right." *New York Times*, January 4. http://www.nytimes.com/.

Clayton. Mark. (2013). "Obama Pressured to Confront China's Xi Jinping on Cyber Spying." *Christian Science Monitor*, June 7. http://www.csmonitor.com/.

Cookson, R. (2013). "Anti-Piracy Drive Sees Premier League Mistakenly Block Websites." *Financial Times*, August 15, 2013.

Dilanian, Ken. (2011a). "Russian and China Accused of Cyber-Spying Campaign to Steal U.S. Secrets." *Los Angeles Times*, August 12. http://articles.latimes.com/.

———. (2011b). "U.S. Lawmakers Demand Action over Alleged China Cyber Attacks." *Los Angeles Times*, October 4. http://articles.latimes.com/.

Dilanian, Ken, and Parsons, Christi. (2013). "White House Adopts New Strategy to Safeguard Intellectual Property." *Los Angeles Times*, February 20. http://articles.latimes.com/.

Emert, Monika. (2011). "Filtering and Blocking Closer to the Core of the Internet?" *Intellectual Property Watch*, November 20, 2011.

Everett-Church, R. (1999). "The Spam That Started It All." *Wired*, April. http://www.wired.com/.

Fox-Brewster, Tom. (2014). "Check the Permissions: Android Flashlight Apps Criticized over Privacy." *Guardian*, October 3.

Fram, Alan. (2012). "SOPA and PIPA Bills: Online Companies Win Piracy Fight." *Huffington Post*, January 21. http://www.huffingtonpost.com/.

Franceschi-Bicchierai, Lorenzo. (2015). "Islamist Hackers Deface French Sites in Response to 'Operation Charlie Hebdo.'" Mashable, January 13. http://mashable.com/.

Ghannoushi, Soumaya. (2011). "Tunisians Must Dismantle the Monster Ben Ali Built." *Guardian*, January 18. http://www.guardian.co.uk/.

Gorman, Siobhan. (2014). "NSA Director Warns of 'Dramatic' Cyberattack in Next Decade." *Wall Street Journal*, November 20. http://www.wsj.com/.

Greenwald, Glenn. (2013). "NSA Collecting Phone Records of Millions of Verizon Customers Daily." *Guardian*, June 5. http://www.theguardian.com/.

Greenwald, Glenn, and MacAskill, Ewen. (2013a). "Boundless Informant: The NSA's Secret Tool to Track Global Surveillance Data." *Guardian*, June 11. http://www.theguardian.com/.

———. (2013b). "NSA Prism Program Taps in to User Data of Apple, Google and Others." *Guardian*, June 7. http://www.theguardian.com/.

———. (2013c). "Obama Orders US to Draw Up Overseas Target List for Cyber-Attacks." *Guardian*, June 7. http://www.theguardian.com/.

Grisham, Lori. (2015). "Timeline: North Korea and the Sony Pictures Hack." *USA Today*, January 5. http://www.usatoday.com/.

Guardian. (2013). "New York Times, Wall Street Journal and Washington Post Hacked." February 20. http://www.theguardian.com/.

Hannigan, R. (2014). "The Web Is a Terrorist's Command-and-Control Network of Choice." *Financial Times*, November 3, 2014.

Jackson, William. (2012). "McCain's Retooled Secure IT Act Still a Privacy Threat, Critics Say." *GCN*, July 2. http://gcn.com/.

Landler, Mark. (2010). "Clinton Urges Global Response to Internet Attacks." *New York Times*, January 21. http://www.nytimes.com/.

Landler, Mark, and Sanger, David E. (2013). "U.S. Demands China Block Cyberattacks and Agree to Rules." *New York Times*, March 11. http://www.nytimes.com/.

Latour, Bruno. (2007). "Beware, Your Imagination Leaves Digital Traces." *Times Higher Literary Supplement*, April 6. http://docs.google.com/.

Lee, Dave. (2012). "Flame: Massive Cyber-Attack Discovered." *BBC News*, May 28. http://www.bbc.com/.

Line, Harriet. (2015). "Charlie Hebdo Attack: Anonymous Claims First Victory in 'War' on Jihadi Websites." *Telegraph*, January 14. http://www.telegraph.co.uk/.

Liptak, Adam. (2008). "A Wave of the Watchlist and Speech Disappears." *New York Times*, March 4, 2008.

Madhani, Aamer. (2013). "Cybersecurity Will Loom Large at Obama-Xi Summit." *USA Today*, June 5. http://www.usatoday.com/.

Markoff, John. (2011). "Malware Aimed at Iran Hit Five Sites, Report Says." *New York Times*, February 11. http://www.nytimes.com/.

Martinez, Jennifer, and Romm, Tony. (2012). "SOPA Blackout Leads Co-sponsors to Defect." *Politico*, January 18. http://www.politico.com/.

McConnell, Mike. (2010). "Mike McConnell on How to Win the Cyber-War We're Losing." Editorial, *Washington Post*, February 28. http://www.washingtonpost.com/.

McConnell, Mike, Chertoff, Michael, and Lynn, William. (2012). "China's Cyber Thievery Is National Policy—And Must Be Challenged." *Wall Street Journal*, January 27. http://www.wsj.com/.

McMillan, Robert. (2014). "The Hidden Privacy Threat of . . . Flashlight Apps?" *Wired*, October 21.

Nakashima, Ellen. (2011). "Report on 'Operation Shady RAT' Identifies Widespread Cyber-Spying." *Washington Post*, August 3.

———. (2014). "White House Says Sony Hack Is a Serious National Security Matter." *Washington Post*, December 18. http://www.washingtonpost.com/.

Newsweek. (2008). "Highlights: Newsweek's Special Elections Project." November 4. http://www.newsweek.com/.

Nye, Joseph S., Jr. (2005). "How to Counter Terrorism's Online Generation." *Financial Times*, October 13.

Paganini, Pierluigi. (2014). "ISIS Is Ramping Up Efforts to Mount a Massive Cyber Attack." *Security Affairs* (blog), September 14. http://securityaffairs.co/.

Perlroth, Nicole. (2013). "Hackers in China Attacked the Times for Last 4 Months." *New York Times*, January 30. http://www.nytimes.com/.

Perlroth, Nicole, and Quentin, Hardy. (2013). "Bank Hacking Was the Work of Iranians, Officials Say." *New York Times*, January 8. http://www.nytimes.com/.

Poulson, Kevin. (2014). "Visit the Wrong Website, and the FBI Could End Up in Your Computer." *Wired*, August 5. http://www.wired.com/.

Riley, Michael A., and Robertson, Jordan. (2014). "Why Would Chinese Hackers Steal Millions of Medical Records?" BloombergBusiness, August 18. http://www.bloomberg.com/.

———. (2015). "Chinese State-Sponsored Hackers Suspected in Anthem Attack." BloombergBusiness, February 5. http://www.bloomberg.com/.

Rogin, Josh. (2012). "NSA Chief: Cybercrime Constitutes the 'Greatest Transfer of Wealth in History.'" *Foreign Policy*, July 9.

Sanger, David E. (2012). "Obama Order Sped Up Wave of Cyberattacks against Iran." *New York Times*, June 1. http://www.nytimes.com/.

Sanger, David E., Barboza, David, and Perlroth, Nicole. (2013). "Chinese Army Unit Is Seen as Tied to Hacking against U.S." *New York Times*, February 18. http://www.nytimes.com/.

Sanger, David E., and Landler, Mark. (2013). "U.S. and China Agree to Hold Regular Talks on Hacking." *New York Times*, June 1. http://www.nytimes.com/.

Sanger, David E., and Perlroth, Nicole. (2013). "Hackers from China Resume Attacks on U.S. Targets." *New York Times*, May 19. http://www.nytimes.com/.

Schiemenz, Juliane. (2014). "US-Bürger wehren sich gegen Stromzähler: Widerstand im Wohnwagen." *Spiegel Online*, May 8. http://www.spiegel.de/.

Shalal-Esa, Andrea. (2013). "Iran Strengthened Cyber Capabilities after Stuxnet." *Reuters*, January 17. http://www.reuters.com/.

Singh, Parminder Jeet. (2012). "Hyping One Threat to Hide Another." *Hindu*, November 28. http://www.thehindu.com/.

Smith, Dave. (2013a). "CISPA 2013: Google, Apple Top Massive List of Supporters Favoring the Controversial Cybersecurity Bill." *International Business Times*, April 12. http://www.ibtimes.com/.

———. (2013b). "RIP CISPA: Senate Expected to Kill 2013 Cybersecurity Bill." *International Business Times*, April 26. http://www.ibtimes.com/.

Smith, Gerry. (2013). "Senate Won't Vote on CISPA, Deals Blow to Controversial Cyber Bill." *Huffington Post*, April 25. http://www.huffingtonpost.com/.

Smith, Josh. (2011). "Rogers: U.S. Must Confront 'Intolerable' Chinese Cyberespionage." *National Journal*, October 4. http://www.nationaljournal.com/.

Smith, Patrick. (2011). "Stealing America: China's Busy Cyber-Spies." *Fiscal Times*, November 7. http://www.thefiscaltimes.com/.

SnoopWall. (2014). "Consumer Digital Privacy Protection Advisory: Top Mobile Flashlight Applications Spy on Users, Warn SnoopWall Cybersecurity Experts." October 2. http://www.snoopwall.com/.

Talaga, Tanya. (2015). "How Social Media Is Fuelling Ukraine's Protests." *Star.com*, March 4. http://www.thestar.com/.

Ukraine Today. (2014). "Ukrainian Volunteers Join Cyberspace War in Bid to Stop Insurgency Funding." November 20. http://uatoday.tv/.

Weaver, Courtney, and Clover, Charles. (2012). "Russia's 'Internet Blacklist' Sparks Fears." *Financial Times*, July 11, 2012.

Wilson, Scott, and Wan, William. (2013). "Obama, Xi Summit Could Help Define U.S.-China Relationship for Years to Come." *Washington Post*, June 5.

Worth, R. F. (2005). "Iraqi Insurgents Put the Web in Their Arsenal." *International Herald Tribune*, March 12.

Wortham, Jenna. (2012). "With Twitter, Blackouts and Demonstrations, Web Flexes Its Muscle." *New York Times*, January 18. http://www.nytimes.com/.

Zetter, Kim. (2010). "Google Asks NSA to Help Secure Its Network." *Wired*, February 4. http://www.wired.com/.

Index

Index

About the Editors and Contributors

Roy Balleste, JSD, is law library director and professor of law at St. Thomas University, in Miami Gardens, Florida. Balleste has concentrated his scholarship in the areas of Internet governance, human rights, and the relationship among information, technology, and people. He teaches Internet-governance and cybersecurity policy at St. Thomas University School of Law. In November 2007, he participated in the Second UN Internet Governance Forum (IGF) in Rio de Janeiro. He also participated in the Fifth UN Internet Governance Forum in Vilnius, Lithuania, in September 2010. Before attending the meeting in Vilnius, he submitted a comment supporting the continuation of the IGF beyond its original five-year mandate. Balleste is a member of the Global Internet Governance Academic Network (GigaNet) where he served as secretary of the Steering Committee from December 2010 to December 2012. Balleste is a member of the Internet Corporation for Assigned Names and Numbers' (ICANN) Non-Commercial Stakeholder Group (NCSG) and the Non-Commercial Users Constituency (NCUC) of the Generic Names Supporting Organization (GNSO). He served as a member of the NCUC's executive committee as the representative for North America. His primary focus has been on GNSO issues that deal with the protection of the user. His book, *Internet Governance: Origins, Current Issues, and Future Possibilities*, was published by Rowman & Littlefield in March 2015.

Joanna Kulesza, PhD, is assistant professor of international public law at the Faculty of Law and Administration, University of Lodz, Poland. She specializes in international Internet law. She is the author of five monographs, including *International Internet Law* (2012) and over fifty peer-reviewed articles on international and Internet law, dealing in particular with human rights protection and cybersecurity challenges online. She has been a visiting professor with the Oxford Internet Institute, Norwegian Research Center for Computers and Law, Institut für Informations-, Telekommunikations- und Medienrecht, Westfälische Wilhelms Universität Münster, and Justus-Liebig-Universität Gießen. She was a postdoctoral researcher at the University of Cambridge and Ludwig-Maximilians-Universität München. Her research was funded by the Robert Bosch Stiftung, the Polish Ministry of Foreign Affairs, and the Foundation for Polish Science. She worked for the European Parliament and the Polish Ministry of Foreign Affairs. She has served as an expert for the Council of Europe and for the Paris-based Diplomatic Academy on their projects dealing with online jurisdiction issues.

She currently is the membership committee chair of the Global Internet Governance Academic Network (GigaNet). She is a member of Internet Society, Diplo Internet Governance Community, and the ICANN Non-Commercial Stakeholder Group (NCSG). Kulesza is the Polish reviewer for the World Intermediary Liability Map (WILMap) project done by the Center for Internet and Society at Sanford University, Faculty of Law. She serves as a reviewer for the *Utrecht Journal of International and European Law*, *SCRIPTed—A Journal of Law, Technology and Society*, and *Internet Policy Review*, and is on the academic board of the Communication and Media Research Center.

* * *

Richard B. Andres, PhD, is a senior research fellow at the Institute for National Strategic Studies and full professor at the U.S. National War College. His work focuses on national security strategy and particularly cyberspace. Previously he was associate professor of security studies at the School of Advanced Air and Space Studies. Andres has held a number of posts in government including special advisor to the secretary of the air force and special advisor to the commander of Air University (twenty-four schools, colleges, and think tanks). Andres specializes in developing national security strategy and has led teams of general officers and senior executives developing strategy for the White House, secretary and chief of staff of the air force, commandant of the marine corps, Office of the Secretary of Defense, several combatant commands, and other civilian and military institutions. He was awarded the medal for Meritorious Civilian Service by the secretary of the air force and the Joint Unit Meritorious Service Award by the chairman of the Joint Chiefs of Staff. Andres received his PhD in political science from the University of California, Davis, and wrote his dissertation under Randolph Siverson, Miroslav Nincic, Scott Gartner, and Kenneth Waltz.

Kalliopi Chainoglou, PhD, graduated with an LLB from the University of Essex in 2001 and completed her LLM in public international law at University College London in 2002. She was awarded a PhD in international law from King's College London in 2007. Chainoglou is a human rights lawyer and an academic who has worked since 2007 at universities in Greece and the United Kingdom. She has been appointed by international organizations as an expert for culture-related projects and international peace and security-related projects. Currently she is a lecturer in International and European Institutions at the University of Macedonia (Greece) and a visiting research fellow at the Centre of Human Rights in Conflict of the University of East London (UK). She is the author and editor of books and articles on international peace and security, cyberwarfare, international protection of human rights, intercultural education, transitional justice, and culture-related issues.

Dimitrios Delibasis, PhD, is an adjunct assistant professor in law and in war studies and a defense consultant; he splits his time and interests between the Academia, the Royal United Services Institute (RUSI), and the U.S. Naval Institute. He is an officer in the army reserves and an associated faculty member on the Centre for Critical Studies on Terrorism of the University of Western Ontario. He completed his postgraduate studies in Georgetown University under the supervision of Colonel Gary Sharp USMC (Ret.) and Commander Thomas Wingfield USN (Ret.). He completed his PhD in 2006 in the University of Westminster under the supervision of Professor Antony Carty. His research interests revolve around strategy, law, and the evolution of warfare. He is also interested in air naval and special operations; seabasing and maritime security; and in national security law. His first book, published in 2006 under the title *The Right of States to National Self-Defense in Information Warfare Operations*, was the first ever concerted effort worldwide to codify existing international legal norms on self-defense with regard to information and cyberspace warfare. The main scope of his work lies in exploring in depth whether twenty-first-century networked globalized terrorism is just plain criminal activity or the next stage in the evolution of warfare and if so whether it requires the development of a new regulatory paradigm.

Delibasis is currently working along with Colonel Albert Klein USAF (Ret.) on the book "Ordo ab Chao: Law, Strategy and Cybersecurity in the 21st Century," with an estimated publication date in the second half of 2016. He is also working with Colonel Klein on developing two specialized graduate courses for professionals for the Air University, the NWC, and the University of Westminster. The first is a course on "Cybersecurity Law and Policy" and the second is a course on "Law, Strategy and International Security." They will also be of a modular format, so they can be adapted to the specific requirements and background of those attending, taking full advantage of modern synthetic training techniques. Finally, both courses will be open to participation by selected specialists and institutions from the academia as well as the public and private sectors.

Marianne I. Franklin, PhD (@GloClomm), is professor of global media and politics at Goldsmiths (University of London, UK) and chair of the Global Internet Governance Academic Network (GigaNet). A recipient of research funding from the Social Science Research Council (United States) and Ford Foundation, she is active in human rights advocacy for the Internet; serving as co-Chair of the Internet Rights and Principles Coalition at the UN Internet Governance Forum (2012–2014). Dr. Franklin is currently on the Steering Committee of the IRP Coalition and Steering Group of the Best Bits Network. She is the Chair of the Global Internet Governance Academic Network (GigaNet). Her latest book is *Digital Dilemmas: Power, Resistance and the Internet*.

Monica Horten, PhD, is a visiting fellow at the London School of Economics and Political Science. In January 2014, she was nominated as an independent expert to the Council of Europe's Committee of Experts on Cross-Border Flow of Internet Traffic and Internet Freedom (MSI-INT). She is the author of two books: *A Copyright Masquerade: How Corporate Lobbying Threatens Online Freedoms* and *The Copyright Enforcement Enigma: Internet politics and the Telecoms Package*. Her latest book will be published in 2016. She has also published articles in the *Journal of Intellectual Property, Information Technology, and Electronic Commerce Law* (*JIPITEC*) and *Internet Policy Review*. Horten's chapter is the result of eight years of academic research into copyright enforcement policy, deep packet inspection, and human rights issues related to the Internet.

Horten writes the influential *Iptegrity* blog on European Internet and copyright policy (http://www.iptegrity.com/), attracting an international readership including academics, lawyers, and policy makers. She has a long track record as a writer on telecommunications and Internet matters, and has written for the *Daily Telegraph* and the *Financial Times*. Her extensive portfolio includes articles on telecoms and mobile phone markets, and the Internet. Horten researched her PhD at the University of Westminster from 2007 to 2010. She holds a master's degree with distinction in communications policy, a postgraduate diploma in marketing (DiP M), and a bachelor of arts from the Australian National University.

Francesca Musiani, PhD, is a researcher at the Institute for Communication Sciences, French National Centre for Scientific Research (ISCC-CNRS) and an associate researcher at the Centre for the Sociology of Innovation of MINES ParisTech-PSL. Her research work focuses on Internet governance, in an interdisciplinary perspective that blends, first and foremost, information and communication sciences with science and technology studies (STS). Since 2008, this research has explored the distributed and decentralized approach to the technical architecture of Internet-based services, in order to understand the coshaping of these architectures and of several different dynamics: the articulation between actors and contents, the allocation of responsibilities, the capacity to exert control, and the organization of markets. This work has spanned a doctoral thesis (2008–2012, MINES ParisTech, Prix Informatique et Libertés 2013 awarded by the French Privacy and Data Protection Commission), a research project funded by the French National Agency for Research, ANR (ADAM-Architectures distribuées et applications multimédias, 2010–2014), and the Yahoo! Fellowship (2012–2013).

Musiani is currently a member of the commission to study rights and liberties in the digital age established by the French National Assembly in June 2014; outreach officer for the Global Internet Governance Academic Network (GigaNet); and cochair of the Emerging Scholars Network of the International Association for Media and Communication Research (ESN-IAMCR). She is a member of the editorial board for the (online, green open access) journals *Tecnoscienza*, *RESET*, and the *Journal of Peer Production*, and an author for the *Internet Policy Review*, the online journal of the Berlin-based Humboldt Institut für Internet und Gesellschaft. Musiani was the 2012–2013 Yahoo! Fellow in Residence at Georgetown University and an affiliate of the Berkman Center for Internet and Society at Harvard University.

Dominic N. Staiger was awarded law degrees from Bond University Australia (LLB with honors) and the University of Zurich (MLaw). He is a licensed attorney-at-law (New York) and attended Columbia University (NY) as visiting scholar. His research interests include privacy and data-protection law with a focus on the legal implications of new technologies such as cloud computing, Big Data, and the Internet of Things. Currently he is completing his PhD on "Legal Compliance in the Cloud" under the supervision of Professor Rolf H. Weber whilst conducting research at the University of California, Berkeley.

Rolf H. Weber, PhD, is ordinary professor for civil, commercial and European law at the University of Zurich, Switzerland, and a visiting professor at the University of Hong Kong. His main fields of research are Internet and information technology law, international business law, media law, competition law, and international financial law.

Weber is director of the European Law Institute and the Center for Information and Communication Law at the University of Zurich. Since 2008, Weber has been a member of the steering committee of the Global Internet Governance Academic Network (GigaNet) and of the European Dialogue on Internet Governance (EuroDIG); and since 2009, he has been a member of the High-Level Panel of Advisers of the Global Alliance for Information and

Communication Technologies and Development (GAID). Otherwise, he is engaged as an attorney-at-law. His research focus lies on the mentioned regulatory topics; the publication list is available at http://www.rwi.uzh.ch/.